Teaching Ethics and Values in
Public Administration Programs

SUNY Series in Public Administration
Peter W. Colby, editor

Teaching Ethics and Values in Public Administration Programs

Innovations, Strategies, and Issues

Edited by
JAMES S. BOWMAN
and
DONALD C. MENZEL

State University of New York Press

Published by
State University of New York Press

©1998 State University of New York

For information, address the State University of New York Press,
State University Plaza, Albany, NY 12246

Marketing by Anne Valentine
Production by Bernadine Dawes

Library of Congress Cataloging-in-Publication Data

Teaching ethics and values in public administration programs :
    innovations, strategies, and issues / edited by James S. Bowman and
Donald C. Menzel.
        p.   cm. — (SUNY series in public administration)
    Includes bibliographical references.
    ISBN 0-7914-3509-1 (HC : acid free). — ISBN 0-7914-3510-5 (PB :
acid free)
    1. Political ethics—Study and teaching (Higher)—United States.
2. Public administration—Decision making—Study and teaching
(Higher)—United States.   3. Professional ethics—Study and teaching
(Higher)—United States.   4. Education (Higher)—Moral and ethical
aspects—United States.   I. Bowman, James S., 1945–   .
II. Menzel, Donald C.   III. Series.
JA79.T4   1998
174'.935—dc21   97-30642
                                                                          CIP

10 9 8 7 6 5 4 3 2 1

To a bright, ethical future . . .

Chris, Andy, Lori, Lana, Liz, Len

—JSB

To my grandchildren . . .

Daniel, Rebecca, Dillon, and Derek

—DCM

Contents

Figures and Tables

TABLES Page

Introduction

The past twenty-five years have witnessed a substantial growth of interest in governmental ethics and a formal educational commitment to adding ethics courses to professional programs of graduate study. Indeed, teaching ethics and values in graduate public affairs/administration (PA/A) programs in the United States is a growing, energetic enterprise as the twentieth century comes to a close. There have been several efforts to track developments in teaching ethics in professional schools to answer questions such as: "why has ethics education become important?" (Rohr 1976; Dwivedi and Engelbert 1981); "What factors have influenced decisions to offer ethics courses?" (Lee and Pugh 1987; Lee 1990); "What are/should be the goals of ethics education?" (Fleishman and Payne 1980; Hejka-Ekins 1988); "How does/should a program/department incorporate ethics instruction into the curriculum?" (Catron and Denhardt 1994); "What is/should be the content of ethics courses?" (Catron and Denhardt 1988); and "How do faculty respond to ethics pedagogy?" (Piper, Gentile, and Parks 1993). This book builds on the extant literature by presenting findings from a 1995 national survey on teaching ethics, and then offering in-depth studies on selected innovations, strategies,and issues in ethics instruction.

NATIONAL SURVEY FINDINGS

In the spring of 1995, all National Association of Schools of Public Affairs/Administration (NASPAA) principal representatives (n=229) were mailed a questionnaire; a total of 138 (60 percent) schools responded. The instrument contained items on (1) curriculum, (2) goals of ethics

1

education, (3) conceptual approaches to ethics education, (4) instructional methods/technologies, and (5) consequences of ethics education.

Nearly 60 percent (n=78) of the respondents indicate that their graduate program offers an ethics course. A smaller percentage, 40 percent (n=54), say that they teach "ethics across the curriculum," either in a formal or an informal way and either with or without a course specifically identified as an ethics course. Most say they do not have a formal program but that, as one person put it, "each course addresses ethical issues within the context of the materials." Among programs that offer an identifiable ethics course, one of every four requires it. Perhaps this requirement, in conjunction with a change in NASPAA curriculum requirements in 1989, is responsible for the steady growth in ethics courses (Figure 1.1).

Who teaches ethics courses? They are offered by one full-time faculty member, although in almost one half of programs (47 percent) part-time instructors are given this responsibility. Among respondents who said they were the primary person providing ethics instruction (n=60), most were tenured, white (95 percent), male (73 percent), full professors (57 percent), and had practitioner experience (70 percent). Moreover, they report having membership in two to three professional

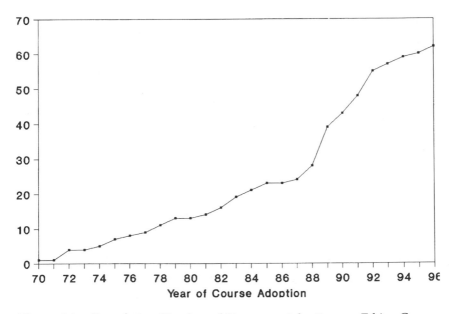

Figure 1.1. Cumulative Number of Programs Adopting an Ethics Course (n = 62)

associations and are very familiar with the American Society for Public Administration (ASPA) code of ethics (fifty-five of the sixty scored their familiarity as either a four or five on a five-point scale).

The goals of ethics education, and the importance that respondents attach to each, are shown in Table 1.1. Ethical awareness, atti-

Table 1.1. Importance of Goals of Ethics Education (Rank Ordered by Average Scores)

	All Respondents (n = 129)	Ethics Instructors (n = 58)
*Foster ethical conduct in the public service	6.45 (1)	6.47 (2)
*Develop an awareness of ethical issues and problems within the field	6.40 (2)	6.48 (1)
*Cultivate an attitude of moral obligation and personal responsibility in pursuing a career in the public service	6.12 (3)	6.15 (4)
*Gain knowledge of ethical standards of public administration	5.95 (4)	5.71 (9)
*Build analytical skills in ethical decision making	5.84 (5)	6.16 (3)
Enable one to resolve ethical dilemmas	5.82 (6)	5.83 (7)
Maintain the integrity of the profession	5.67 (7)	5.73 (8)
*Recognize the discretionary power of the administrator's role	5.60 (8)	5.85 (6)
*Stimulate the moral imagination	5.50 (9)	5.9 (5)
Reduce racial, gender, or ethnic prejudice	5.02 (10)	4.97 (11)
Prevent or minimize illegal behavior	4.98 (11)	4.81 (13)
Better define the public interest	4.97 (12)	5.07 (10)
*Cultivate moral character	4.91 (13)	4.95 (12)
Minimize organizational corruption	4.87 (14)	4.75 (14)
Acquire knowledge of ethical codes	4.56 (15)	4.29 (15.5)
*Become familiar with western traditions in moral philosophy and political thought	4.19 (16)	4.29 (15.5)

Cell values represent average score on scale of 1–7, with 1 = little importance and 7 = extreme importance. Numbers in parentheses represent rank order from high (1) to low (16).

*These goals/items are from Hejka-Ekins (1988).

tudes, knowledge, and behavior lead the list, although those who are the primary person teaching ethics give ethical knowledge a lower priority. Instead, they indicate that building analytical skills in ethical decision making is among the highest four goals. Ranked lower, but certainly not regarded as "unimportant," are objectives such as defining the public interest, acquiring knowledge of ethics codes, and becoming familiar with Western traditions in moral philosophy and political thought. Cultivating moral character also received lower scores. This rank order is consistent with that reported by Hejka-Ekins (1988). None of the sixteen goals received scores at less than the mid-scale value of four; in other words, while there are differences in "importance" attached to ethics goals, the variation is not large.

Regarding conceptual approaches, Table 1.2 reveals that a "moral reasoning" strategy receives the greatest attention, followed closely by

Table 1.2. Emphasis Placed on Conceptual Approaches to Ethics Education (Rank Ordered by Average Scores)

	All Respondents (n = 93)	Ethics Instructors (n = 56)
Moral reasoning	5.66 (1)	5.82 (1)
Democratic thought	5.20 (2)	5.19 (2)
Citizenship	5.16 (3)	5.05 (3)
Professional codes of conduct	4.67 (4)	4.53 (6)
Virtue and character development	4.65 (5)	4.79 (4)
Regime values via constitutionalism	4.59 (6)	4.72 (5)
Utilitarianism	4.26 (7)	4.34 (7)
Principles such as the Golden Rule	3.98 (8)	4.16 (8)
Covenants	3.65 (9)	3.69 (9)

Cell values represent average score on scale of 1–7, with 1 = not emphasized and 7 = emphasized very heavily. Numbers in parentheses represent rank order from high (1) to low (9).

"democratic thought" and "citizenship." Among those least emphasized are "covenants" and "principles," with "virtue and character
development," "constitutional regime values" and "professional codes
of conduct" in the middle-emphasis range. NASPAA schools and ethics instructors are in less agreement about conceptual approaches than
they are about the goals of ethics education.

Even more divergence can be found on instructional methods and
techniques (Table 1.3). Small-group discussion, case studies, decision-

Table 1.3. Instructional Methods and Technologies Used in PA/A Ethics Instruction (Rank Ordered by Average Scores)

	All Respondents (n = 90)	Ethics Instructors (n = 55)
Small-group discussion	6.00 (1)	5.98 (1)
Case studies	5.78 (2)	5.93 (2)
Decision-making scenarios	5.26 (3)	4.98 (4)
Research papers	5.17 (4)	5.22 (3)
Lectures	4.77 (5)	4.67 (5)
Role playing	3.86 (6)	3.51 (7)
Self-assessments	3.70 (7)	3.56 (6)
Videos/movies	3.45 (8)	3.30 (8)
Guest speakers	3.41 (9)	2.76 (11)
Simulations	3.37 (10)	2.92 (10)
Fiction/movies	3.09 (11)	3.08 (9)
Biographies	2.92 (12)	2.73 (12)
Field studies	2.75 (13)	2.53 (13)
PC multimedia material	1.91 (14)	1.73 (14)

Cell values represent average score on scale of 1–7, with 1 = "rarely used" and
7 = "extensively used" in the respondent's program of ethics instruction.
Numbers in parentheses represent rank order from high (1) to low (14).

making scenarios, and research papers are among the most frequently mentioned instructional methods. At the other end are PC multimedia material, field studies, biographies, and fiction. In between are lectures, role playing, self-assessments, videos, guest speakers, and simulations. The average scores varied from a high of 6.00 for small-group discussion to a low of 1.91 for PC multimedia.

Survey participants were also asked, "Do you believe that students who receive ethics instruction in your program (1) Find the subject matter valuable? (2) Feel threatened? (3) Become more ethically sensitive? (4) Use the knowledge gained to resolve ethical dilemmas? (5) Become more ethical persons in terms of behavior? (6) Become moral exemplars? (7) Become self-righteous? (8) Develop an attitude of being more ethical than others?"

Seven out of ten respondents said that students find the subject matter valuable. Nearly all felt that students are *not* threatened by ethics instruction. A two-thirds majority believe that class members become more ethically sensitive, although not necessarily more ethical in their behavior. Indeed, by the same two-thirds margin, respondents say that they do *not* believe that students become more ethical persons. A majority (52 percent), however, believe that those who receive instruction use that knowledge to resolve ethical dilemmas, and even larger proportions (88 percent and more) believe that students do not become "self-righteous" or "develop an attitude of being more ethical than others." These findings, although "soft" in measuring actual outcomes of ethics education, are encouraging. While ethics instructors do not perceive themselves as turning students into moral exemplars or virtuous persons, they do believe that their efforts are having positive and beneficial impact.

In all, the data reveal that ethics is taught in some form, but usually not as a required course. While the goals of ethics education are diverse and comprehensive, ethical awareness is seen as the single most important one. The conceptual approach most often emphasized is moral reasoning using discussion, case, scenario, and paper-writing pedagogies. Finally, most respondents believe that students find the instruction to be valuable.

Catron and Denhardt (1994:60) argue that "We need further progress in developing a shared understanding of the goals of ethics education, greater training opportunities for faculty interested in teaching ethics, and greater coverage and better coordination of ethics in the curriculum." The data reported here point to some success in achieving a shared understanding of the goals of ethics education, although there is no clear consensus. The results also suggest that progress is being made in providing greater coverage and better coordination of ethics in graduate programs. Moreover, Catron and Denhardt's (1994:57) observation that "overall, coverage of ethics in public administration programs is increasing" is supported. There are more ethics courses being taught in the 1990s than ever before, and a small but growing number of schools are teaching "ethics across the curriculum."

Still there are several areas where more work is needed, namely, faculty development and recruitment. Faculty development can be provided by professional associations and universities. The American Society for Public Administration (ASPA) and the American Political Science Association (APSA) offer some assistance through workshops and conferences. ASPA typically convenes one or more ethics panels at its annual conference (Cooper 1994:23–24) and has sponsored one national conference in 1989 which produced two volumes, Bowman (1991) and Lewis (1991). ASPA has also published materials by Mertins, et al. (1994) and Richter, et al. (1990). There has even been discussion of creating an ethics section within ASPA which could benefit faculty who want to develop expertise in ethics pedagogy. The American Political Science Association has a substantial publication division but has published no instructional material dealing with ethics.

At the university level, there have been two efforts to bring interested faculty together. One conference was held in 1991 in Park City, Utah (Frederickson, 1993), and another in 1995 in Tampa, Florida (see below). Each was well attended, attesting to the need for such events. More direct support by universities, however, appears to be limited, according to the 1995 survey data. When asked "Does your department/program support training and faculty development efforts to improve ethics education?" a majority (55 percent) of the respondents said "no." Among those who said "yes," most (87 percent) indicated that their institutions supplied funds to attend workshops or seminars; 68 percent said their schools provided verbal encouragement. Yet only ten professors (less than 20 percent) stated that instructional release time for faculty development was provided.

Concerning faculty recruitment, the other area warranting additional work, the demographic data reported earlier raises a serious question about the composition of the teaching corps. Fewer than one of every four ethics instructors is female, and almost none are nonwhite. In this "age of diversity," an effort should be made to foster a professoriate reflective of society. This will not be easy since most of those who teach ethics (90 percent) were drawn to it by personal interests [other motives included research interests (55 percent), NASPAA requirements (23 percent), and request by the chair (eight percent)].

Despite these concerns, the field of ethics education for public service may indeed be healthy and vibrant overall (Catron and Denhardt, 1994: 60). Nonetheless, there is, much to do and the contributions in this volume help point the way.

BOOK CHAPTERS

Although a variety of useful literature exists on teaching ethics in public administration, until now no one reference has offered a comprehensive selection of the latest work available. This collection of original studies is a product of the 1995 National Symposium on Ethics and Values in the Public Administration Academy convened by the editors. Presented here are a number of substantially revised papers from that meeting as well as one additional study. The result is a book in which each chapter, although written from a particular vantage point, provides fresh insights into a common phenomenon: the revival of interest in ethics instruction and the resulting innovations, strategies, and issues. Most selections proceed by introducing the subject matter, providing necessary background material, developing pedagogical and related themes, and concluding with a set of lessons or implications.

This volume consists of four sections: (1) Program Innovations (2) Teaching Inside the Academy, (3) Teaching Outside the Classroom and (4) Ethical Issues: Programs, Students, Faculty. Part one presents a selection of program innovations from across the nation. Alfred Killilea,

Lynn Pasquerella, and Michael Vocini, in "The Rhode Island Ethics Project," report on the rationale for, origins of, the strategies utilized in developing one of the most innovative programs in the county. Funded by the U.S. Department of Education and subsequentially supported by a local philanthropist, it began with a set of trust-building, agenda-setting and problem-solving workshops involving academicians and state agency leaders. The outcomes proved to be substantial, ranging from a replicable model for use elsewhere to the institutionalization of ethics education in Rhode Island. The authors believe that the key lesson is that there is "a strong undercurrent among state administrators, university faculty, philanthropists, and the general public to do something about preserving the integrity of our public life . . ." They find that such people need only to be asked, and the result will be change in the culture "to support proud, reflective, and ethical public servants."

Chapter 2, "Using an Ethics Matrix in a Master's of Public Administration Program" by Dalmas H. Nelson and Peter J. VanHook of the University of Utah, describes the creation of a pioneering attempt (now twenty years in the making) to infuse ethical concerns throughout the curriculum. As with the Rhode Island experience, this effort was the result of a collaboration between practicing managers and educators. It has been nurtured through the years by consensus-building activities including annual retreats, noncredit faculty-practitioner seminars, and an ongoing relationship with the university's philosophy faculty. The matrix that developed from these activities found formal expression in the early 1980s and recently has been revised in response to the department's NASPAA self-study report. It outlines the ethical dimension in all offerings in the curriculum and is anchored by an ethics seminar. The Utah faculty, like their colleagues elsewhere, recognize a need to determine how much difference their initiative has made "in the attitudes and behavior of MPA students in their careers."

"Reinventing the Master's in Business Administration Curriculum" by Dennis Wittmer and his colleagues provides in Chapter Three an exemplary attempt to redesign an entire degree program at the University of Denver. A number of troubling trends in public administration's sister professional program provided the stimulus to restructure the degree "to balance technical and humanistic skills through an innovative experiential curriculum." With the help of leaders in business and education, and later supported by a philanthropist, twenty-six free-standing courses were replaced by six functionally integrated courses taught by multidisciplinary teams with a "Values in Action" class as the cornerstone. Wittmer and his colleagues delineated the promise, problems, and prospects of this carefully conceived enterprise recognizing that the traditional ways of delivering course content are seriously flawed. If the Rhode Island project is led by one course in ethics, and the Utah initiative is guided by a curriculum-wide matrix to encourage ethics, the Denver innovation reframed how the degree would be conceptualized and identified the major role that ethics would have in it. A public administration program interested in change would be remiss not to examine the approach discussed here.

The final chapter in this section, "An Outcomes-Centered Approach to Teaching Ethics" by philosopher David Ozar from Loyola University of Chicago, describes the nature of an outcomes-focused curriculum for professionals. It then analyzes four categories of outcomes for ethics education: awareness, reasoning/reflective skills, implementation, and motivation/conviction. Ozar examines curriculum assessment designs as well as teaching strategies. Such an approach to evaluating instruction would be useful not only for the program-wide innovations discussed in this section, but also for individual courses both inside and outside academe—the subjects of the next two parts of this volume.

Selections in part two examine pedagogical methods with substantial relevance to on-campus teaching. The initial two contributions focus on the learner, the first with the type of student desired as a program graduate and the second with the practicalities encountered in teaching a common kind of student thinker. These selections are followed by three chapters which address the fine arts, codes of conduct, and the comparative method as teaching tools.

Jeffrey Mayer and Robert Seidel, in "Citizenship and the Policy Professional," describe the signature experience in the Master's policy studies degree at Johns Hopkins University. It is dedicated to training "professional citizens," that is, people who devote their careers to developing solutions to public problems. The assumption is that such individuals engage in sustained contemplation of the public good akin to that of the classical amateur citizen, an activity that most of the general public finds difficult to engage in today. The program features a course entitled "Citizenship" that explores the American political tradition and develops the ideas of professional citizenship and the nature of the bureaucratic role within which many professionals operate. A subtext of the course is the value of life involved with public issues, including obstacles to effective consideration of the greater good. The chapter concludes with an assessment of the authors' progress and the distance to be traveled to reach their ideal destination. Since most students in public administration/affairs programs either are now serving or will serve the public interest in some capacity, the significance of this type of class cannot be underestimated.

Purdue economist John G. Pomery, in "Teaching Professional Ethics," describes a teaching method to encourage moral sensitivity among quantitatively oriented students from technical backgrounds. Such learners are typically trained to believe that important questions have unambiguous answers and are consequently impatient with the perceived inconclusiveness of moral reasoning. Pomery identifies the assumptions undergirding an "indirect approach" to ethical thinking, shows how it has been implemented in several courses, and reports the results.

In chapter 7, Georgia College's Henry T. Edmondson III uses a Greek tragedy to provide a dramatic example of the damage done by a morally zealous but imprudent person. "*The Hyppolytus*, Public Administration, and the Need for Prudence" focuses less on the need for ideals to guide behavior than on the challenge to effectively implement such ideals. That is, one must not only recognize a moral goal but also determine how best to achieve it. The lesson from Euripides' play *The Hyppolytus* is clear: a prudence that teaches tolerance of imperfection is the key virtue for the effective, moral manager. The pedagogical implication is that instructors can use characters portrayed in fine arts, and contemporary analogs such as U.S. Surgeon General C. Everett Koop, to cultivate this virtue in their students.

"Using Codes of Ethics in Teaching Public Administration" by Pennsylvania State University's Jeremy Plant shows how effective such documents "can be when combined with instruction in moral reasoning and the ethical dilemmas endemic to modern governance." As imperfect but real artifacts, codes become useful teaching tools to make ethical discourse more practical, as well as to "elevate the work of the public servant and link it to the higher vision of democracy." This, for Plant, is the ultimate task of teaching ethics in public management, and strategies for using professional association codes are also discussed.

Finally, the contemplation of the commonweal can be retarded as privatization of government services and shared partnerships between public and private sectors increase. Accordingly, practitioner-student Robert W. Smith of the State University of New York at Albany compares how ethics is taught in business and public administration programs. In an extensive review of the literature, "Teaching Public and Private Sector Ethics" examines major themes found in the two arenas and calls for an intersectoral approach that draws upon and enhances the teaching of ethics in both sectors.

Part three, "Teaching Strategies: Outside the Academy," provides three examples of ethics training in the field with three different kinds of student-managers in three different parts of the nation. "Ethics Workshops in State Government" by William D. Richardson and his colleagues at Georgia State University describes an attempt to introduce managers to pertinent material on ethics and to develop an agency ethics code. Conducting such training in a highly politicized environment and in a troubled department, no matter how great the need, is a difficult challenge. The resistance encountered, and the modifications to and devolution of the program are reviewed. The lessons drawn from this effort, including reasons why public agencies are reluctant to have ethics training evaluated, are valuable to anyone interested in teaching outside the halls of academe.

Louis C. Zuccarello of Marist College, informs us of his experience in conducting seminars with volunteer and part-time public servants. His "Ethics, Values, and Part-Time Civic Leaders" confirms the dwindling public consensus on core societal values. Yet it also demonstrates that these individuals welcome the opportunity to consider ethical concerns, and that the seminars serve as an initial step in identifying common ground for ethical decision making.

"Ethics Education in Municipal Government" contributes to the empirically based body of knowledge on ethics by reporting results of the national survey of municipal clerks. Willa Bruce of the University of Nebraska at Omaha finds that significant attitudinal differences exist between those who received ethics training and those who did not. She is quick to recognize that cause-and-effect relationships, while reasonably posited, are difficult to specify. The need for additional research is apparent as the self-reported perceptions are not confirmed by objective outcome measures. Nonetheless, it is encouraging to have confirmation that ethics education seems to have a real-world impact.

The professional roles enacted by faculty in the public administration/affairs academy offer a rich environment in which to explore ethical activity. Part three therefore deals with the following professorial responsibilities such as program management, faculty-student relations, research, and consulting and their often overlooked ethical ramifications. Charles Fox, director of the Texas Tech University MPA program, presents a provocative critique of management of graduate PA/A programs. "Post-modernity, Fads, and Program Management" takes aim at symbolic reform movements in academe and argues that accrediting bodies undermine the intellectual independence of individual programs. The conflict between the knowledge production ("truth") and the imperatives of program maintenance (power), as seen through the NASPAA accreditation process, is resolved by power trumping knowledge, a process that Fox labels "presumptive consequentialism." The analysis offers recommendations designed to combat this phenomenon in the name of fostering a more authentic decision-making process.

Recognizing that a part of program management is faculty-student interaction, Marcia Lynn Whicker of Rutgers University argues that competence and fairness are the key criteria for judging ethical behavior in faculty-student relations. The implementation of these two principles is complicated and can be easily confounded by a number of constraints, such as professionalism, the use of an industrial (rather than a medical) model in dealing with students, the decision-making processes typical in universities, tenure, and friendships between professors and students. In light of these circumstances, the line between ethical and unethical behavior is frequently unclear. Her chapter, "The Ethics of Faculty-Student Relations," recommends that professors internalize the standards of competence and fairness.

Since advising can be one of the most important dimensions of student-faculty relations, George Cox of Georgia Southern University takes a rare look at the ethical dimensions of this crucial activity. His "The Ethics of Graduate Student Advising" discusses three roles in the advisor/student relationship (teacher/pupil, mentor/protege, artisan/ apprentice) as well as corresponding values for each (concern and credibility, trust and authenticity, collegiality). Interpersonal challenges to these values, such as indifference, intimacy, and exploitation, are examined. Cox offers a set of voluntary restraints in order to protect the advisor and the advisee and to ensure that socialization into the profession is as effective as possible.

One of the concerns that both Whicker and Cox note is the role of students and faculty in research. In "Ethical Principles for Public Administration Research," Jerry Mitchell of the City University of New York identifies truthfulness, thoroughness, objectivity, and relevance as benchmarks. A cogent analysis follows of the difficulties involved in putting these ideals into practice. Mitchell, for instance, asks how is it possible for research to be objective when so much of it is derived from normative theory? For a variety of reasons, he argues that "ethical reflection has not been important to public administration research" despite the fact that ethical issues are, indeed, important in scholarly inquiry. The chapter concludes with a discussion of how research ethics can be fostered in the profession.

The final chapter of this section, much like those that preceded it, attempts to "map a black hole." Thomas H. Roback of the Virginia Polytechnic Institute and State University points out that consulting in the field has received little attention in the literature. The need to better understand this activity derives from the unique professional milieu of the PA/A faculty "where lines dividing scholarship, public service, sponsored research, and personal consulting are intertwined and blurred." Roback presents four ideal-type consulting roles (Lone Ranger, Rainmaker, Salaryman, Altruist) and the ethical ramifications for each. He analyzes the ethical dilemmas involved in university policies and procedures, as well as the question of whether public administration faculty have a higher ethical responsibility to government clients than other consultants. The "Ethics of Consulting in the Public Administration Academy" concludes with a discussion of future consulting trends and their ethical implications in universities.

CONCLUSION

Throughout, the book offers specific ethics innovations, strategies, and issues found in the public affairs and administration academy. As such, it represents the state of the art and suggests how faculty can assist each other in best serving students and the public at large. In so doing, the volume contributes to understanding the ethos of government management in a democracy. By emphasizing educational and ethical standards, it seeks to foster the growth and development of the virtuous practice of administration.

Certainly no single compendium of current work in an multidisciplinary field such as public administration can or should be complete. Yet a timely study of ethical issues in academia can be found in these chapters. The role of ethics in American democracy and how it is taught are crucial subjects for inquiry. As a presentation of recent advances in these areas, this volume will have achieved its purpose if greater ethical reflection and action occur in the future.

ACKNOWLEDGMENTS

Many people have contributed to *Teaching Ethics and Values*. First, of course, gratitude is extended to the chapter authors who educated us with their thoughtful papers. They worked to produce a book representative of contemporary thinking. Their readiness to revise and resubmit their draft manuscripts attests to their respect for the subject and their skill in mastering it.

This task was facilitated by the thorough, insightful, and prompt reviews of draft chapters by more than two dozen referees, including Stuart Gilman (U.S. Office of Government Ethics); John Rohr (Virginia Polytechnic and State University); Gerald Pops (West Virginia

University); April Hejka-Ekins (California State University); Jonathan West (University of Miami); Montgomery Van Wart (Arizona State University); Mary Ellen Guy (University of Alabama); David Coursey (Florida State University); Harold Gortner (George Mason University); Vera Vogelsang-Coombs (Cleveland State University); Dalton S. Lee (San Diego State University); as well as the contributors to this volume. Menzel would like to thank the following persons and programs for their assistance: Travis Dorsey, the Research and Creative Scholarship Grant Program of the University of South Florida, and NASPAA representatives who responded to the questionnaire. Many thanks are also owed to our families for their support.

James S. Bowman
Donald C. Menzel

REFERENCES

Bowman, James S. 1991. *Ethical Frontiers in Public Management.* San Francisco: Jossey-Bass.

Catron, Bayard L. and Kathryn G. Denhardt. 1988. *Ethics Education in Public Administration and Affairs.* Washington, D.C.: American Society for Public Administration.

Catron, Bayard L. and Kathryn G. Denhardt. 1994. "Ethics Education in Public Administration," in *Handbook of Administrative Ethics,* edited by Terry L. Cooper. New York: Marcel Dekker, Inc., pp. 49–61.

Cooper, Terry L. 1994. "The Emergence of Administrative Ethics," *Handbook of Administrative Ethics,* edited by Terry L. Cooper. New York: Marcel Dekker, Inc., pp. 3–30.

Dwivedi, O.P., and E. A. Engelbert. 1981. "Education and Training for Values and Ethics in the Public Service: An International Perspective," *Public Personnel Management* 10 (Special Issue):140–145.

Hejki-Ekins, April. 1988. "Teaching Ethics in Public Administration," *Public Administration Review* 48 (September/October):885–891.

Frederickson, George H. 1993. *Ethics and Public Administration.* New York: ME Sharpe.

Fleishman, Joel L., and Bruce L. Payne. 1980. *Ethical Dilemmas and the Education of Policymakers.* Hastings on Hudson, New York: The Hastings Center.

Lee, Dalton S. and Darrell Pugh. 1987. "Codes of Ethics, Education, and the Making of a Profession." Paper presented at the Western Social Science Association Annual Meeting.

Lewis, Carol W. 1991. *The Ethics Challenge in Public Service.* San Francisco: Jossey-Bass, Inc.

Mertins, Herman Jr., Francis Burke, Robert W. Kweit, and Gerald Pops. 1994. *Applying Professional Standards and Ethics in the Nineties: A Workbook and Study Guide for Public Administrators.* Washington, D.C.: American Society for Public Administration.

Piper, Thomas R., Mary C. Gentile, and Sharon Daloz Parks. 1993. *Can Ethics Be Taught?* Boston: Harvard Business School.

Richter, William L., Frances Burke, and Jameson W. Doig, Eds. 1990. *Combating Corruption/Encouraging Ethics.* Washington, D.C.: American Society for Public Administration.

Rohr, John. 1976. "The Study of Ethics in the PA Curriculum," *Public Administration Review* 36 (July/August):398–406.

PART I

Program Innovations

The Rhode Island Ethics Project: A Model for Integrating Ethics into a Master of Public Administration Program

ALFRED G. KILLILEA, LYNN PASQUERELLA,
AND MICHAEL VOCINO

This chapter describes and analyzes an unusual effort to integrate the teaching of ethics throughout a Master of Public Administration (M.P.A.) Program. The Rhode Island Ethics Project, supported by the U.S. Department of Education's Fund for the Improvement of Post-Secondary Education (FIPSE), provides a model not only for other M.P.A. programs in teaching ethics but also for instigating change in the culture to support proud, reflective, and ethical public servants.

A surprise finding of the project was how few obstacles there are to bringing state agency leaders and faculty together to talk about ethics. Indeed, the role of the practitioners enlarged significantly as these encounters continued and as they produced some remarkable results. The experiences of the administrators not only enlightened and encouraged the faculty in teaching ethics in all of the M.P.A. core courses, but these experiences also provided fascinating case studies which the group has published in a new book. These workshops proved so successful that a philanthropist has endowed a new ethics center at the University of Rhode Island to institutionalize and assure the continuance of these encounters. The pages that follow detail the genesis, strategies, successes, and occasional pitfalls of this project, which produced enormous returns in professional and personal insights and relationships.

BACKGROUND

The model which emerged from the Rhode Island Ethics Project is the result of a rare collaboration between Rhode Island academicians and public administrators. The group initially came together in the fall of 1993, in the aftermath of the collapse of many of the state's banks and credit unions and the virtual collapse of the public's confidence in the ethics of public officials. The chief justice of the State Supreme Court had just become the second consecutive official in that position to resign under the threat of almost certain impeachment for ethics violations. The demoralization of the public was increased by revelations of widespread misuse of the state employees' pension fund and a succession of state regulatory failures. An ethics task force appointed by the governor had recently detailed in its first report nothing less than a moral hemorrhaging in the state:

> Nowhere have the results of a betrayal of trust, and the unethical conduct it manifests, been more devastating than here in Rhode Island. In recent months, the very civility that in the past ensured reasonable public discourse has been lost as the intensity of the anger and despair some Rhode Islanders feel grows over their government's failure to perform its duties and keep faith with the people.

> An atmosphere of greed and an environment of indulgence among the corrupt and connected that accept, excuse, and participate in unethical behavior as part of "the price of doing business" in Rhode Island have diminished the people's bond of trust. (Report, 1991; 2)

The participants in the project gathered in an effort to dispel one small part of the ethical gloom that had descended on Rhode Island. Two of the authors of this chapter, University of Rhode Island Professors Michael Vocino and Alfred Killilea, had proposed a plan for brightening the future of the state government service by initiating the teaching of ethics throughout the M.P.A. program which is jointly offered by the University of Rhode Island, Providence College, and

Rhode Island College. Funded by a grant of $180,000 from FIPSE, this proposal emphasized the importance of teaching faculty members about ethics as a way of reinforcing a concern for ethics in the core courses of the M.P.A. Program. In addition to initiating a seminar on "Ethics in Public Administration," we hoped to keep ethics from being viewed as an isolated side dish to the meatier and more essential offerings on such matters as budgets and personnel.

Integrated curricula that stress decision making and the formulation of values and moral choice are nothing new in postsecondary education. Indeed, the efforts of others to integrate ethics throughout the curriculum have been well documented (Pascarella and Terenzini, 1991). However, comprehensive attempts have not been undertaken to integrate ethics across a Master of Public Administration program, although teaching and even requiring a public ethics course in such programs has become more commonplace (Cleary, 1990 and Hejka-Ekins, 1988).

The Rhode Island M.P.A. program was ideally situated for making the point that public administrators need training in ethics. After all, it was Rhode Island that was featured in the *Wall Street Journal* and on a national news program as "Rogue's Island," a state with a history of corrupt government. And outsiders were not the only ones pointing fingers. Many government officials, educators, and academics within the state stressed the need for ethics education (Moakley and Cornwall 1996; Report 1991). The success of this project was due in part to its being perceived as essential for Rhode Island, and this, in turn, accounts for much of its success in attracting moral and financial support.

The project began with a series of six day-long workshops conducted by national experts on public ethics with the eleven faculty members connected with the M.P.A. program, plus a like number of state agency leaders who held positions at either the director or assistant-director levels. The latter group consisted of the directors of the departments of Corrections; Transportation; Elderly Affairs; and Mental Health, Rehabilitation, and Hospitals; plus assistant directors from Human Services; Children, Youth and their Families; Environmental Management; Corrections; Education; and Administration. The selection of administrators involved a mixture of invitation and self-selection; we invited about twenty-five leaders, but with short notice. The fifteen practitioners who participated made considerable sacrifices by increasing their workloads to attend the all-day Friday sessions. There was no perceptible difference in contribution or commitment between the politically appointed directors and the career civil servants. All seemed eager to participate, and all indicated a desire to affect the education on ethics of their future colleagues currently in the M.P.A. program.

The initial motive for including the practitioners in the workshops was for them to provide "reality testing" for ideas on ethics that faculty members might pursue in their courses. However, as bonds of trust and mutual respect developed among participants, an interesting shift occured in the focus of the workshops. The experiences of the administrators came to be seen as valuable teaching tools, and the workshops increasingly concentrated on grappling with the ethical issues raised by these experiences. Faculty members provided "theory testing" whether and how one could generalize from these concrete issues for pedagogical purposes. Of the six workshops, the first two were overnight and focused on the philosophical foundation of ethics, the third and fourth dealt with ethics and personnel and budgetary issues, and the last two were devoted to changing the ethical culture in public agencies.

A book, *Ethical Dilemmas in Public Administration* (Pasquerella, Killilea, and Vocino 1996), emerged naturally from the process of discussing the experiences of practitioners facing ethical dilemmas. Two-person teams, composed of an administrator and an academic, described a particularly trying ethical dilemma that the administrator had confronted and analyzed that experience. The two members of these writing teams seemed to complement each other perfectly. The administrators had abundant experiences of ethical successes and failures but almost no time to react to these experiences or probe their wider implications. The faculty members often regretted how far they were from the firing line, but were skilled in exploring the insights in practitioners' combat experiences. Both groups wanted to extend the learning that occured in the workshops to a wider audience who might take advantage of these experiences.

It seemed especially important to provide students and young professionals with practice in reacting to ethical conflicts. All of the cases in the resulting book invite the reader to weigh the alternatives faced by the public administrators and to critique the decisions made in those cases. The fact that the cases are based on actual experiences heightens their interest and credibility. The fact that almost all of the participating administrators and faculty commentators are from Rhode Island made this collaboration feasible and friendly but should not limit the relevance of these cases to other geographical locations.

Even as we describe in some of these cases discouraging and longstanding impediments to pursuing the public interest, we believe that this project itself is part of a new seriousness about public ethics in Rhode Island. Moreover, the satisfaction and mutual support we have found in collaborating in the workshops and in the writing of the book suggest that it may be easier than commonly supposed for public officials and citizens to take concrete steps to reassert a concern for ethics in public life. We are encouraged by the recent endowment of the John Hazen White, Sr., Center for Ethics and Public Service at the University of Rhode Island, which will make our experimental workshops on ethics for public administrators more numerous and more permanent. The Center has sponsored the first-ever seminars on ethics for both houses of the state legislature. The first executive order of the new governor was that all state agency directors will attend ethics workshops run by the Center.

The book and the workshops have had little to say about ethics violations stemming from simple greed and seeking to enrich the office holder at the expense of the public. These offenses are serious and common but rather easily identified as legal and ethical violations. The state's Ethics Commission is making a strong effort to educate public officials at all levels concerning their legal duties and liabilities. We are more interested here in ethical dilemmas in which the law provides little guidance and where the administrator must first have the sensitivity to perceive the conflict and then the judgment to make the hard choice among various imperfect solutions. We believe these are the more trying and more important ethical challenges confronting public officials. We offer no dogmas in settling these issues, but rather encouragement, practice, and examples from people who have known the pressure and discomfort of these dilemmas.

DEVELOPING THE CURRICULUM FOR THE WORKSHOPS

This approach of developing cases as practice for facilitating ethical analysis served as the basis for the curriculum. To provide participants with the conceptual tools necessary to engage in ethical decisionmaking, we used a case-based approach throughout the ethics workshops. These tools include the ability to identify positions, construct and evaluate arguments, expose hidden assumptions, recognize the presuppositions and implications of various positions, and to use reason in drawing conclusions concerning what to believe or do. We chose this method in a conscious effort to promote collaborative learning which would encourage critical and analytical problem solving by having individuals work together in small groups or teams on substantive issues. Those who employ collaborative learning seek to shift the focus of classroom authority from the teacher to the participants. Given the desire we had to dispel the notion that some of the participants were experts and others were only there to learn, applying this technique proved to be central to our mission. In fact, the only leaders in this kind of learning are those chosen by the group members to record and report back to the larger group whatever resolutions they have generated.

Because dissent often serves as a powerful tool for fostering understanding of ethical issues, we wanted to provide a forum that would encourage the free exchange of ideas. By immediately engaging participants in an interactive process, we hoped to allay any fears that dissention means disruption of a process whereby experts disseminate information. Collaborative learning appeared to be well suited to a program whose focus was on ethical decisionmaking in public administration. Ethical dilemmas by their nature involve circumstances under which some ethical principle will be violated no matter what course of action is taken. Since no single response can be determined the correct solution to such problems, collaborative learning provided the means for a comprehensive analysis of the dilemmas that were encountered.

In addition, by forcing group members to seek consensus regarding what constitutes ethical behavior under a certain set of conditions, we hoped to encourage the open-mindedness and willingness to entertain alternative points of view that are necessary to engage in critical thinking. While consensus-seeking may seem to be at odds with the encouragement of dissent, meaningful discourse can take place only when one truly understands the opponent's point of view. Because group members are asked to defend a single position, it is likely that at least some of the participants will be defending a position with which they disagree. The value of this exercise is the encouragement of argumentation skills which include anticipating and responding to objections to one's own views.

We identified two primary obstacles to the success of these workshops. First, from pre-workshop interviews and discussions with participants we knew that several of the public administrators tended to view faculty as operating solely on a theoretical plane and scrutinizing administrators' ethical decisionmaking from their ivory towers. Faculty members, on the other hand, had gleaned their perceptions of the quality of administrative ethical decisionmaking largely from reading newspaper headlines frequently written by "troubleshooters." The first obstacle, then, was the need to overcome stereotypes. Since we wanted participants to learn from one another, we set out to create a learning environment in which these ill-formed judgments would be quickly challenged and eventually dissipated. We were optimistic that collaborative learning would be effective in this regard.

The second obstacle was the fear of repercussions. Workshop participants represented a great number of administrators at a variety of levels. The willingness to share their professional experiences was an essential component of the proposed project. Yet detailing the kinds of ethical dilemmas encountered in daily activities could result in the identification of co-workers both inside and outside state agencies. These confidentiality considerations prompted a realistic concern about the possibility of a "chilling effect" on discussion. The focus on collaborative learning was intended, in part, to address these concerns by fostering an environment of mutual respect and trust. Admittedly, while we were astounded by the willingness of participants to share their ethical dilemmas in the context of our discussion sessions, many of the most revealing dilemmas in terms of their complexity and transferability across agencies could not be written about by the administrators due to pending administrative action. Nevertheless, participants constructed a broad range of cases highlighting issues of conflict of interest, confidentiality, sexual harassment, truth telling, whistle blowing, and attempts to reform the organizational culture, without finding the need to go to great lengths to disguise agencies or individuals.

While our emphasis has been on the pedagogy involved in conducting the workshops, we were convinced of the need to provide some theoretical background to serve as a framework for discussion. For this reason, the workshops began with an interactive lecture on the tasks of normative ethics in general and applied normative ethics in particular. Because ethical analysis is a philosophical endeavor, we modeled the process of doing philosophy by taking participants through the steps of resolving an ethical dilemma in public administration. This involved engaging discussants in the two broad stages of doing philosophy, consisting of identification and clarification of issues in the first stage and argumentation in the second. The discussion of the second stage included a brief overview of the methods of evaluating arguments supporting and opposing a given position. We then discussed how an application of competing normative ethical principles, exemplifying various deontological and consequentialist perspectives, might lead to contradictory conclusions concerning the correct course of action.

Finally, we considered two primary challenges confronting this approach to ethical decision making. These challenges come in the form of relativism and arguments from strong role differentiation. The latter position seemed particularly important for administrators who may view their professional roles as exempting them from certain common standards of morality in order to preserve an institution which is deemed an overriding social good.

After this brief introduction to normative ethics, participants were asked to work in small groups to resolve a broad range of ethical dilemmas faced by administrators at various levels of different agencies. For instance:

(a)   Suppose you are a middle manager in charge of making a recom-
       mendation for an opening in your organization. You have formed
       a committee and appointed a chair to conduct the search process.
       Shortly after the process begins, you receive a call from your
       supervisor telling you that a family friend is one of the candi-
       dates. Your superior assures you that the call is in no way an
       attempt to influence the process but reiterates the closeness of
       their relationship and comments about the person's excellent
       qualifications for this position. The search committee recommends
       a rank order of three persons. As it turns out, your supervisor's
       friend is ranked number two in what was, by the chair's own
       account, a close and difficult ranking process. Would you recom-
       mend your supervisor's friend under these circumstances? Would
       it be morally permissible to do so? Why or why not? Suppose
       you are the supervisor in this case. Have you done anything
       wrong? Please explain.

(b)   Your agency has been given a state grant. At the end of the
       fiscal year you face a decision whether to return unspent por-
       tions of the grant to a state that is in dire need; to spend the
       money on nonessentials; or to encourage employees doing valu-
       able work on other projects to list their unfunded work under
       the budget for this grant, thereby zeroing-out the grant. You
       know that if the money is not all spent, the next year's grant
       will be reduced by a substantial amount. What should you
       do?

(c)   It is brought to your attention as manager that someone in your
       department took a sick day to attend the funeral of an uncle. The
       bereavement policy in your agency does not provide paid leave
       covering this relationship. A co-worker discovers that the person
       is being paid for an unauthorized personal leave day and comes
       to you as the supervisor. What action should be taken? Should
       you use coercion to discourage this type of whistle blowing, or
       should you praise the behavior? Is this a genuine ethical di-
       lemma? Why or why not?

Reporting back on these dilemmas allowed participants to observe how their colleagues in other agencies, along with those in the academy, would respond to the typical crises they face.

In the afternoon, participants worked in teams, consisting of one faculty member and one administrator, who were responsible for drafting a table of contents to be used for developing a code of ethics for the administrator's own agency. We proceeded to compare the issues outlined by different administrators as central components of a comprehensive guide for an ethics training manual. Samples included statements of expectations by the director, codes of conduct, agency goals, sections on employer/employee relations (identifying common ethical problems such as union issues, harassment, power issues, and whistle blowing), worker/client issues, agency to agency issues, opportunities for continuing discussion of ethics, and enforcement procedures.

During the evening of the first workshop, which was an overnight session, we had a study-circle discussion of issues surrounding sexual harassment. The next day was focused on sources of corruption in the state and strategies for improving the state's ethical climate. The discussions highlighted the different strengths administrators and faculty bring to bear on these complex issues. The openness of the discussions was clearly prized by the administrators. One commented on an evaluation sheet, "I have not had an opportunity before to discuss these issues *freely*—nice job of creating an open environment."

Administrators left the workshops with renewed confidence in their own abilities to identify and resolve ethical dilemmas within their agencies. Agency leaders revealed that the types of dilemmas with which they are confronted are not substantially different from those faced by other agency directors. For instance, the director of a large social service agency spoke of the difficulties of trying singlehandedly to make a change in the ethical climate. He had an employee who also worked as a fireman; when his shift was changed at the fire station, creating a conflict with his agency job, the employee asked for a leave of absence. Such leave is normally granted only for medical reasons, and so the director refused the request. The employee's close connections to union officials and powerful state legislators led to explicit threats of vengeance upon the director's job and the agency's budget.

The director stood by his decision and weathered the political storm, but at great cost to his time and energy. He felt these costs were worth paying, because he saw this challenge not as an isolated issue but as an opportunity to maintain a standard of ethics for the entire state service. It was crucial for him to have the support and encouragement of other administrators in the state The easy solution for him personally would have been to accommodate the employee, avoid a series of grievances, and perpetuate a culture where state employment is seen as an entitlement to employment and shallow commitment.

That culture will be changed by one decision after another by administrators who are able to see the ripple effect of each decision made, with the assurance that colleagues are prepared to make the same commitment to uphold ethics in public service. By sharing such cases, administrators also share the sense that they are not alone in their efforts to undertake ethical reform in an occasionally unresponsive bureaucracy. In fact, administrators across the state have strengthened their ties by exercising their ability to engage in the meaningful discourse that is necessary to create a political culture in which ethics is of paramount importance.

Faculty also forged new relationships with colleagues that continue to generate research and teaching projects. One consequence of the project is that faculty members from different departments and institutions have come together to work on grants, conduct training sessions, write articles, and team-teach courses. In addition, because we established writing teams which paired one faculty member with one administrator, faculty were able to experience administrative decision making from within the institutions. This has proved extremely valuable for those faculty members teaching both public policy and public administration courses.

Finally, both groups were able to take advantage of the case studies generated by workshop participants. Some agency directors used the cases to conduct ethics training workshops for the employees in their organizations, and faculty used the cases in the classroom. By including practical assignments in a case-based approach to ethics training, we encouraged agency leaders and M.P.A. faculty to address ethical issues frequently and consistently.

MAJOR OUTCOMES TO DATE

The following are the most significant outcomes of the three-year Rhode Island Ethics Project:

A Working Model for Teaching and Studying Ethics

The workshops on ethics for public managers can be replicated in virtually any state by other M.P.A. programs interested in cultivating a concern for ethics in public officials. With a very low budget, faculty can invite practitioners to meet on a regular basis to discuss case studies the participants create from their own experience. They probably would find colleagues with experience in applied ethics very willing to serve as facilitators for these discussions. Once begun, these dialogues will develop a style and purpose of their own, but they are almost certain to be valuable for all involved.

Core Ethics Course Institutionalized in M.P.A. Program

PSC 504—Ethics in Public Administration—was developed as a discrete ethics course following directly from the FIPSE grant. The course was offered for the first time in the fall of 1993 and is taught annually. By means of a case study method, class discussion, films, and readings, this course explores how ethical deliberation in the public sector is an essential commitment and skill for public administrators.

Anthology of Cases and Comments

This book, *Ethical Dilemmas in Public Administration* (Pasquerella, Killilea, and Vocino 1995) comprises original chapters written by participants in our workshops. Eleven working groups, pairing a state agency leader with an academician, were organized midway through our seminars.

Each group produced a chapter dealing with an ethical dilemma experienced by the administrator. The academic worked with the administrator to analyze the decision-making process, their options, and outcomes.

John Hazen White Center for Ethics and Public Service

This center is probably the most dramatic and noteworthy outcome of the project. It demonstrates the university's commitment to institutionalizing a permanent ethics workshop program, not only for public managers but elected public officials and court administrators as well. A proposal for a $5,000,000 endowment was developed by the university, and a local philanthropist, interested in improving the quality of Rhode Island's public life, provided the endowment. The center will house a permanent ethics education program for public officials, which our project initiated. The center has already conducted a series of three day-long workshops on ethics for the directors of all state departments.

Programs dealing with professional ethics and public service are being developed for graduate students as well as undergraduates. Seventy University of Rhode Island faculty members have expressed written interest in attending next year's Professional Ethics for Academics workshops. The center has also provided the impetus for further grant-writing and as a focal point for those interested in exploring ethics education in a variety of settings.

Community Awareness

Publicity about the project has resulted in invitations to develop ethics presentations in a variety of forums. A panel on public ethics sponsored by the URI Alumni Association was held in November 1994 at the Warwick City Hall as part of a community outreach program. An audience of at least two hundred citizens attended. Participants in our workshops have described the benefits of the project at an ASPA regional conference in Vermont, and in conferences in Washington, D.C., and Florida.

The Development of Professional Relationships Around the Issue of Ethics

Working together in the project's seminars has facilitated bonding among faculty participants and state administrative leaders. Many of the faculty and administrators, in turn, have led and will continue to lead workshops sponsored by the new Center for Ethics. The project has identified a critical mass of motivated professionals who will work together to try to change the ethical culture of state service.

EVALUATION OF THE PROJECT

Review of an undertaking such as the Rhode Island Ethics Project requires mention of evaluation methods. Measuring the success of the project's intervention has been an ongoing process. The evaluation process has had some preliminary results, mostly qualitative, which are very encouraging. The pre- and post-testing of workshop participants has been particularly encouraging. Most of the previous three years have been spent collecting quantitative data for analysis at the end of the project. Professor Jon Wergin of Virginia Commonwealth University and Glenn Erickson and Bette L. Erickson of the Instructional Development Program have served as external and internal reviewers. FIPSE requires a full evaluation of each project it funds and that the final results be published. It is expected that the effects of the Rhode Island Ethics Project will be long-term, and therefore the benefits of ethics education modeled by this project will be best measured by longitudinal studies. Structural and cultural change will not be immediately apparent. The project is viewed as an investment in facilitating the moral development of public managers in Rhode Island.

CONCLUSION

It is not lost on the authors that the unique success of the Rhode Island Ethics Project has a great deal to do with the fact that the project took place in Rhode Island. Many of our ethical problems stem from the reality that, in a cozy city-state of one million people with perhaps only two degrees of separation from each other, everyone is "connected." At the same time, in a state of this scale change is possible.

It is believed that this uniqueness does not mean that larger states cannot learn from our experience, but rather that the project provides a microcosm for trying out ideas and for changing attitudes from which other states can extrapolate. This modest experiment did not so much change people as identify them and invite them to come together for collective thought and action. Once together, they provided their own agenda and momentum. We would never have guessed how generous colleagues in the M.P.A. program would be in allowing philosophers to share their turf and curriculum, or how receptive overworked agency leaders would be to collaborate with faculty on problems of public ethics.

There is serendipity in every discovery, and the fact that not all the outcomes of this project were planned does not mean others cannot profit mightily from the lessons stumbled upon. Perhaps the key lesson has to do with the strong undercurrent that exists among state administrators, university faculty, philanthropists, and the general public who are determined to do something about preserving the integrity of our public life, if only they can find an effective vehicle. We believe we have found such a vehicle for various groups in our state. Our specific strategies may be directly relevant in other locations, but the vehicle is not as important as the fact that many professionals in public administration (which, after all, does not tend to attract tycoons or narcissists) are primed to take extraordinary steps to create a culture where refining ethical judgment is a central professional and governmental concern.

The major discovery of our project is that there are many professionals and public servants who need only to be asked in order to make a substantial commitment to learn from each other about ethics and to take action together. They want to create a culture that is not only intolerant of sleaze, but also is sensitive to the more subtle ethical dilemmas every well intentioned public servant encounters as an inherent part of the job. We believe that facilitating an exchange among faculty and practitioners that sharpens their capacity to resolve dilemmas by examining how others have maneuvered through various ethical thickets is ethics education that will gain the enthusiastic support of citizens and administrators in many states.

REFERENCES

Cleary, Robert E., 1990. "What Do Public Administration Masters Programs Look Like? Do They Do What is Needed?" *Public Administration Review*, vol. 50, no.6 (November/December), 668–72.

Hejka-Ekins, April. 1988. "Teaching Ethics in Public Administration." *Public Administration Review*, vol. 48, no. 5 (September/October), 885–91.

Moakley, Maureen, and Elmer Cornwall. 1996. *Politics in Rhode Island*. Lincoln: University of Nebraska Press.

Pascarella, Ernest T., and Patrick T. Terenzini. 1991. *How College Affects Students: Findings and Insights from Twenty Years of Research*. San Francisco: Jossey-Bass.

Pasquerella, Lynn, Alfred Killilea, and Michael Vocino. 1996. *Ethical Dilemmas in Public Administration*. Westport, CT: Praeger Press.

Report of the Governor's Ethics Task Force. 1991. Providence, R.I.: Governor's Office.

Schlaefli, Andre, James R. Rest, and Stephen J. Thoma. 1985. "Does Moral Education Improve Moral Judgment? A Meta-Analysis of Intervention Studies Using the Defining Issues Test." *Review of Educational Research*, vol. 55, no. 3 (Fall), 319-52. This piece includes a comprehensive bibliography on the subject of ethics integration into the curriculum.

CHAPTER 2

Using An Ethics Matrix in a Master of Public Administration Program

DALMAS H. NELSON AND PETER J. VAN HOOK

In responding to the difficult challenge of how to cultivate ethical attitudes and behavior among public administration students, one possible approach is the development and use of an ethics matrix. This chapter discusses the experience of the University of Utah's Master of Public Administration (MPA) program with such efforts. The policy device discussed here is called a "matrix" because it has been intended to structure the role of ethics in the content of MPA core courses, to nurture the development and viability of that role, and to facilitate the viewing and reviewing of relationships among those courses regarding the role of ethics.

This chapter analyzes the gradual genesis of the matrix, including (a) evolutionary factors contributing to its formation, (b) ways of helping faculty members fulfill their responsibilities in implementing the matrix, (c) characteristics of the design, (d) its modification, and (e) experience with the central course for the matrix—the ethics seminar. It also makes some assessment of the impacts of the approach and identifies some major continuing issues concerning it.

BACKGROUND

In this section we look at the history and development of the matrix within the university's MPA program, which began in 1976. From the start substantial attention was given to ethics as an important program component. The idea of an ethics matrix gradually emerged out of struggles by faculty members, staff, students, and contributing outsiders with the question of how best to make ethics one of the living themes in the program.

The central course for the matrix has been the ethics seminar. Until 1988 it bore the title, "Seminar: Public Administration." As of 1984–85, the university catalog course description read: "Taken at end of student core course work; seeks to integrate that work; focuses especially on ethics; substantial research and writing project and student oral presentation." The course was intended in part to draw upon students' practical administrative experience and relate·it to the core courses, thus linking aspects of theory and practice, while maintaining a prime focus on ethics. As it happened, from its beginning until the early 1990s, three faculty members were by turns the instructors for the ethics seminar. Assignment of these three was informally derived and based mainly on their expressed interest in the course. None of these three felt well prepared by training, intellectual grasp, or instinct to deal with such complex, arguably interdisciplinary subject as ethics. Those well-founded feelings of insecurity lay behind much of the subsequent series of efforts to build the program's capacity to deal well with the ethics component, including the development of an ethics matrix.[1]

Many factors sparked attention to ethics in the late 1970s in the early years of university's program. Certainly there was repeated evidence of major ethical problems in American society, not only in its institutions but among the people. James Q. Wilson (1985, 3), for example, referred to "a deepening concern for the development of character in the citizenry." In the mid-1970s the American Society for Public Administration (ASPA) began to put "greater emphasis on professional standards and ethics in public service" (A. Lee Fritschler, quoted in Mertins and Hennigan, 1982, iii). ASPA's initial workbook on ethics (Professional Standards and Ethics Committee, 1979) was an indicator of this emphasis, and literature in public administration on ethics was beginning to emerge at this time (well described by Rohr 1990, 97–123).

The university's faculty and administrative staff members, anxious that the program's graduates serve honorably in their professional callings, gradually came to believe that ethics, as a topic, cannot be given sufficient attention by merely one course, and that ethics, as an element in a range of courses, has to be planned course by course. Various scholars' advocacy of a matrix approach was noted. For example, Donald Warwick declared, "the teaching of ethics should be integrated into all forms of teaching rather than confined to a separate course" (1980, 49). Joel Fleishman and Bruce Payne argued, "without focused curricular attention, the pervasiveness of values in policy studies and policy analysis does not go very far in teaching students about ethical analysis" (1980, 4).

The National Association of Schools of Public Affairs and Administration (NASPAA) served as an example by formulating standards which provided reference points in the examination of individual courses. These standards included the requirement that accredited programs would "develop in students a demonstrated ability to . . . implement an effective and ethical course of action . . ." (NASPAA 1981, 3). Warwick (1980, 50) asserted that "graduate programs in the social sciences should offer a course devoted wholly or substantially to questions of ethics."

In its relatively early attention to and emphasis on ethics, the Utah program probably was ahead of the predominant national patterns regarding this topic (Fleishman and Payne 1980, 2, 57n). The broad context of MPA education in the United States, then, has supported the Utah program's concern for ethical practice in its graduates, and it remains a principal consideration of the faculty.

EMPHASIZING ETHICS AS A PROGRAM ELEMENT

Several activities have facilitated the emphasis on and the creation of the matrix, including: annual faculty retreats, faculty/practitioner seminars on ethics, and an ongoing relationship with the university's Department of Philosophy.

Retreats

Utilizing a time frame of several days, the summer faculty retreat has involved nearly all of the core faculty in the MPA program, as well as program staff, student representatives, and a group of guests whose composition has varied across the years. Each retreat has afforded opportunity for in-depth thought and discussion about program goals and methods, quite free from the diverting pull of daily academic pressures. Retreats have been conducted with carefully developed agendas involving advance preparation of materials. In significant degree retreats have been mutual training sessions, as different faculty members and guests made presentations and led discussions on important topics.

A continuing hallmark has been the willingness of the individual faculty members to submit their versions of courses to sometimes intense scrutiny by participants. Faculty members involved have been fairly nondefensive in responding to often frank queries, comments, and suggestions, reflecting their commitment to program quality and collegiality. This has greatly aided the effort to make program development fruitful.

Timing of the retreats by design has enabled participants to attend a different Shakespeare play each of three nights at the Utah Shakespearean Festival. Usually a professor of English has discussed the evening's play at each of three luncheons, and these plays often raise large moral issues germane to our concerns.

The first annual Public Administration Retreat was held in 1978. A major part of it consisted of applying a matrix for evaluating the still quite new program, in relation to the standards set by NASPAA. The second retreat, in 1979, focused mainly on ethics and rhetoric. The third annual retreat included an ethics workshop led by Professor of Philosophy Bruce Landesman for the equivalent of a full day. It included readings and discussion about methodological challenges that drew upon several of the Hastings Center volumes on the Teaching of Ethics (Fleishman and Payne 1980; Hastings Center 1980; Warwick 1980). That workshop also saw further efforts to develop a matrix design for the teaching of ethics, relating it to the ethics seminar and to other courses.

The matrix was also on the agenda for various later retreats.[2] However, after its implementation it did not receive the degree of scrutiny it had at earlier retreats, until the 1990s. Development of the current version of the matrix is discussed below. An example of a recent retreat dealing with ethics was in 1990, when much of one session focused on approaches to combatting corruption in government.

The 1981 Faculty/Practitioner Seminar

The second important activity leading to the development of the matrix was the faculty/practitioner seminar titled "Ethics and the Public Administrator." This ad hoc, noncredit course consisted of eleven sessions held across Winter and Spring Quarters in 1981 and conducted by Professor Landesman with several of his philosophy colleagues as guest instructors. The nineteen students included a political theorist from the Political Science Department, the core faculty, and administrators from the university and from all levels of government in Utah. Substantial readings were provided, and the seminar constituted a fine learning opportunity. Selected session titles are suggestive of the philosophical orientation:

Morality and Rules: Limiting the Appeal to Consequences

Moral Knowledge and Moral Skepticism: Why Be Moral?

Theories of Justice, the Nature of Rights, and Varieties of Liberty

Social, Political, and Administrative Roles: Role-Morality vs. Ordinary Morality?

Truth Telling, Lying, and Deception in the Public Sector

The Moral Uses of Administrative Discretion

Public Sector Paternalism: Protecting People from Their Own Mistakes

Confidentiality and Secrecy in Government: Their Nature, Functions, and Moral Limits

Discussions in class were lively, informed, and enhanced by the range of backgrounds and perspectives. The building of faculty members' understanding of theories of ethics, as well as an increased understanding of practitioner perspectives on moral issues in government, contributed to their ability to incorporate ethics into the core courses, and to draw upon philosophical writings in the seminar.

Relationships with the Philosophy Department

Given their background in ethics, several philosophy faculty members have been viewed as resources that are important to the MPA program. This they have proven to be. Their capacity to assist public administration faculty was enhanced by their involvement in the Philosophy Department's "Course Program in Professional Ethics," out of which came a reader in professional ethics (Windt, et al. 1989).

Linking philosophers with a public administration ethics program is not without controversy. Mark Lilla (1981, 9–17) has expressed strong skepticism about its desirability, reasoning that philosophy may make students better able to give justifications for their actions as administrators without actually making them more ethical. Over the years philosophy professors' participation has taken a variety of forms, including publications (e.g., Francis and Francis 1976; Huefner and Battin 1992), summer retreats, seminar offerings, syllabus reviews, teaching resources (Windt 1992), guest lectures, and joint administration of a "graduate research program in political thought" (University of Utah 1994–95, 280). This collaboration has helped to broaden the perspectives of the MPA faculty, strengthened their conceptual understanding, increased interdisciplinary aspects of the program, provided needed external input to reviews of program quality, and enhanced student enjoyment of the ethics seminar.

THE ETHICS MATRIX

The matrix was made possible by utilizing ties to political scientists with interests in political theory and public law. It also used, directly or indirectly, other people involved in the retreats, the 1981 Faculty/Practitioner Seminar, and the at least quarterly meetings of the Public Administration Committee of the Political Science Department. Before it received expression in a formal document in the early 1980s, the matrix existed informally as a conscious effort to nurture attention to ethics in all of the core courses and to build a strong ethics seminar. It listed each of the core courses in the program and the primary expectations for attention to ethics within each course. Components were grouped under four general categories, shown below in the 1993 version currently in use. Each of the core courses (and some prerequisites) were individually associated with certain aspects of ethics analysis. Group approaches were employed in matrix development in order to take advantage of viewpoints of participants and to build faculty member commitment to the matrix.

Development of the matrix was based on several assumptions: that it could help instructors see that ethics is much too large a subject to be confined to one course; that particular types of ethical issues arise in the special fields dealt with by other courses; and that conscious efforts to respond to those issues are likely to enhance course quality. Furthermore, it was believed that this approach could help faculty identify and deal with significant gaps, see course interrelationships regarding ethics, and respond to the continuing need for course improvement.

The 1983 *NASPAA Self-Study Report* from the University of Utah program provides evidence of faculty and staff members' perspectives on the ethics emphasis at that time: "Cultural, Ethical, and Social Values. This NASPAA standard is addressed to at least some degree in nearly every required course and prerequisite." The report expressed the view that a strength of the program was the extent to which faculty members had "coordinated the offerings of the core courses and had been able to work together ... in integrating throughout the core courses the development of fundamental skills in communication, quantitative techniques, and ethical sensitivity" (Center for Public Affairs and Administration and Department of Political Science, 1983, 32, 128).

The 1990 Self-Study

In the view of the faculty members circa 1990, the ethics matrix had worked quite well. This is the general perspective provided in the 1990 *NASPAA Self-Study Report* on Ethics in the Curriculum:

> The MPA program's approach to enhancing the student's values, knowledge, and skills to act ethically is best understood by reference to the program's "ethics matrix." Faculty

have identified specific formal standards, style, accountability, and purpose components of administrative ethics and structured the curriculum and course content to address these topics. In addition, the curriculum includes the core course, Seminar: Public Administration and Ethics, in which students consider formal ethical systems and their application to decision making in public administration. Attention also is given to codes of ethics written to apply to public administrators. Finally, in the Seminar all students prepare and orally defend a major research paper on a topic in administrative ethics.

a. *Management of public and, as appropriate, third sector organizations.* Examination of the ethics matrix reveals many critical management ethics topics . . . receiving attention . . . are the Administrative Procedure Act, fiduciary responsibility, application of ethics in affirmative action and merit systems, codes of ethics, personnel evaluations, constitutional rights and obligations to protect them, and the conflict of rights to information versus privacy.

b. *Application of quantitative techniques of analysis.* Core courses in the curriculum address such topics as the uses that can be made (and sometimes are made) to distort with statistics, the conflicts between rational-comprehensive and incremental decision making, the use of "ploys" in the budgetary process, professional responsibility of statisticians and quantitative analysts, accountability in service delivery (e.g., comparisons of direct provision and contracting-out), and ethical concerns in social research (informed consent, privacy, confidentiality).

c. *With an understanding of the public policy and organizational environment.* Because consideration of ethics is accomplished in the context of substantive courses, that consideration includes the policy and organizational environment in which ethical decisions are confronted. Further, in their required paper written in Seminar: Public Administration and Ethics, students address ethical issues as they have been faced by practicing administrators. By doing so, they are able to test the applicability of philosophical ethical systems or codes of ethics to "real world" issues. ([re-named] Center for Public Policy and Administration/Department of Political Science, 1990)

In the NASPAA Site Visit Committee's Report on the program in 1991, the Committee remarked that "the content of individual courses is much like those courses anywhere except for a stronger emphasis on ethics (which predated the current national focus on ethics). . . ." The Committee said it "strongly encourages the program to continue . . . the emphasis on ethics. . . ."

1993 Revision of the Ethics Matrix

The matrix statement was significantly revised in 1993 (see Table 2.1). Several new faculty members had been added who had ideas which needed consideration. The model needed revisiting in light of experience and of developments in government and in the literature. Some changes had occurred in the particulars of the core courses and prerequisites.

An introductory paragraph was added at the beginning of the matrix to indicate its general nature and purposes. Various changes were made among the four section headings to clarify, elaborate, reduce complexity, or indicate a partial shift of focus. A small paragraph of introductory comments was added at the beginning of each of the four sections. "E.g." was inserted at the beginning of the listing for each course to remove any possible implication that the listings were regarded as comprehensive. A core course, Administrative Practice, which had been left out of the initial matrix, was included, and a core course, Politics and the American Economy, created and adopted since the initial matrix, was added.

The revision reflected in part an updating to take account of new concerns and emphases, as indicated by such changes as the name of the Public Personnel Administration course to Public Human Resource

Table 2.1. The Ethics Matrix (Revised)

All wording which is different from the initial version is indicated by italics.

This statement is intended to remind regular faculty and adjuncts of the MPA program's commitment to give appropriate attention to ethics in the content of the core courses; to help stimulate thought about ethics in reference to individual courses; to provide examples of ways in which the core courses may relate to different aspects of ethics; and to provide a framework for faculty discussion.

A. Persons and groups

Assumptions about their value and treatment: American culture's attachment of significance to the idea of the worth of the individual has impacted what the society expects of government and how government performs and behaves. Likewise, group concerns, claims, and conflicts have greatly influenced government. The dynamic interplay of focus on the individual and focus on the group implicates aspects of ethics.

P. S. 523 *Administrative Law*	*E.g.: Public employee constitutional rights and interests versus organizational needs*
P. S. 536 *Public Human Resource Management*	*E.g.: Diversity as a value; employee assistance programs; employee health and safety; pay equity*
P. S. 538 *Politics and the American Economy*	*E.g.: Regulatory policy and social equity; individual freedom as a consideration in economic policy*
P. S. 622 *Constitutional Law*	*E.g.: Assumptions about the value of each individual as they affect constitutional interpretation*
P. S. 630 *Administrative Theory*	*E.g.: Individualism as a social value; the organization versus the individual; participative management's theoretical and practical justifications; distributive justice and corrective justice*
P. S. 633 *Administrative Practice*	*E.g.: Importance of and sanctity of individual values, beliefs, and attitudes, and their relevance to "intentions to behave"; assumptions about human behavior relative to person in context considerations; group dynamics and importance of norms; organizational change and ethical implications; leadership, motivation, and individual considerations*

Table 2.1. *continued*

P. S. 638
*Planning, Budgeting,
and Control*

*E.g.: Estimating budgetary and revenue policy
impacts on individual well-being*

P. S. 687
*Seminar: Public
Administration and
Ethics*

*E.g.: Responses to ethical issues in policymaking;
ethics of character, utilitarianism, rights-based
ethics, etc.; the "public interest" as a criterion; case
studies*

Quantitative Skills

*E.g.: Limits of benefit-cost analysis; moral inade-
quacies of reliance on aggregate numbers; significance of qualitative research*

B. Formal standards: Responsibilities to law and rules

*Seeking prospectivity, generality, impartiality, and fairness. I.e.: Conventional
(or "legal") justice—right action as following the rules. America's official
governmental traditions have included major emphasis on the "rule of law,"
modified in practice by the considerable scope of administrative discretion and
by informal organization norms.*

P. S. 523
Administrative Law

*E.g.: Constitution; Administrative Procedure Act;
legislative intent as a norm for action; ex-parte
contacts; disqualifying bias*

P. S. 536
*Public Human
Resource Management*

*E.g.: Objectivity, fairness, and merit systems;
affirmative action; diversity; testing, selection, and
evaluation*

P. S. 538
*Politics and the
American Economy*

*E.g.: Efficiency; open market; standardization
(accuracy, scheduled releases, and public accessi-
bility) of economic indicators; obedience to law in
conducting regulatory programs*

P. S. 622
Constitutional Law

*E.g.: Substantive and procedural limits on
governmental power as moral guide*

P. S. 630
*Administrative
Theory*

*E.g.: Weber's rational-legal vs. patriarchal ideal
types: role of law in former; bureau pathology;
informal organization norms*

P. S. 633
*Administrative
Practice*

*E.g.: Norms; expectations; standards of conduct;
group dynamics and importance of norms;
performance management; goal setting*

Table 2.1. *continued*

P. S. 638 *Planning, Budgeting,* *and Control*	*E.g.: Fiduciary responsibility; Schick's "control";* *financial and compliance audits*
P. S. 687 *Seminar: Public* *Administration and* *Ethics*	*E.g.: Codes of ethics; conflict of interest laws;* *corruption; Constitution, statutes, and agency rules* *as norms; using law and policy for moral social* *ends*
Quantitative Skills	*E.g.: Logic (e.g., significant figures) and conventions* *(e.g., levels of significance); reliability; application of the* *same tests to similar problems*

C. Administrative discretion and accountability

To whom or what are public servants responsible, by what means? The question of appropriateness of institutional structures and processes; identifying responsibility for results; the problem of expertise. Our governmental setting is characterized by separated branches with overlapping powers and functions; the interfacing of changing political administrations and continuing bureaucracy; and the complex and interrelated impacts of the media, interest groups, professional norms, and public opinion. These are some of the reasons why enforcing accountability of public servants is a considerably challenging task.

P. S. 523 *Administrative Law*	*E.g.: Conflicts and reconciliations between rights* *and agency effectiveness; institutional checks on agency* *wrongs; constitutional rights of public employees;* *government agency and officer tort liability.*
P. S. 536 *Public Human* *Resource Management*	*E.g.: Personnelists' roles; performance appraisal;* *disciplinary case handling*
P. S. 630 *Administrative Theory*	*E.g.: Professional vs. political accountability* *(comparison of US and UK systems especially helpful);* *moral controversies in motivation theory; ethical* *controversies in leadership theory*
P. S. 633 *Administrative* *Practice*	*E.g.: Performance management; psychological* *contract*

Table 2.1. *continued*

P. S. 638 *Planning, Budgeting,* *and Control*	*E.g.: Rational/comprehensive vs. incremental/* *political; alternative service delivery systems* *accountability and contracting out: Is accountability (or* *impartiality and trust) lessened?*
P. S. 687 *Seminar: Public*	*E.g.: Political process and professional standards* *(Rohr); Waldo's ethical map of diverse obligations; role* *conflicts; T. Cooper's "doing creative ethics"; resigna-* *tions in protest; whistleblowing*
Quantitative Skills	*E.g.: Statisticians' responsibility to their profession and* *to their citizen audience; ethical concerns in social* *research: Informed consent, privacy, confidentiality*

D. Conduct

Integrity, forthrightness, and trust; ploys (bluffing, cajoling, threatening, bribing, etc.); honesty, faithfulness to values. The individual public servant brings to the workplace internalized values which are affected by the organizational culture. But the individual's values interacting with that culture also may influence responses to contingencies, agency policy choices, bureaucratic politics, and the struggle for personal and organizational survival and fulfillment.

P. S. 523 *Administrative Law*	*E.g.: Openness of procedures, deliberations, and* *determinations; records management; self-disqualifica-* *tion of officials*
P. S. 536 *Public Human* *Resource Management*	*E.g.: Effective use of personnel evaluations; pro-* *fessional standards vs. "political" expectations*
P. S. 538 *Politics and the* *American Economy*	*E.g.: Objectivity of releases and interpretations of* *economic indicators*
P. S. 622 *Constitutional Law*	*E.g.: Procedural limits (from Constitution) on* *governmental power as moral guides*
P. S. 630 *Administrative Theory*	*E.g.: The budget maximization imperative: Can* *ethics make a difference? Public versus private organi-* *zation ethics; cooptation; groupthink; diffusion of moral* *responsibility in bureaucracy; Shklar's defense of* *hypocrisy*

Table 2.1. *continued*

P. S. 633 *Administrative* *Practice*	*E.g.: Leadership; patterns of communication; style of communication; decision making/problem solving*
P. S. 638 *Planning, Budgeting,* *and Control*	*E.g.: Wildavsky: Confidence as the basis for dealing with complexity, "strategies," and "expected" roles; Anthony's "ploys" and responses*
P. S. 687 *Seminar: Public* *Administration and* *Ethics*	*E.g.: Bok's Lying and Secrets; why be ml; objective vs. subjective administrative responsibility; whistleblowing*
Quantitative Skills	*E.g.: Wheeler's Lies, Damn Lies, and Statistics; strengths and especially limitations of economic and social indicators*

Management and the adding of references in that course's listing to diversity, employee assistance programs, and pay equity. The adding of "records management" for the Administrative Law course and several items for the Administrative Theory and Budgeting courses also indicate changes of focus. The name of the ethics seminar was also modified, but this did not signal a change of focus.

Matrix Implementation in Courses

In the Administrative Law course, the matrix term "legislative intent as a norm for action" has been applied by incorporation of a segment on the roles of a statute as well as cases interpreting statutory requirements. The matrix phrase "institutional checks on agency wrongs" has been applied by a segment on judicial review, among other ways. The matrix words "openness of procedures, deliberations, and determinations" are applied by attention to the federal Freedom of Information Act and two Utah statutes, the Open Meetings Act and the Government Records Access and Management Act.

In the Public Human Resource Management course, the matrix phrase "pay equity" is applied by attention to issues on comparable worth. The matrix words "performance appraisal" are given life by exploration of inadequacies of performance evaluation systems as a type of moral criticism. The phrase "disciplinary case handling" is applied by facing the difficult issues of doing justice in dealing with employee problem cases.

In the Administrative Theory course, the matrix phrase "ethical controversies in leadership theory" is applied by use of Wallace Stegner's book (1953) on John Wesley Powell as a leader. The matrix statement "Weber's rational-legal vs. patriarchal ideal types: Role of law in former" is applied by the use of John Rohr's book (1986) on the legitimizing impact of the Constitution on the administrative state.

Judging Significance

The matrix is intended to be a guiding policy document whose application provides for a high degree of individual teacher autonomy in course design and delivery. Assessing how much difference the ethics matrix really has made is very difficult. One of the chapter authors (Van Hook) surveyed a large proportion of the regular and adjunct faculty who have taught core courses in the program in roughly the past ten years. There was a distinct contrast between the two groups in their knowledge and use of the ethics matrix. Regular faculty knew the matrix, and each reported having been influenced to some extent by its provisions. On the other hand, none of the adjuncts could recall ever having seen a copy of the matrix, although each noted that ethics had been included as an important element in the course they taught. All indicated their desire to see, make use of, and contribute to the further development of the matrix.

The connection between the ethics matrix as policy guidance and individual students taking particular core courses is very indirect. The design of forms used for student evaluations of courses has not thus far included assessment of the matrix. However, the central course for the matrix has been quite steadily evaluated, as noted below.

The Ethics Seminar as Central to the Matrix

The ethics seminar, P.S. 687, has played a central role in the application of an ethics matrix.[3] The 1983 *NASPAA Self-Study Report* broadly described the course this way (32):

> P.S. 687 is designed to confront the student with ethical issues which arise in public service and provide an understanding of the ethical public servant. The seminar explores the reasoning processes and precepts for handling ethical dimensions of major decisions that are likely to confront public administrators.

To a substantial extent the seminar research project represents implementation of another program matrix on "Communication." Thus, student preparation of a paper is to be followed by an oral presentation.

The seminar's title was changed in 1988 and appeared in the *Bulletin of the University of Utah General Catalog* in the 1989–90 issue. The new title, "Seminar: Public Administration and Ethics," was in part a response by the faculty to learning that a national survey of ethics courses had not counted the program as having such a course. The new course description read: "Integration of courses and administrative experience; application of ethical theories to public administration practice; required major research paper on ethical issues in government."

The seminar is taken by students near the completion of their other core courses and has regularly been divided into two main phases: discussion of assigned readings and oral presentations of students' papers. Instructors select the readings for their own version of the course. Traditionally they have shared syllabi and other materials with each other and worked together in a collegial spirit to review periodically the ethics seminar in retreats.

Some of the basic skills instructors have sought to nurture include the ability to engage in critical and analytical thinking, the ability to use ethical theory and philosophical criteria to recognize different types of dilemmas and other ethical problems which arise in government, and the ability to apply ethical reasoning to resolve such problems. The seminar has sought to enhance student skills in oral expression through vigorous discussions and presentations, as well as research and writing skills and skill in evaluating the seminar paper of at least one fellow student.

The course has attempted to develop deeper student understanding of a substantial amount of material concerning ethics. Assigned readings have included attention to multiple, sometimes conflicting, moral obligations of public servants; contrasting approaches in philosophies of ethics; normative ethical criteria, such as regime values, expressed in the U.S. Constitution and other laws; democratic tests of the public will; professional expertise and concepts of the "public interest"; institutional safeguards against corruption and error and the limitations of such safeguards; and major types of moral issues in government service. Students have been taught that not only particular individuals' attitudes and behavior, but also organizational structures, processes, informal norms, and social policies can be sources of moral problems and sources of improvement.

Examinations rarely have been used in the seminar. In most versions students have been graded in part on the quality of their discussion of the readings, on their oral presentation, and on the paper itself. In many of its incarnations, the course has required students to rewrite their papers.

Capstone Aspects of the Seminar

Virtually from the start the seminar has served as a "capstone" in several senses. It focuses mainly on ethics as the centerpiece of the matrix. Part of the time has been devoted to reviewing highlights of other core courses, in order to help students integrate and reinforce their substance in preparation for the comprehensive examination. Preliminary data from a 1993 survey of NASPAA schools by Steven Hays and Sandy Schneider (1994) on "capstone courses and their relationship to the comprehensive examination" suggest that the Utah program's capstone is quite unusual. A large proportion of MPA programs do not use comprehensive examinations, and capstone courses can be used for a considerable variety of other purposes.

The ethics seminar continues to be regarded by faculty as an essential component of the matrix. Beyond the consideration given to ethics in other core courses, devoting an entire course largely to ethics greatly helps to ensure sufficient attention to ethical aspects of student's overall educational development. The format, with smaller class size and emphasis on group discussion, seems especially suited to reasoned exploration of ethics.

Case Studies, Ethics Codes, and Poetry

The case-study approach has had a significant role in the seminar. Case studies based on actual events in administrative history help to provide students with a concrete, "real-world" context for in-depth analysis of the often ambiguous ethical circumstances.[4] Several fine works are available (Gutmann and Thompson 1984, 1990; Moore and Sparrow 1990; Richter, et al. 1990).

Ethics codes usually have been a topic in the seminar. Assigned reading and discussion often has included ASPA's Code of Ethics. The importance of codes has been stressed by a number of scholars, including Ralph Clark Chandler (1983, 32–39) and Darrel Pugh (in Bowman 1991, 9–30). A survey of practicing administrators found that a majority attach substantial significance to a code of ethics while recognizing its limitations (Bowman 1990). Faculty members have had the benefit of ethical guides concerning themselves as academicians, including the American Political Science Association's *A Guide to Professional Ethics in Political Science* (Schier 1985).

Selected works of poetry such as those by William Shakespeare, William Blake, Ralph Waldo Emerson, and Walt Whitman have been employed in some versions of the seminar. The arts, including poetry and other literary forms, can reach a person's feelings as well as their intellect and therefore connect public administration with the full drama of human life. The arts in general have largely untapped potential to provide images of healthy and unhealthy organizations, insights about human nature and behavior, value systems, motivation, and the power of imagination in administration.[5]

Variations in Teaching Approaches

Many of the syllabi used during the history of the seminar were re-viewed by the authors. We found that practices among different in-structors have varied significantly in the handling of certain aspects of the seminar.[6] In assigned readings, for example, inclusion of writers from the field of philosophy has fluctuated, as has the degree of emphasis on the study of corruption in government, as compared with other focuses such as social policy. Over the almost two decades in which the seminar has been offered, assigned books have included a variety of texts.[7] Besides its ethics codes, several works from ASPA have played a role (1979a, 1979b; Mertins and Hennigan 1982). Often instructors have supplemented assigned books with collections of indi-vidually-selected journal articles and book chapters.

Perspectives on Seminar Quality

To the extent that student evaluations of the seminar are an indicator of its quality, the data are very encouraging. The course has been well received by students and given relatively high marks in formal evalu-ations over the years. Given the significant variations in the ways different instructors have taught the seminar, the basic framework has been consistent: discussion of assigned readings and researching, writing, and oral presentation of the seminar paper. The formula works.

A number of other conclusions can be drawn from the experi-ence. Grading the quality of their participation in class discussions helps to give students an extra incentive to do the reading. Students in general can find ethics literature intellectually interesting, stimulat-ing, and challenging. The seminar affords an additional concrete op-portunity for students to learn first hand that integrity in the research and writing of a paper is a crucial part of ethical behavior.

Several valuable devices are available to enhance student abili-ties in oral communication besides participation in group discussion. Forbidding students to simply read their papers to the class encour-ages them to identify and describe the paper's highlights. That prohi-bition, as well as limiting presentation time and expecting presenters to answer questions, gives them an experience parallel to what they would face in a professional administrative setting. Moreover, videotaping each presentation is an instructive developmental process. Although students often resist in advance the idea of being videotaped, experience has shown the process to be unobtrusive.

We have the impression, supported by student feedback, that the majority of students have found the modest portions of the seminar devoted to reviewing other core courses to be significantly helpful to their preparation for the comprehensive examination. It can be a truly integrative process.

Student's seminar papers often have been an effective foundation for the final research project in the program, the MPA Research Paper. This strategy has been encouraged in recent years as giving the student more intensive, in-depth experience with a particular topic.

The intensive review of the course as the capstone seminar has demonstrated that it has been a positive and constructive part of the program. While the matrix itself needs to be better known, the emphasis on ethics has helped to create and maintain the quality of the program.

CONCLUSIONS

The University of Utah has been unusual in its approach to incorporating ethics in the MPA program. An ethics matrix has been central to these efforts. Its development and use have been made possible by several interrelated devices: early on, a seminar on ethics for faculty members and practitioners; some close working relationships with Philosophy Department faculty members; annual retreats; and the ethics seminar.

We believe that experience has shown the necessity for continuing assessment of courses and faculty teaching efforts. The willingness and ability of faculty to lay their syllabi on the table for examination is fundamental to any success the program may have had regarding the role of ethics.

The largest uncertainty concerns how much difference the ethics matrix and the ethics seminar have made in student attitudes and behavior. Faculty and staff members need to develop and apply better means for assessing this impact, at least from the perspective of the students themselves. Adjunct faculty who teach core courses must become better acquainted with the ethics matrix, its nature and purposes. Additional steps could be taken to further institutionalize the ethics matrix with the practices of regular faculty members. Maintenance of the traditionally strong collegiality among faculty is crucial.

Faculty members recognize that large differences of opinion exist in public administration and political science nationally about the best ways of teaching ethics. As Kathryn Denhardt has noted (in Bowman 1991, 91):

> Despite recent attention to ethics . . . and many improvements in the effort to teach ethics . . . , a significant problem remains. Every recent study of ethics education and even a "state-of-the-discipline" report on ethics in public administration have concluded that the field is marked by diversity bordering on chaos, a lack of clarity about what ethics in public administration means, and ambivalence about teaching or approaching a subject with such a lack of coherence. . . .

Many appealing approaches to ethics education are available which might deserve more consideration in the program as it confronts the challenges of the future.[8] Ethics education, with all its difficult issues and problems, should continue to be of major importance in MPA programs. The story of Utah's struggle with it can be instructive to others so engaged.

NOTES

1. Two additional instructors had significant backgrounds in ethics, both in training and professional experience, which greatly influenced their being invited to teach the Seminar starting in the early 1990s.

2. After the first few years, when a particularly large array of issues needed resolving, the standard time frame for the retreat at Cedar City tended to be two and one-half days, plus travel time. Starting in the early 1990s the location of the retreat usually has been much closer to Salt Lake City.

3. Copies of the syllabi for the current versions of the seminar are available from the authors.

4. Case studies have included such classics as John Bartlow Martin, "The Blast in Centralia No. 5: A Mine Disaster No One Stopped" (1947) (Stillman 1983, 25–39); Peter Schuck, "The Curious Case of the Indicted Meat Inspectors" (1972) (Stillman 1983, 338–49); Walter D. Broadnax, "The Tuskegee Health Experiment: A Question of Bureaucratic Morality?" (1975) (Uveges 1978, 201–09); Graham T. Allison and Lance M. Liebman, "Lying in Office" (1980) (Gutmann and Thompson 1984, 38–43; 1990, 39–45); Jeremy Paul, "The New York City Fiscal Crisis" (1979) (Gutmann and Thompson 1984, 44–58; 1990, 60–74); Henry L. Stimson, "The Decision to Use the Atomic Bomb" (1947) (Gutmann and Thompson 1990, 3–15; also Stillman); and Elliot Richardson, "The Saturday Night Massacre" (Richardson 1976). Cynthia Massie has provided a helpful recent analysis of the case method's useful features (1995).

5. Employment of the arts in ethics teaching has various advocates (e.g., Edmondson 1995, 226–29; Marini 1992, 420–26). Charles Goodsell and Nancy Murray recently have identified numerous ways in which the arts can assist the study, teaching, and practice of public administration (1995, ix–xi, 3–23).

6. Variations in content have included selection and amount of assigned reading for discussion; the degree to which such reading was ethics literature; the degree of emphasis on case studies; the scope of information provided in the course syllabi about course goals, methods, grading criteria, and possible research projects; the usage of guest lecturers; the degree to which student papers were expected to be strictly on an ethics topic (in contrast to including some attention to moral aspects of another topic); the extent of commitment of instructor time for discussing with individual students their projected research projects; the scope of efforts by instructors to coach students about oral and written communication; the number of other students' papers each student was expected to read and critique; the amount of class session time allotted to each student's presentation of his/her paper; the amount of class time provided for discussion of a paper; the extent to which of videotaping of student presentations was used (adopted as MPA program policy regarding the seminar); particular grading practices; and the scope of efforts to include class time for integrative overview of other core courses.

7. Each of the following has been used at least once: Cooper (1982, 1990), Denhardt (1988), Frankena (1973), Gutmann and Thompson (1984, 1990), Lewis (1991), Madsen and Shafritz (1992), Rawls (1971), Rohr (1978), Solomon (1984), Thompson (1987), and Waldo (1980).

8. Examples of the rich variety of avenues of possible emphasis include the positive cases of government administrators as moral exemplars (Cooper and Wright 1992); the administrator as citizen in "the ethical tradition of American citizenship" (Cooper 1991, 202 and generally); the nature and causes

of "bureaupathology" (Caiden 1991); cultivating virtue, building on humanity's degrees of shared "moral sentiments" (Wilson 1993; Galston 1988); and enhancing the role of ethics considerations in policy making (e.g., Schelling 1981; 't Hart 1990).

REFERENCES

American Society for Public Administration (ASPA). 1984. *Code of Ethics and Implementation Guidelines.* Washington, DC: ASPA.
————. 1994. *Code of Ethics.*
American National Council. 1979a. *Whistle Blowing: A Time to Listen . . . a Time to Hear.* Washington, DC: ASPA.
American Professional Standards and Ethics Committee, Herman Mertins, Jr., ed. 1979b. *Professional Standards and Ethics: A Workbook for Public Administrators.* Washington, DC: ASPA.
Bowman, James S., ed. 1991. *Ethical Frontiers in Public Management: Seeking New Strategies for Resolving Ethical Dilemmas.* San Francisco: Jossey-Bass Publishers.
————. 1990. "Ethics in Government: A National Survey of Public Administrators," *Public Administration Review*, 50 (May/June), 345–53.
Bruce, Willa. 1995. "Ideals and Conventions: Ethics for Public Administrators" (book review), *Public Administration Review*, 55 (Jan./Feb.), 111–16.
Caiden, Gerald E. 1991. "What Really Is Public Maladministration?" *Public Administration Review*, 51 (Nov./Dec.), 486–93.
Center for Public Affairs and Administration and Department of Political Science. 1983. *Master of Public Administration, NASPAA Self-Study Report*, Vols. I, I:A, and II. Salt Lake City: University of Utah.
Center for Public Policy and Administration/Department of Political Science. 1990. *NASPAA Self-Study Report, Master of Public Administration Program.* Salt Lake City: University of Utah.
Chandler, Ralph Clark. 1983. "The Problem of Moral Reasoning in American Public Administration: The Case for a Code of Ethics," *Public Administration Review*, 43 (Jan./Feb. 1983), 32–39.
Cooper, Terry L. 1991. *An Ethic of Citizenship for Public Administration.* Englewood Cliffs, NJ: Prentice Hall.
————. 1982. *The Responsible Administrator: An Approach to Ethics for the Administrative Role.* Port Washington, NY: Kennikat Press.
————. 1990. *The Responsible Administrator: An Approach to Ethics for the Administrative Role*, 3rd ed. San Francisco: Jossey-Bass Publishers.
Cooper, Terry L., and N. Dale, Wright, eds. 1992. *Exemplary Public Administrators: Character and Leadership in Government.* San Francisco: Jossey-Bass Publishers.

Denhardt, Kathryn G. 1988. *The Ethics of Public Service: Resolving Moral Dilemmas in Public Organizations*. Westport, CT: Greenwood Press.

Edmondson, Henry T. III. 1995. "Teaching Administrative Ethics with Help from Jefferson," *PS: Political Science and Politics*, 28 (June), 226–29.

Fleishman, Joel L., and Bruce L. Payne. 1980. *Ethical Dilemmas and the Education of Policymakers*. Hastings–on-Hudson, NY: Institute of Society, Ethics, and the Life Sciences, The Hastings Center.

Francis, Leslie Pickering, and John Gregory Francis. 1976. "Nozick's Theory of Rights: A Critical Assessment," *Western Political Quarterly*, 29 (Dec.), 634–44.

Frankena, William K. 1973. *Ethics*, 2d ed. Englewood Cliffs, NJ: Prentice-Hall.

Galston, William A. 1988. "Liberal Virtues," *American Political Science Review*, 82 (Dec.).

Goodsell, Charles T., and Nancy Murray, eds. 1995. *Public Administration Illuminated and Inspired by the Arts*. Westport, CT: Praeger Publishers.

Gutmann, Amy, and Dennis F. Thompson, eds., 1984, 1990. *Ethics and Politics: Cases and Comments*, 1st and 2d editions. Chicago: Nelson-Hall Publishers.

Hastings Center. 1980. *The Teaching of Ethics in Higher Education*. Hastings-on-Hudson, NY: Institute of Society, Ethics, and the Life Sciences, The Hastings Center.

Hays, Steven W., and Sandy Schneider. 1994. Memo to "Respondents to . . . Capstone Course Survey." Columbia, SC: University of South Carolina, Feb. 10.

Huefner, Robert P., and Margaret P. Battin, eds. 1992. *Changing to National Health Care: Ethical and Policy Issues*. Salt Lake City: University of Utah Press.

Lewis, Carol W. 1991. *The Ethics Challenge in Public Service: A Problem Solving Guide*. San Francisco: Jossey-Bass Publishers.

Lilla, Mark T. 1981. "Ethos, `Ethics,' and Public Service," *Public Interest*, No. 68 (Spring), 3–17.

Madsen, Peter, and Jay Shafritz, eds. 1992. *Essentials of Government Ethics*. New York: Meridian.

Marini, Frank. 1992. "The Uses of Literature in the Exploration of Public Administration Ethics: The Example of *Antigone*," *Public Administration Review*, 52 (Sept./Oct.), 420–26.

Massie, Cynthia Z. 1995. "Teaching Introduction to Public Administration Via the Case Method," *Proceedings of the Eighteenth National Conference on Teaching Public Administration*, Seattle, WA, Mar. 23–25.

Mertins, Herman, Jr., and Patrick J. Hennigan, eds. 1982. *Applying Professional Standards and Ethics in the 80s*. Washington, DC: ASPA.

Moore, Mark H., and Malcolm K. Sparrow, eds. 1990. *The Moral Challenge of Public Leadership*. Englewood Cliffs, NJ: Prentice Hall.

National Association of Schools of Public Affairs and Administration. 1981. *Standards for Professional Master's Degree Programs in Public Affairs and Administration*. Washington, DC: NASPAA.

Rawls, John. 1971. *A Theory of Justice*. Cambridge, MA: The Belknap Press of Harvard University Press.

Richardson, Elliot. 1976. "The Saturday Night Massacre," *Atlantic Monthly*, 237 (March), 40–44.

Richter, William L., Frances Burke, and Jameson W. Doig, eds. 1990. *Combatting Corruption, Encouraging Ethics: A Sourcebook for Public Service Ethics*. Washington, DC: American Society for Public Administration.

Rohr, John A. 1978. *Ethics for Bureaucrats: An Essay on Law and Values*. New York: Marcel Dekker, Inc.

———. 1986. *To Run a Constitution: The Legitimacy of the Administrative State*. Lawrence: University Press of Kansas.

———. 1990. "Ethics in Public Administration: A State-of-the-Discipline Report." Naomi B. Lynn and Aaron Wildavsky, eds. *Public Administration—The State of the Discipline*. Chatham, NJ: Chatham House Publishers, Inc., 97–123.

Schelling, Thomas C. 1981. "Economic Reasoning and the Ethics of Policy," *Public Interest*, No. 68 (Spring), 37–61.

Schier, Richard F., ed. 1985. *A Guide to Professional Ethics in Political Science*. Washington, DC: The American Political Science Association.

Solomon, Robert C. 1984. *Ethics: A Brief Introduction*. New York: McGraw-Hill Book Co.

Stegner, Wallace. 1953. *Beyond the Hundredth Meridian: John Wesley Powell and the Second Opening of the West*. Boston: Houghton-Mifflin Company.

Stillman, Richard J. II, ed. 1983. *Public Administration: Concepts and Cases*, 3rd ed. Boston: Houghton Mifflin Company.

't Hart, Paul. 1990. *Groupthink in Government: A Study of Small Groups and Policy Failure*. Amsterdam/Lisse: Swets & Zeitlinger B.V.

Thompson, Dennis F. 1987. *Political Ethics and Public Office*. Cambridge, MA: Harvard University Press.

University of Utah. 1989, 1992, 1994. *Bulletin—University of Utah General Catalog*. Salt Lake City: University of Utah.

Uveges, Joseph A., Jr., ed. 1978. *Cases in Public Administration: Narratives in Administrative Problems*. Boston: Holbrook Press, Inc.

Waldo, Dwight. 1980. *The Enterprise of Public Administration*. Novato, CA: Chandler & Sharp Publishers, Inc.

Warwick, Donald P. 1980. *The Teaching of Ethics in the Social Sciences*. Hastings-on-Hudson, NY: Institute of Society, Ethics, and the Life Sciences, The Hastings Center.

Wilson, James Q. 1985. "The Rediscovery of Character: Private Virtue and Public Policy," *Public Interest*, No. 81 (Fall), 3–16.

———. 1993. *The Moral Sense*. New York: The Free Press.

Windt, Peter Y., Peter C. Appleby, Margaret P. Battin, Leslie P. Francis, and Bruce M. Landesman. 1989. *Ethical Issues in the Professions*. Englewood Cliffs, NJ: Prentice Hall.

Windt, Peter. 1992. "Notes on Ethical Theories." Mimeo. Salt Lake City: University of Utah.

CHAPTER 3

Reinventing the Master of Business Administration Curriculum: Integrating Ethics, Law, and Public Policy

DENNIS WITTMER, JOHN HOLCOMB,
BRUCE HUTTON, AND DONALD R. NELSON

This chapter describes one college's evolution from a traditional, technical skill delivery system for MBA education to a program whose core is six functionally integrated megacourses. This represents the University of Denver's response to the current wave of criticism of business education. These courses include critical experiential learning opportunities, which balance technical skills such as accounting, economics, finance, and marketing with humanistic skills, including ethics, communication, entrepreneurship, creativity, and international and multicultural perspectives. The focus of this paper is the Values in Action course, designed as an issues-based business course developed by integrating three required, independently taught courses in public policy, the legal environment of business, and ethics and social responsibility. Additionally, a required community service component was included in this integrated framework.

BACKGROUND

Historical Context

Criticisms of business schools are not new. Since 1881 when a Philadelphia businessman, Joseph Wharton, gave $100,000 to the University of Pennsylvania to establish the first school of business and commerce in the United States, the concept of business education has been questioned, criticized, and subjected to several major reexaminations.

Initially, the critics questioned whether or not such a school even belonged in a university. The concern in 1881 was whether the curriculum was too vocational. This criticism persisted until the middle of this century, most notably expressed in two Ford and Carnegie Foundation reports (Gordon & Howell 1959; Pierson 1959). At the same time, the number of business school graduates was growing so swiftly that by 1955 business administration had become the most popular undergraduate major.

Over the years, business schools responded to this criticism by raising standards, producing more academically trained faculty, requiring more rigorous course work, increasing graduate work, and decreasing undergraduate specialization. In fact, business schools responded so well to the vocational school criticism that the current round of criticism is ironically the opposite. That is, business schools currently are criticized as too academic, too technical, too narrow, and therefore not preparing graduates to be leaders in the kind of environment in which organizations currently operate. For example, a study commissioned by the American Assembly of Collegiate Schools of Business (AACSB), the accrediting body for business schools, summarized the major criticisms of business education as: "Insufficient attention to the external (legal, social, political) environment . . . Insufficient attention to ethics . . . Too much emphasis on quanitative analytical techniques" (Porter & McKibben, 1988, pp. 65–66).

The Current Crisis

Thus the 1980s found business education, and particularly the Masters of Business Administration (MBA) programs, at a significant crossroads. The envy of its peers in other parts of the university community, the MBA had grown both in status and number of student applicants for thirty years. In 1960 there were 4,646 MBA degrees granted. By 1983 there were 63,000 MBAs, with the number of degree-granting institutions more than doubling to 600. Since that time, however, the MBA student population began shrinking. Jobs became harder to find, the educational needs of business and society changed measurably, and business school curricula and faculty were being criticized for being insular and unresponsive to the needs of students and the business community. "The loss of U.S. dominance in the world market has been caused less by a lack of technical skill than by flaws in judgment, character, and values," wrote one critic (Leonard 1984).

The criticism of business schools came from a variety of directions. Media, corporate officers, deans, students, and all too often unemployed graduates. "I tell my MBA friends, 'We're the lawyers of the nineties, there are too many of us'" (Linden, et al. 1992). Three issues appeared to drive these disturbing trends. First, business school curricula failed to match the needs of the market. Demographic changes, globalization, and the relentless advance of technology had begun to put a premium on the need to balance all those technical and analytical skills with an equally important set of humanistic skills, including values clarification, interpersonal communication, creative entrepreneurism, and multicultural perspectives. Second, as business searched for both its soul and the bottom line, it was increasingly going global, downsizing, reengineering, adopting TQM, flattening, and teambuilding. Business schools, on the other hand, continued to deliver a product focusing on quantitative analysis, theoretical and bureaucratic management, and independent technical skill development.

Contributing to both of these issues was a third, the increasingly narrow (and many would say irrelevant) definition of scholarship being embraced by the academy. At precisely the time when the business world needed broader perspectives, integrated knowledge, and critical thinking, the universities had come to regard scholarship as primarily the production of discipline-focused publications. There was a passing acknowledgement of teaching and even less value placed on community service, including the application of knowledge to real-world problems.

As a new decade began, business schools again were forced to examine their curriculum and value. One response was the 1990 Keystone Project Conference, sponsored by the University of Denver's College of Business. The conference brought together for the first time leaders of business and education to discuss corporate social policy. Keynote speaker James Parkel of IBM said,

> Customers don't want to do business with companies which pollute the environment, or which are notorious for shoddy products and practices; employees don't want to work for companies which have no social conscience; nations and communities don't roll out the welcome mat for companies which take everything out of a community and put nothing back in; students and faculty want to be part of institutions which have a vision of the world as it ought to be, not just as they inherited it; finally, voters and shareholders rally in favor of causes that are socially responsible—and powerfully against those which are not. (Parkel 1991)

It was against this background that the University of Denver began a fundamental and philosophical reexamination of its MBA curriculum.

Program Evolution

The University of Denver's initial response to the environment described by Parkel was a traditional overhaul of existing courses offered in the MBA program. Following lengthy literature reviews in management education while surveying the local business community, the following six new courses were moved into the core MBA program:

(1) Logic and Reasoning—to develop in the student a greater ability to think logically, to assimilate information and place it within a meaningful framework for analysis, and to improve reasoning skills.

(2) Organizational Communications—to develop skills in human interaction, persuasion, written communications (when, how, why), and handling interfaces with subordinates, peers, customers, suppliers, governmental agencies, the media, etc.

(3) Negotiations and Dispute Resolution—to develop the ability to recognize and manage conflict and the skills necessary to resolve such conflict, especially through negotiation and mediation.

(4)   Business Ethics—to develop a frameworks for distinguishing right from wrong, and for helping the student to determine propriety in the "gray areas."

(5)   Human Resources Management—to develop an understanding within the general manager of linkages between organizational problems, such as turnover, absenteeism, poor attitudes, and low motivation, and organizational policies and procedures regarding employee influence, recruitment, development, rewards mechanisms, and work systems.

(6)   Two courses in the international sphere: International Management Issues—to elevate student awareness of cultural differences and their importance to organizational success and world stability; and International Economics and Finance—to develop a better understanding of currency fluctuations, balance of trade issues, and the effects of foreign investment.

These program changes caught the attention of a local businessman and philanthropist. Working with the chancellor of the university, the business school developed a proposal to fundamentally restructure the MBA program to balance technical and humanistic skills through an innovative experiential curriculum. The proposal was funded with an eleven million dollar matching gift.

The second phase of the MBA program's evolution began with a five-person Program Development Team whose first task was to determine what additional outcome attributes students needed in order to complement their technical knowledge. More than forty such attributes were identified and organized into the three broad focus areas of values, communication, and creativity, with an additional focus, international/cross-cultural, integrated into these three (Table 3.1). Knowledge related to these attributes was subsequently delivered through a variety of free-standing courses (e.g., Ethics and Social Responsibility), experiences outside the classroom (e.g., Outward Bound), and workshops and seminars (e.g., diversity and etiquette).

The third and current phase of MBA evolution began when it was realized that the curriculum changes did not deliver in two important

Table 3.1. Areas of Emphasis

Outcome Attributes	Type	Focus Area
• Honest, principled, humane, possess integrity	• A1 Ethical	A. Values
• Courteous, respectful, reliable, accountable, dedicated, loyal, enthusiastic, organized, punctual, committed to excellence	• A2 Professional	
• Community-minded, socially aware and responsive	• A3 Social	
• Self-awareness, coping skills, logic/reasoning skills, a sense of perspective	• B1 Interpersonal Skills	B. Communication
• Good listener; effective interviewer, counselor, negotiator, appropriate appearance	• B2 Intrapersonal Skills	
• Leadership; effective in consensus-building, group dynamics, and conflict resolution	• B3 Group Process Skills	
• Articulate, persuasive, effective presenter, effective media skills	• B4 Oral Communication Skills	
• Effective writer of reports, memos, and executive summaries	• B5 Written Communication Skills	
• Innovative/inventive, effective problem solver, imaginative, good risk assessor, risk receptive, courageous	Regarding: • C1 People • C2 Processes • C3 Products	C. Creativity and Entrepreneurial Spirit

areas. First, students had a hard time seeing the relevance of the more humanistic components (e.g., community service) to their functional courses (e.g, marketing). Second, feedback from the business community informed us that the delivery modes (e.g., independent, nonintegrated courses) were out of sync with how businesses operates today. The result, after another year and one half of intensive curriculum design work, is a new educational model based on four key features: (1) the replacement of twenty free-standing discipline-focused courses with six functionally integrated megacourses plus a capstone internship; (2) the use of multidisciplinary faculty teams, ranging from two to five persons, to deliver the courses; (3) imbedding within the megacourses several experiential learning elements; and (4) The rigid use of student cohorts for the first two terms. In this new configuration, the Values in Action Course is a keystone.

ORGANIZATION AND DESIGN OF THE VALUES COURSE

Goals and Objectives

The two-quarter course Values in Action uses the idea of "community" as its central organizing concept, focusing on the relationships of managers and business organizations in their communities. By analyzing issues that managers are likely to face in the 1990s, the course examines the roles and responsibilities of managers and business firms in a way that is topical and relevant. Current issues are examined in terms of their legal, public policy, and ethical dimensions, with a goal of providing students with generalized understanding and skills that can be employed in dealing with other issues that may emerge in their business careers.

An assumption of the course design is that students must learn to function effectively in a world where legal compliance, political pressures, and ethical choices are shifting from reactive processes to proactive and strategic approaches. Incorporating such a shift into strategic decisions allows the firm to gain competitive advantage while contributing to community health, whether that community be the local neighborhood, the organization itself, or the global community. The course is intended to develop and strengthen the following skills, capacities, and competencies:

(1)　Awareness and Sensitivity: To develop greater awareness of and sensitivity to the importance of ethical, legal, and public policy components inherent in managerial decision making.

(2)　Analytical Skills: To provide students with conceptual tools and frameworks necessary for analyzing business decisions, practices, and policies in terms of their legal, ethical, and public policy dimensions.

(3)　Adaptation: To prepare future managers and leaders to meet their social obligations, function within organizational realities, and manage the complex interrelationships with other groups and institutions.

(4)　Application and Implementation: To apply creatively the learned frameworks, perspectives, and skills to critical business issues of the 1990s. To make the process of translating knowledge to practice an integral part of the course experience.

Organization of the Course Content

Values I.　The newly integrated values course replaces three required, self-standing courses (Business Ethics and Social Responsibility, Public Policy and Business, and the Legal Environment of Business). The new two-quarter sequence is divided in terms of a career life cycle and a micro/macro perspective. The first quarter is intended to address issues that managers are likely to face in the early stages of their careers, focusing more on individual (micro) decision making. Relationships of managers to members of the community are explored by examining current issues. For example, as seen in Figure 3.1, relationships to employees, shareholders, customers, and competitors are examined in the first quarter. Issues explored for each relationship have included the following: (1) Employees: privacy, sexual harassment, employment discrimination, employment at will, and whistleblowing; (2) Customers/Consumers: product liability, deception in marketing and advertising, sales responsibilities, and database marketing and privacy; (3) competitors: intellectual property and trade secrets, pricing and antitrust, and aggressive practices; (4) Shareholders: insider trading.

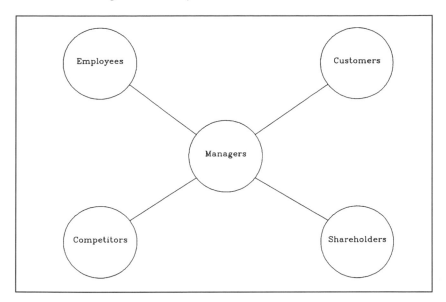

Figure 3.1. Managerial Relationships

Before exploring the above issues and relationships, three weeks are spent laying the groundwork for discussion providing conceptual frameworks for analyzing the issues. Included in this phase are: prisoner dilemma exercises, an introduction to social contract theory and theories of jurisprudence, public policy lifecycle and managerial strategies, normative ethical frameworks including Aristotle's theory of moral virtue, an introduction to cultural relativism, and community service as it relates to citizen participation.

Community Service.   A required community service component is central to the course. Experiential learning through community service is considered essential for acquiring an understanding of the interdependent relationships within and between social institutions. This component is premised on the Aristotelian notion that moral virtue and citizenship are acquired from practice and habit. Students read selections from both Aristotle and Benjamin Barber's *An Aristocracy for All.* Goals of the community service component include enhanced sensitivity to humanitarian needs; an understanding of the nature of nonprofit organizations and the issues confronting them; and a better understanding of the relationships between governmental organizations, business, and nonprofit organizations.

Community service is a component of the course during both quarters. The requirement for the first quarter is eight hours of service for a local nonprofit or public service organization. Students may fulfill this requirement individually or as a member of a group. Organizations are identified individually by students from projects and contacts maintained by either the college's Institute for Professional Excellence (a unit created to administer various enhancements of the graduate school), or GIVE Graduates Involved in Voluntary Experiences (GIVE) a volunteer organization of graduate students.

Values II.   The second quarter is intended to examine issues that managers are likely to face in more senior positions, focusing on organizational (macro) strategies and positioning in the community. Relationships at this point shift to the larger community and include relationships with government agencies, elected officials, business associations, advocacy groups, citizen groups, the media, and the larger society (Figure 3.2).

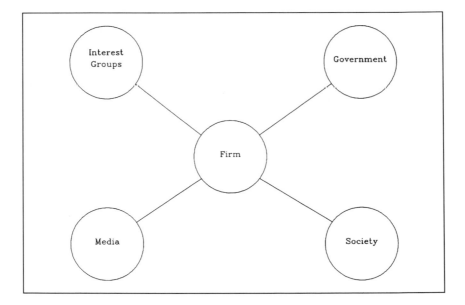

Figure 3.2.   Firm Relationships

During the first two weeks of the course, discussions of background frameworks and concepts include communitarian perspectives, stakeholder theory, corporate social responsibility, and corporate rights in order to provide an analytical and social paradigm. Issues and topics examined during this quarter have included: corporate governance and executive pay, organizational liability, community involvement, corporate social performance, corporate philanthropy, government regulation and self-regulation, industrial policy, lobbying, PACs and campaign finance reform, citizen group pressures, dealing with the media, and crisis management.

Community service is fulfilled with a group project. The class self-selects into groups of three by topic interest. Groups then explore a topic by examining the perspectives of all three sectors (business, government, and nonprofit). The assumption here is that community problems are increasingly being solved through new and emerging relationships among government, business and nonprofit organizations, and their leaders. Hence, the project is intended to prepare students for their roles as business leaders and community members. Examples of project topics include: school violence, sexual orientation and discrimination, immigration policy, NAFTA, health care reform, economic development, violence in the media, toxic waste policy, product liability reform, and campaign finance reform.

Organization of Faculty Resources and Pedagogical Approaches

Since the new two-quarter course replaced three required, self-standing courses in the old curriculum, and since the content and approach were designed to address issues by integrating legal, ethical, and public policy dimensions, a team approach to teaching was seen as the most logical and effective (albeit not most efficient) alternative. Moreover, team teaching was viewed as an essential part of the larger curriculum change.

Two types of teams were formed for the design and implementation of the Values course. In order to make the course truly interdisciplinary, a college-wide review team was created provide to representation from each of the traditional disciplines and programs. In addition to those who traditionally teach in law, public policy, and ethics, it was deemed important to include the perspectives of scholars in accounting, finance, statistics, and other traditional core business disciplines.

The second team was the core teaching team. Since Values in Action integrates three required courses from the previous curriculum (business ethics, business law, public policy and business), individual faculty members were selected for these teams from among those who had taught two of the three required courses, thus maximizing continuity, integration, and overlap. Core teams of two were created, and these pairs functioned as "true teaching teams" as opposed to "tag teams" or sequential teaching, with both instructors being present for virtually all classes. Members of the larger design and review team provide spot lectures and participants for topics appropriate to their area of interest and expertise. For example, for the topic of drug testing, the statistics member developed a reference table concerning the conditional probability that a positive screen was a false positive. Students see the applicability of statistics, the implications for managerial strategies, and the ethical and legal issues that complicate the adoption of company drug testing policies.

Change and integration were required of faculty as well as students. Faculty themselves were required to integrate knowledge, attack problems from multiple perspectives, communicate effectively with others having different disciplinary languages, listen to customers and stakeholders, negotiate and compromise in order to achieve a common purpose, learn from one another, and build something new by learning and utilizing the strengths of other faculty (team members). In effect, the steps and skills required for building the Values course paralleled the skills to be taught in the new, integrated program.

Pedagogical approaches are varied. There has been a combination of lecture and discussion, case discussion, student group presentations, video clips and discussion, in-class exercises, and guest speakers. One of the benefits of team teaching from a faculty point of view is the opportunity to watch other faculty members and their unique styles and pedagogical approaches, which stimulates growth and development in teachers as well as students. One of the other elements has been a group project that requires students to engage in research into the current state of issues. This project requires students to use current technology (e.g., Lexis/Nexis and presentation software such as Powerpoint), contact responsible government agencies (e.g., EEOC for sexual harrassment), and assess corporate policies and strategies. Although structuring the projects has been challenging, the great benefits intended for students have been engaging in integration of theory and practice, appreciating the shifting and evolving nature of business issues, and developing skills that can be transferred to other emerging issues.

EXAMPLES OF ISSUES AND APPROACHES

Both segments of the Values in Action course interweave the public policy, legal, and ethical aspects of each issue or case examined. In focusing on the public policy aspects, students are often challenged to apply the stages of the public policy cycle discussed in the first week of the Values I course. They are expected to identify the stage at which the issue now resides in the cycle, e.g., at the agenda setting, policy formulation, or implementation stage (Baumgartner and Jones 1993; Kingdon 1984), and to explain how and when the issue travelled through previous stages in the cycle. Students may also discuss the alignment of the various political interests on the issue and their relative power, as well as the roles of the formal institutional actors, such as Congress or state legislatures. As state and local governments have become more activist on many of the public policy issues addressed in the course, it is important that students appreciate the roles played by the various levels of government in advancing the issues discussed.

Beyond cultivating an understanding of the political forces surrounding each issue, the course also examines the relevant case law and legal doctrines applied by courts to the issue. In so doing, the instructors attempt to expose the legal reasoning and theories of law applied by the courts in adjudicating the issue, again based on material discussed early in Values I (Smith 1993; Posner 1990). Moreover, the course attempts to impart an understanding to the students of how judicial interpretations of the issue have evolved, as well as possible future directions of judicial thinking.

Finally, after analyzing a case or issue from public policy and legal perspectives, students then apply appropriate normative theories (from among utilitarianism, deontology, rights, and justice) to engage in ethical analysis of the case at hand (Beauchamp and Bowie 1993). Even though a corporation or manager might overcome legal obstacles and have the legal right to pursue a course of action, this phase of the analysis poses the question, "Is it the right thing to do?." Occasionally, the students might also be prompted to apply concepts of virtue ethics in addressing that question.

By way of demonstrating how the public policy, legal, and ethical aspects of the course blend together on any given case or issue analysis, this chapter will examine the application of those aspects to four issues discussed in the course, two drawn from the first segment of the course and two drawn from the second. Table 3.2 portrays the application of the three fundamental components of the course to those four issues.

Sexual Harassment

In the course of discussing sexual harassment, various political factors and elements of the public policy process are apt to emerge. The role of feminist and women's rights organizations in placing the issue on the agenda, and the way in which the Clarence Thomas hearings may have propelled the issue forward, are likely to surface (Phelps and Winternitz 1992; Brock 1993; Mauer and Abramson 1994). Regarding cultural factors and international trends, the growing sensitivity of other cultures to the issue, including even Japan, will emerge in the discussion. The role of the Equal Employment Opportunity Commission (EEOC) in defining and regulating sexual harassment will be a focal point of class discussion, especially in distinguishing between quid pro quo offenses and hostile environment offenses. Moreover, the role of the U.S. Supreme Court and lower courts in adjudicating key cases, such as *Meritor Savings Bank v. Vinson* and *Harris v. Forklift Systems*, is discussed, including the competing legal theories applied by the majority, concurring, and dissenting opinions. Elements of agency law addressed in those cases are also discussed. The emerging political backlash to what is perceived as an over-extension of hostile envi-

Table 3.2. Sample Course Components

	Topic	Law	Ethics	Public Policy
Values I	→Sexual harassment	→Key court cases →Vinson & Harris cases →Backlash cases	→Duties →Organizational efficiency →Conflicting rights	→Title VII →EEOC regulations →Women's groups →Male backlash
	→Product liability	→Recovery theories Contract theories →Negligence →Strict liability →Market share liability	→Duties →Competitive costs →Risk sharing →Punitive damages	→State reforms →Failure of federal reforms →Numerous political actors
Values II	→Corporate governance	→Corporation law →Business judgment rule	→Institutional shareholders →Stakeholder management	→State anti-takeover laws →Federal laws/regulations on executive pay
	→Executive Pay		→Efficiency aspects →Justice aspects	→Governance reforms
	→Corporate political activities	→Cases on speech on issues →Cases on speech on candidates	→Deontology →Distributive justice →Rights →Corruption	→Federal laws →State laws →Competing reforms →Diverse political actors

ronment theory may also surface in class discussion, along with the attendant clash between fair employment on one hand and free speech on the other (Hayes 1991; Johnson 1994; Leatherman 1994).

Normative theories are also applied to the different varieties of sexual harassment. Not only are the rights of potential victims addressed, but also the rights of other employees within the same office environment and the overall consequences to business productivity. Duties to fellow workers will also emerge in class discussion, along with the free speech rights of potential offending managers. Finally, the types of systems and internal controls that a firm can adopt to protect itself from liability, or even go beyond the law, are important features of the case and issue analysis (Deutschman 1991; Sandorff 1992).

Product Liability

On the issue of product liability, it makes more sense to start with a legal and ethical analysis and then apply public policy concepts in the context of addressing reforms in product liability law. In first explaining relevant case law, the course explores the evolution of theories of recovery, from contract and negligence theories through strict liability and more modern concepts, like market share liability (Spiro 1993; Velasquez 1993). Along the way, students explore the ways in which different jurisdictions have applied the concepts differently. Students also discuss the ways in which a business can protect itself from inherent liability risks, including the due care that can be exercised from the production through the distribution processes. This segment of the course also applies normative theories in analyzing the ethics of strict liability, market share liability, and punitive damages, all aspects of product liability that are rich in ethical implications (Brenkert 1993).

After examining cases that surface the relevant legal and ethical questions, public policy concepts are applied in the context of the debate over product liability reform. Initiatives at the state and federal levels are discussed, along with the political forces in the business community that have placed the issue on the public policy agenda. The countervailing forces from consumer groups and the plaintiff's bar that have stymied the issue at the federal level for the past decade are also addressed, and questions about the failures of business political strategy then emerge (Moore 1991).

In the second half of the Values course, as the focus shifts from the micro (managerial) level to the macro (corporate) level, the issues of corporate governance and (corporate) political activities provide ample opportunity to apply concepts of law, ethics, and public policy in an integrated fashion.

Corporate Governance

The law surrounding corporate governance involves traditional corporation law concepts that define the fiduciary duties of board members and managers and the rights of shareholders. Major cases involving the constraints that the business judgment rule imposes on officers and directors are addressed, especially in the context of corporate takeovers (*Unocal Corp. v. Mesa Petroleum Co.*, 493 A.2d946 [Del. 1985]). State statutes passed to regulate takeovers are also addressed (*CTS Corp. v. Dynamics Corp. of America*, 481 U.S. 69 [1987]), and the issue poses the further opportunity to explore the stakeholder management approach, along with the ethics of considering the interests of employees, suppliers, and local communities in corporate decisionmaking (Evan and Freeman 1993; Goodpaster 1993). The growth of activism by institutional shareholders, along with their agenda of changes in corporate governance, are also explored (Dobrzynski 1992; Wayne 1993; Wayne 1994). Particular attention is paid to the issue of executive compensation, which affords a ripe opportunity to once again engage in normative analysis, especially probing the efficiency and justice aspects of the issue (Byrne and Hawkins 1993).

Moreover, since Congress and the Securities and Exchange Commission (SEC) have both promoted initiatives on the issue, executive compensation provides a handle for once again applying public policy concepts and discussing the various political forces and actors concerned with the issue. Finally, cases of responsible and innovative corporate policies and practices on executive pay emerge in this segment of the course (Cowan 1992).

Corporate Political Activities

Corporate political activities, and especially corporate political action committees (PACs) and campaign finance, provide another useful focus for applying a blend of legal, ethical, and public policy analysis. It also proves to be an ongoing issue rich in complexity and of great interest to students. Regarding statutory law at the federal level, the evolution from the Tillman Act of 1907 to the 1974 Federal Election Campaign Act, to various regulations enacted by the Federal Elections

Commission (FEC), enables students to understand how and why issues emerge and return to the public policy agenda. The competing positions of interests like businesses, labor unions, Common Cause, the American Civil Liberties Union, and the political parties tend to provoke strong reactions, and in so doing also promote an understanding of the roles played by the various political actors in the public policy process (McFarland 1984; Malbin 1980; Magleby and Nelson 1990; Nugent and Johannes 1990; Sabato 1984). The polarized views of such interests also help students to understand the difficulties of achieving consensus on any public policy reform.

Discussion of the flow of First Amendment decisions by the Supreme Court, with particular emphasis on four leading cases, enables the students to understand the crucial differences between the higher level of protection provided for speech on issues and the lower level of protection provided for corporate speech on candidates. These cases also contain a lively debate on fundamental interests of liberty and equality, as they starkly demonstrate how the law embodies a tension between key normative concepts. The cases also address the critical issues of corruption, the potential for economic interests to contribute to corruption, and the need therefore to limit them.

Since the internal dynamics of PAC decisionmaking and the external impacts of PAC activities raise different kinds of normative questions, the subject is one that poses numerous ethical issues (Clawson, Neustadtl, and Scott 1992; Sorauf 1992). The multidimensional relationships between PACs and their contributors in executive ranks and the candidates whom they support pose deontological issues and issues of rights and distributive justice. Finally, managerial decisions confronting PACs regarding which candidates to support and which reforms to endorse raise questions of political strategy for students to ponder.

CONCLUSION

In a managerial environment that is experiencing constant change, business education must be able to be both responsive and proactive. As discussed earlier, business education and business ethics education in particular are at a significant crossroads. We have argued that traditional ways of delivering course content are seriously flawed in a number of ways.

In the traditional curriculum the student is left to discern whether and to what extent discipline-based courses of study intersect or address similar issues. For example, curricula generally contain separate courses in law, ethics, or public policy. These courses study similar issues but each with a different focus. However, they all are deeply concerned with examining ways in which we define the terms of social cooperation on a societal and individual level. One attribute of the integrated approach, using case and legislative law, is the explicit, continuous demonstration of intersections and issues of joint concern by law, ethics, and public policy within a business context.

Our integrated values course has evolved as an issues-based course that attempts to engage students in understanding the relationships and responsibilities in their communities. The course continues to evolve, incorporating new ideas and approaches with each iteration of the class. We currently adopt a shrink wrap of texts as well as a course packet for new materials. One of the long-range goals of the teaching teams is to develop a text suited to this approach, since no single book currently contains all of the needed materials.

The integrated approach is conceptually and philosophically sound. However, implementation has uncovered a number of concerns and challenges. Among these are:

(1) Efficient Utilization of Faculty Resources. While this approach may be very effective in demonstrating multiple perspectives for a variety of issues, it has not been efficient. The course has generally required a team of two to overlap substantially in the classroom, and there is a heightened need for coordination in all aspects of the course. Thus inefficiencies exist in utilizing faculty at the level of individual faculty time and at the college.

(2) Positioning of the Course. The values courses are currently taken about halfway into a student's course of study in order to have maximum value. Exposure, especially to ethical issues, might be better placed earlier in the curriculum. Indeed, we have

experimented with placing a separate ethics course as the first course in another MBA program, and this has been effective in terms focusing on the notion of a learning community and students' responsibilities to one another.

(3)   Alternative Models for Content and Delivery. While the micro/macro organization has appeared to be well received, there likely are other models of delivery that should be explored. The call for business education reform continues unabated. A recent article deemed business education largely irrelevant by virtue of continuing to push arcane and unintelligible technical models as being the essential component of business curriculum while dismissing applied knowledge (Jennings 1994). In another call for reform, Trevino and McCabe (1994) advocate integrating ethics education into fuctional area courses and expanding ethics education to the program's "hidden curriculum" by developing and building just communities and "honorable business school communities."

Criticism persists and challenges remain. Given the current business and education environments, the only thing worse that failing in reform is not attempting reform at all. As Lawrence Kohlberg is reported to have said, "Anything worth doing is worth doing poorly." Of course, Kohlberg's observation is not advice to do poorly. Rather, it is to accept the inherent risk of doing poorly a project that is significant enough to explore areas where road maps do not exist. We have not done poorly, but have we have explored a new and serious landscape. Hopefully, we have left guideposts for those who follow.

REFERENCES

Barber, B. R. 1992. *An Aristocracy of Everyone: The Politics of Education and the Future of America*. New York: Ballantine Books.

Baumgartner, F. R., and B. G. Jones. 1993. *Agendas and Instability in American Politics*. Chicago: The University of Chicago Press.

Beauchamp, T. L., and N. E. Bowie, (eds.) 1993. *Ethical Theory and Business*. Englewood Cliffs, NJ: Prentice Hall.

Brenkert, G. G. 1993. "Strict Products Liability and Compensatory Justice." In T. L. Beauchamp and N. E. Bowie, eds., *Ethical Theory and Business*, 198–203. Englewood Cliffs, NJ: Prentice Hall.

Brock, D. 1993. *The Real Anita Hill: The Untold Story*. New York: The Free Press.

Byrne, J. A., and C. Hawkins. 1993, April 26. Executive Pay: The Party Ain't Over Yet. *Business Week*, 56–64.

Clawson, D., A. Neutsadtl, and D. Scott. 1992. *Money Talks: Corporate PACs and Political Influence*. New York: Basic Books.

Cowan, A. L. 1992, September 18. "Coming Clean on Executive Pay." *New York Times*, C1, C10.

De George, R. T. 1994. "Business as a Humanity: A Contradiction in Terms?" In T. L. Donaldson and R. E. Freeman, eds., *Business as a Humanity*, 11–32. New York: Oxford University Press.

Deutschman, A. 1991, Nov 4. "Dealing with Sexual Harassment." *Fortune*, 145, 148.

Dobrzynski, J. H. 1992, Mar 30. "Calpers Is Ready to Roar, but Will CEOs Listen?" *Business Week*, 44–45.

Evan, W. M., and R. E. Freeman. 1993. "A Stakeholder Theory of the Modern Corporation: Kantian capitalism." In T. L. Beauchamp and N. E. Bowie, eds., *Ethical Theory and Business*, 75–84. Englewood Cliffs, NJ: Prentice-Hall.

Goodpaster, K. E. 1993. "Business Ethics and Stakeholder Analysis." In T.L. Beauchamp and N.E. Bowie, eds., *Ethical Theory and Business*, 85–93. Englewood Cliffs, NJ: Prentice-Hall.

Gordon, R. A., and J. E. Howell. 1959. *Higher Education for Business*. New York: Columbia University Press.

Hayes, A. S. 1991, November 14. "Stroh's Harassment Suit Pits Feminists Against Groups That Defend Free Speech." *Wall Street Journal*, p. B5.

Johnson, D. 1994, May 11. "A Sexual Harassment Case to Test Academic Freedom." *New York Times*, p. A13.

Kingdon, J. W. 1984. *Agendas, Alternatives, and Public Policies*. New York: Harper Collins.

Leatherman, C. 1994, September 28. "Free Speech or Harassment?" *Chronicle of Higher Education*, p. A22.

Leonard, G. 1984, April. "The Great School Reform Hoax." *Esquire*.

Linden, B., and Lane. 1992, January 20. "Another Boom Ends." *Forbes*.

Magleby, D. B., and C. J. Nelson. 1990. *The Money Chase: Congressional Campaign Finance Reform*. Washington, D.C.: The Brookings Institution.

Malbin, M. J., ed. 1980. *Parties, Interest Groups, and Campaign Finance Laws*. Washington, D.C.: American Enterprise Institute for Public Policy Research.

Mayer, J., and J. Abramson. 1994. *Strange Justice: The Selling of Clarence Thomas*. Boston: Houghton Mifflin.

McFarland, A. S. 1984. *Common Cause: Lobbying in the Public Interest*. Chatham, NJ: Chatham House Publishers, Inc.

Moore, W. J. 1991, November 23. "Knocking the System." *National Journal*, 2844–49.

Nugent, M. L., and J. R. Johannes, eds. 1990. *Money, Elections and Democracy: Reforming Congressional Campaign Finance.* Boulder, CO: Westview Press, Inc.

Parkel, J. 1990. "Corporate Social Policy: The New Dimensions." In R. B. Hutton, ed., *The Keystone Project Proceedings.*

Phelps, T. M., and H. Winternitz. 1992. *Capitol Games: Clarence Thomas, Anita Hill, and the Story of a Supreme Court Nomination.* New York: Hyperion.

Pierson, F. C. 1959. *The Education of American Businessmen.* New York: McGraw-Hill.

Porter, L., and L. McKibben. 1988. *Management Education and Development: Drift or Thrust into the 21st Century.* New York: McGraw-Hill.

Posner, R. A. 1990. *The Problems of Jurisprudence.* Cambridge, MA: Harvard University Press.

Sabato, L. J. 1984. *PAC Power: Inside the World of Political Action Committees.* New York: W. W. Norton and Company, Inc.

Sandroff, R. 1992, June. "Sexual Harassment: The Inside Story." *Working Woman,* 47–51, 78.

Smith, P., ed. 1993. *The Nature and Process of Law: An Introduction to Legal Philosophy.* New York: Oxford University Press.

Sorauf, F. J. 1992. *Inside Campaign Finance: Myths and Realities.* New Haven, CT: Yale University Press.

Spiro, G. W. 1993. *The Legal Environment of Business: Principles and Cases.* Englewood Cliffs, NJ: Prentice Hall.

Trevino, L. K., and D. McCabe. 1994. "Meta-Learning about Business Ethics: Building Honorable Business School Communities." *Journal of Business Ethics,* 13, 405–16.

Velasquez, M. G. 1993. "The Ethics of Consumer Production." In T. L. Beauchamp and N. E. Bowie, eds., *Ethical Theory and Business,* 189–97. Englewood Cliffs, NJ: Prentice Hall.

Wayne, L. 1993, July 16. "Exporting Shareholder Activism." *New York Times,* C1–C2.

Wayne, L. 1994, January 30. "Have Shareholder Activists Lost Their Edge?" *New York Times,* F7.

CHAPTER 4

An Outcomes-Centered Approach to Teaching Public-Sector Ethics

DAVID T. OZAR

Little communication has taken place between academic philosophers who specialize in ethics and public administration ethics faculty. The distance is unfortunate because they could likely learn a lot from each other, as the Utah experience discussed in chapter 2 shows. There are, for example, important patterns to be observed in how practitioners learn about ethical matters, and these patterns in moral learning have important implications for teaching.

This chapter offers a proposal regarding the appropriate outcomes for the teaching of public-sector ethics by identifying similarities between ethics teaching in that arena and the teaching of ethics in other parts of the academy (in my case medicine, nursing, dentistry, and additional health professions, see, e.g., Ozar, 1993) as well as professional groups such as lawyers, engineers, court employees, court managers, and child welfare workers in the public sector. The analysis focuses on outcomes because one of the fruits of reflecting on teaching, especially when combined with work done by my spouse (Ozar, L., 1994), is a set of steps for curriculum design.

BACKGROUND

The outcomes-centered approach focuses the teacher's attention on *outcomes,* a term that is here used without the behaviorist and quantitative connotations that many faculty in ethics will want to resist. What the focus means is that the professor begins the process of designing an educational activity—whether a single class, a unit, a course, or a whole degree program—by asking what the students ought to be able to do, or do better, when they finish it that they could not do, or do as well, when they began. This is the first step in an outcomes-centered process for curriculum design.

The second step is for the professor to ask how he or she will know whether the students have accomplished the outcomes aimed at in the class, unit, course, or program. Clearly if professors do not know how to tell if the students have accomplished the intended outcomes, they have no dependable way of knowing if the students accomplish them. In practice, professors are often quite confident that their students are accomplishing the intended learning, especially if the students do well on tests. But such confidence would be much more justified if professors were clear and articulate about the basis of these judgments, since many of the tests used are designed without any direct reference to the intended learning outcomes.

This assessment step is by far the hardest. The effort to articulate how one will know that one's students are achieving the intended outcomes often forces an instructor to return to the first step and reexamine the proposed outcomes. It frequently forces a person engaged in curriculum planning to become much more precise and concrete about the outcomes intended, in order for them to be the sorts of things about which the teacher can answer the assessment question; that is, the kind of activities whose presence or absence the instructor can in fact dependably assess. I can no longer be content, for example, with saying that I want ethics students to understand some approach to moral reflection. This is a worthy aim for a unit, but it is not precise or concrete enough to be an assessable outcome.

Instead, they now need to be able to explain that approach, to identify features of a concrete case that are relevant to that approach, and to articulate a reasoned judgment about the case that uses that approach. These three activities—explaining, identifying, and articulating a reasoning process—are assessable activities in a way that understanding is not. It is often valuable to have stated aims, but such statements frequently cannot effectively identify outcomes until they are translated into assessable activities about which the professor can dependably determine the student's ability.

Assessable activities are not limited to the overly-narrow range of observable, countable behaviors that the behaviorists attend to. In particular, many of the activities assessed in outcomes-centered teaching are instances of discourse, both interpersonal communication and an individual's expression of his or her own thoughts. So the worries about behaviorism and quantification that the language of "outcomes" sometimes prompts are unfounded in this approach. Notice also that the chief purpose of assessing of student performances is to determine how effectively the students are learning and the professor is teaching, not to rank the students into grades so they can be duly credentialed (or not) when the course is over. The outcomes-centered approach tries to keep a sharp distinction between the professor's efforts to assess student learning in order to enhance it further, and the activities of grading and credentialing which are not chiefly educational in their aims.

The third step of this curriculum-design process is the development of appropriate teaching strategies to help the students achieve the outcomes. But only when the first two steps have been carefully undertaken is one ready to proceed to this third step. It is only when the professor has identified appropriate outcomes for the learning activity, and then determined how to assess the students' achievement of these outcomes, that the professor is ready to focus narrowly on the means available for helping students achieve these outcomes. To select textbooks, develop a syllabus, determine what will be the order and content of individual assignments, and so on, prior to this point in the process makes no sense. This does not mean, of course, that looking at potential textbooks, readings, or assignments before this juncture would be foolish. It does mean that looking at them before this point should be for the purpose of identifying appropriate learning outcomes and assessment tools, for it is literally aimless to begin developing teaching strategies if the first two steps of the process have not been completed.

This approach turns what appears to be standard practice on its head. Many faculty first ask what material and what books will be taught, then they teach these materials, and subsequently they design the tests to match what has been taught. They look at the course's outcomes, if at all, only when the term is over and the course is being evaluated. That approach may have been more or less effective for many, but as a plan for coherent curriculum design, it makes no sense at all. If professors want to proceed coherently and efficiently, they have to begin with the outcomes. Instructors have to begin by asking what the students ought to be able to do or do better when they finish the class, unit, course, or program that they could not do or do as well when they began.

PROFESSIONAL AND PUBLIC-SECTOR ETHICS EDUCATION

With this set of steps for curriculum design as a guide, this chapter will examine what sorts of outcomes are appropriate for ethics teaching programs for public employees. Some parts of the answer will pertain to an employee's activities in a particular job or role in a given bureau, and these matters will be too specific for careful consideration here. But there are important general patterns in the learning of ethics by, and the teaching of ethics to, members of the professions that can shed light on the question.

There are two important similarities for present purposes between the members of a profession and public-sector employees. The first similarity is that the members of both groups perform in a specific and fairly well defined social role. Because of this, there are standards of conduct to which they are held responsible whose content is not chiefly for them to determine. Instead the content of these standards is the product of complex processes, some quite overt and others extremely subtle, by which that role is defined and proper conduct within it is identified within the community that has this role. In a similar way, within each of the professions, the current content of the ethic of that profession is the product of an ongoing dialogue, sometimes very clear but often informal and nearly invisible, between members of the community whom the profession serves and members of the expert group that makes up the profession.

This point is akin to that which Rohr (1989) makes when he speaks of "regime" values. This chapter will use the expression *conventional standards* to refer to the fact that the particular values, principles, and ideals that are to guide the conduct of persons who undertake a particular social role are determined by the members of the community. These determinations may be overt or covert, simple or complex, relatively stable or easily changed; but they are the source of the content of the standards of conduct of the members of professional and public-sector employees.

This means that the moral understanding and reflective skills of the ordinary adult, which students ideally bring to the professional or public-sector educational enterprise, are not likely to be sufficient. It will not do, in other words, to focus simply on the traits of character and the modes of moral reflection that enable an adult to be a decent ethical person in his or her ordinary life. There is a distinct set of conventional standards to be applied in that role, and therefore there is an additional set of skills that will be needed. Nor is this simply a matter of learning a new set of rules and then following them. The values, principles, and ideals that serve as the standards of any social role, if that role is important enough to educate for, cannot be compiled in a behavioral code or a set of simple algorithms. The aim should be that students learn how to discern these conventional standards and apply them in a manner that goes beyond mere conformity to the simplest strictures among them.

To make this point in the language of "aims" or "objectives," which will be translated into outcomes in a moment, leading public administration students from ignorance to compliance certainly is important. But we want to lead them further. When they move from compliance to understanding and support, they will see the reasons for what is required and what is restricted and what is striven for. When they move from understanding and support to conviction and good judgment, they will affirm the values that ground those reasons and can thus make judgments that support them in conflicted situations.

The second point of similarity between members of professions and public-sector employees is that both groups are in positions of power; they affect the lives of others in ways over which those so affected have little capacity for timely oversight or effective control. Physicians, nurses, and dentists, for example, possess the expertise to relieve pain and suffering, and patients depend on them in order to regain or retain control over important aspects of their physical—and

possibly psycho-social—functioning. Rohr (1989) has argued effectively
that public sector employees similarly have power to affect the lives
of people outside the government. One reason for this, he argues, is
that public sector employees who are employed and evaluated on the
basis of merit are not subject to election and so are not subject to the
oversight and control of those whose lives they affect.

In both instances, among professionals and within the public
sector, the larger community would be unwise to permit such power
to be exercised altogether unobserved and unchecked. But the mechanisms of oversight and control that are employed in relation to elected
officials, for example, would produce profound costs and inefficiencies if applied to either the professions or the vast numbers of public-
sector employees needed to carry out the work of government. Luckily
there is an alternative check on the misuse of this power, which has
proven remarkably efficient in protecting the larger community from
harm at the hands of expert groups and merit system public employees. It consists in the community's establishing a set of conventional
standards for those who undertake these roles and in educating the
whole community, from their mothers' and fathers' knees onward,
that anyone who undertakes such a role is bound by the conventional
standards of that role.

Because the community as a whole accepts the general convention
that these particular social roles shall be governed by specific conventional values, principles, and ideals, it follows that anyone who undertakes one of these roles is so obligated. Much more could be said about
these points of similarity and what they can teach us about aims or
objectives for ethics education for these two groups, and in turn about
appropriate outcomes. But now it is time to discuss outcomes directly.

OUTCOMES FOR ROLE-BASED ETHICS EDUCATION

The developmental psychologist James Rest has distinguished four
deficits that moral education is striving to help learners overcome and
that also serve as the principal explanations for people's inappropriate
conduct (Rest 1983, 1984, 1989). With some interpretive additions, the
first three deficits are (1) Awareness (lack of sensitivity to what is

ethically at stake in the situation); (2) Reasoning and other reflective skills (leading to incorrect judgments about what ought to be done); and (3) Motivation/Conviction (deficits in the person's willingness to give priority over other considerations to the values, principles, or ideals that prompt the action that ought to be done). To these, I add (4) Implementation (inability to implement the course of action that one has judged ought to be done).

It is easy to say that the aim of role-based ethics education ought to be that students overcome each of these deficits in relation to their role-based conduct, insofar as they presently suffer them. But that suggests a question of great importance that can be addressed only briefly here. The first step in identifying outcomes has to be identifying the baseline from which the learning begins. What is it that the students can already do, to which this new learning adds and on which it will be built?

The answer is based on the author's generalizations from teaching students in the health professions, most of whom have not had a rich, well-rounded liberal education as an undergraduate, but have rather fulfilled undergraduate distribution requirements while focusing on preprofessional courses. It seems likely that many students in public administration would come to a public sector ethics course or program with comparable background. But the reader should make appropriate adjustments if the baseline of his or her students is typically different from what is described. The student envisioned here is an adult with at least the following baseline "credentials" in the four areas just identified:

(1) Awareness: The students have a significant (that is, conduct-affecting) awareness of such general values as life, health, personal autonomy or self-determination, integrity, and social cooperation, together with Rohr's three "regime" principles of equality, freedom, and respect for property, and personal ideals consistent with these values and principles.

(2) Reasoning/Reflective Skills: They have the ability to reason logically on simple issues and an understanding of the general relation of premises to conclusions, but little grasp of the characteristic

modes, elements, or patterned contents of moral reasoning/re-
flection in terms that are either communicable to others or functional as tests of the quality of their own reasoning/reflection.

(3)   Motivation/Conviction: The students have given little thought
       to the reasons for having conventional role-based standards, much
       less to the specific values, principles, and ideals grounding the
       actual standards of typical public-sector roles, and so they have
       little effective motivation/conviction regarding these standards
       specifically; yet they understand that there are such conventional
       standards for these roles, and ordinarily they are sincerely moti-
       vated, from a variety of forms of both personal and possibly
       social motivation/conviction, to later perform such roles success-
       fully and therefore to learn to do so now.

(4)   Implementation: Since implementation depends on concrete un-
       derstanding of the practice setting in some detail, the students
       have little grasp of any situation-specific challenges to imple-
       mentation of their role-specific obligations or of the situation-
       specific resources available in typical public sector roles; but they
       do have ordinary young-adult abilities to resolve impediments
       to appropriate action.

If these are the baseline characteristics of the students in professional or public sector ethics, then the following learning outcomes
seem appropriate for an ethics curriculum, divided again into the four
categories with the second category further subdivided and the third
and fourth reversed:

(1)   Awareness: The students' awareness of the values, principles,
       and ideals, already indicated as the baseline, should grow to be
       an articulate awareness of these values, principles, and ideals.
       The students should be able to identify which of them are at
       stake in a wide range of typical cases and issues in a variety of
       public-sector employment situations. The students should also
       become articulately aware that these values, principles, and ide-
       als are often mutually exclusive in concrete situations requiring

action (that is, aware of moral/ethical "dilemmas"), and so become aware of the value of moral reflection in addressing such situations. The students' articulate awareness should also include any other values, principles, or ideals that are relevant to any more specific or more specialized role within public service for which a particular group of students is specifically preparing.

(2) (a) Reasoning/Reflective Skills, Content, and Limits: *Skills.* The students should become capable of giving articulate examples of ethical reasoning which is: logical (the conclusion follows from the reasons given and no important steps among the reasons are omitted), clear (key terms and concepts explained if necessary and used consistently), and careful (key presuppositions of the reasoning are articulated; familiar and important objections are acknowledged and answered if possible). Their examples of reasoning should take explicit account of the values, principles, and ideals already mentioned, as well as any other moral considerations not directly related to their role but potentially competing with the values, principles, and ideals that ground it, and should offer reasons in terms of those values, principles, and ideals for the conclusion proposed. The cases/issues discussed should include a wide range of typical cases and issues in a variety of public-sector employment situations. In student discussions of cases/issues, they should correctly and usefully employ the various conceptual tools provided them to assist their moral reasoning/reflection.[1]

(b) Reasoning/Reflective Skills: *Content.* The student should be able to identify the more specialized standards of conduct relevant to typical public-sector roles and explain how the values, principles, and ideals which ground the standards of conduct of public-sector roles serve to ground specific standards for these roles. They should be able to explain the implications of these standards in typical cases drawn from practice in these roles. The student should be able to identify (but not from memory) sections of the Standards of Ethical Conduct for Employees of the Executive Branch, or some other standard code of conduct, that are relevant to typical cases in the practice of typical public-sector roles (or from the relevant code of conduct, if one exists, for any specific or specialized public-sector role for which a particular group of students is being specifically prepared.) The student should also be able to explain, in general but clear terms, the reasons for the existence of conventional standards of conduct for public-sector employees in general.

(c)   Reasoning/Reflective Skills: *Recognition of Limits.* The student should be able to identify situations, from cases and issues discussed, in which his or her ability to reasonably resolve the ethical issues involved is at its limits and should be able to articulate a reasonable plan (of appropriate consultation, appropriate referring to higher authority, and so on) about how a person ought to proceed under such circumstances.

(3)   Implementation: Students should be prepared to describe typical hindrances to implementation of their moral judgments in typical public-sector roles and to describe typical resources available to public-sector employees for resolving these hindrances. Students preparing for a specific or specialized role should also be able to describe typical hindrances to implementation within that role and typical resources for resolving them there.

(4)   Motivation/Conviction: This is the hardest set of outcomes to describe because it is the hardest set of outcomes to assess. Assessment of affective outcomes is often more difficult than assessment of cognitive outcomes. Although awareness is an affective trait, one valued test of awareness is in discourse, so assessments of reasoning/reflective skills simultaneously yield assessments of awareness. But the most effective test of motivation/conviction is action, especially habituated action. Nevertheless, the following outcomes are at least a starting point for assessing students' achievement of outcomes in the category of motivation/conviction.

First, building on their baseline motivation/conviction to perform the role successfully, student discourse should indicate that respect for the relevant conventional standards is a matter of high priority for them, as are the general reasons for conventional standards for public sector employees' conduct and the reasons for typical examples of more specific standards.

Second, student discourse should indicate a similar concern regarding the relevant standards of conduct governing their lives, and they should act in accordance with those standards. That is, the relevant values, principles, and ideals should not only be evident in their discourse about their future lives in public service and about hypothetical situations, but also in the way they act. Third, they should typically respond to cases, issues, and other scenarios in ways supportive of other actors acting consistently with these priorities.

ASSESSMENT

Assessment of cognitive outcomes is done by way of eliciting relevant forms of discourse and evaluating it to see that the desired skills, content, and awareness of limits are evident. This can occur in both oral and written form, individually or in the forum of the class in discussion, or by some other mechanism. It is much more difficult to assess the student's achievement of affective outcomes. But as was just mentioned, awareness of moral values, principles, and ideals is significantly assessable through the role they play for the student in reasoning and other forms of moral reflection which are revealed in discourse. Consequently, students' achievement of awareness outcomes can be assessed in significant measure by means of the same discourse elicited to assess the student's achievement of cognitive outcomes, namely the categories of reasoning/reflective skills and implementation.

Most of the criteria employed in these assessments have already been identified in the statements of outcomes above. One complicating factor is that some students' limited writing and/or speaking skills, together with some shyness about speaking in class, prevents them from articulating their achievements, both cognitive and affective, as fully as they otherwise might. Proper preparation for their roles requires us to expect students to become articulate in these matters; that is why the outcomes are stated explicitly in terms of an *articulated* awareness of values and reasoning processes, and so on. This is especially true if we are genuinely committed to the objective of moving students past compliance to understanding and support, and past understanding and support to conviction and good judgment.

Here again we face the difficulty of assessing motivation/conviction. One's discourse is only a partial sign of these affective traits, although spontaneous discourse over a long period of time is a fairly dependable indicator, because it is ordinarily a sign of habituated views and values and so of conviction. But it is hard to make dependable judgments of motivation/conviction without evidence from conduct, and individual instances of conduct are not as dependable evidence of motivation/conviction as are patterns of conduct over time.

This is why the second outcome under motivation/conviction explicitly mentions the students' conduct in their present role as students. We need explicitly to link their conduct as students of a conventional role with the grounds for the standards of the role itself. This is not easily done when so many different roles are available in the public sector, so only the most general of grounds of public-sector standards are relevant to all students. It is made more difficult when the student in society is so readily conceptualized in terms of a market relationship in which the student is a consumer buying a product from the professor and the school. This state of affairs leads to the conviction that we have to seriously rethink the roles of student, teacher, and school to pursue outcomes in the realm of motivation/conviction effectively. This point is connected to an important component of moral education which has not been mentioned so far, namely, the powerful impact of role models in the formation of professional and other role-based values and ideals. This is a theme that would need to be developed in a fuller treatment of motivation/conviction in an outcomes-centered account of role-based ethics education.

TEACHING STRATEGIES

Finally, a few words on how to help students reach these outcomes, how to "teach to" these outcomes, are appropriate. The ethics teacher is not someone who tells other people how they ought to act in specific situations. He or she is first and last able to offer student only two things, though both are of substantial value for moral learning. First, the teacher can offer the conceptual tools to facilitate moral reasoning and reflection, and can model the use of these tools. This can be and should be done in many ways. It can be done by explaining the conceptual tool, employing it on a case or issue to model its use, coaching an individual student orally to use it in his or her own thinking, coaching a group of students or a whole class in its use by structuring a discussion of a case or issue to model the tool's proper use, and so on. Many of these same techniques can be used on students' written work as well.

Many of the most important decisions in the design of teaching strategies concern which of the many available sorts of conceptual tools to offer the students, and how much of the students' time and energy to devote to each, since that will ordinarily determine their degree of mastery of each. Also relevant is the determination of what sort of cases/issues to use, how many to use, and to what degree(s) of complexity. Staging the use of these materials properly is also a subtle matter, since some sets of conceptual tools or cases/issues will build more effectively on others. All of these matters need to be addressed with the fact centrally in mind that the teacher's aim is not to "finish the material." These decisions are strategic judgments meant to facilitate as much as possible student achievement of the intended outcomes.

Second, the professor is a role-model for the students, whether he or she wants it or not. Affective learning by adults occurs as a consequence of contact with a human model of a value, principle, or ideal (whether this model is actually living, or deceased, or fictional). The teacher is the students' primary model of the value of careful moral reasoning and reflection. In addition, teachers are models of the values, principles, and ideals that are the grounds of the community's conventional standards for its public-sector employees in general, as well as the more specific standards of conduct of more specific public-sector roles. The instructor may judge that some of those standards, and even some of those grounds, ought to be challenged. But even such challenges, and all aspects of the standards supported by the teacher, must always be in terms of moral grounds genuinely espoused and so modeled in his or her discourse and conduct.

In this respect, ethics teaching cannot be viewed as merely a strategic enterprise, for no one can dissemble to a whole class of students about his or her most genuine moral convictions for a whole term. The only possible strategy is genuinely to be yourself; if you are not convinced of the value of moral reasoning and reflection, if you believe it leads humankind nowhere valuable, or if you are not convinced of the general value of conventional institutions and of public-sector employment as one of them, then you must not teach in this field if you value integrity at all.

CONCLUSION

These reflections are certainly not a finished product, much less a thorough program for curriculum design in government ethics. They represent an attempt to outline the steps of an outcomes-centered process of curriculum design and to sketch the content of these steps in relation to a course or program in public-sector ethics. There are surely many gaps in this employment of the outcomes-centered approach; and the use made here of the author's teaching experience in the health professions may require professors of public-sector ethics to revise the proposed outcomes and assessments significantly. But the hope is that much of what has been offered here will translate into useful insights, that the outcomes-centered approach will prove a useful tool for their efforts at curriculum design, and that productive dialogue among teachers of ethics in many practical and professional fields will thereby be enhanced.

NOTE

1. Contact the author for "Model of Role-Based Ethical Decision-Making" as an example of the conceptual tools available.

REFERENCES

American Judicature Society. 1989. "AJS Model Code of Conduct for Non-Judicial Court Employees," drafted by D. T. Ozar, C. Kelly, and Y. Begue, *Judicature*, 73, 138–40.

Ozar, David T. 1993. "Building Awareness of Ethical Standards and Conduct," in Lynn Curry and Jon Wergin, eds., *Educating Professionals.* San Francisco: Jossey-Bass.

Ozar, Lorraine A. 1994. *Creating a Curriculum That Works: A Guide to Outcomes-Centered Curriculum Decision Making.* Washington, D.C.: National Catholic Education Association.

Rest, James R. 1994. "Background: Theory and Research," in James R. Rest and Dacia Narvaez, eds., *Moral Development in the Professions.* Hillsdale, N.J.: Lawrence Erlbaum Associates.

Rest, James R. 1984. "The Major Components of Morality," in W. Kurtines and J. Gewirtz, eds., *Morality, Moral Behavior, and Moral Development.* New York: Wiley.

Rest, James R. 1983. "Morality," in J. Flavell, E. Markham, and P. H. Mussen, eds., *Handbook of Child Psychology: Vol. 3, Cognitive Development.* New York: Wiley.

Rohr, John A. 1989. *Ethics for Bureaucrats,* 2nd ed. New York: Marcel Dekker, Inc.

PART II

Teaching Strategies: Inside the Academy

CHAPTER 5

Citizenship and the Policy Professional

JEFFREY MAYER AND ROBERT SEIDEL

The "Citizenship" course at Johns Hopkins University's Institute for Policy Studies (JHU/IPS) should be the signature academic experience in a Master's degree program that is dedicated to "training professional citizens." Like all good courses, however, IPS's citizenship course, as we presented it initially in the spring of 1994, is a work in progress. This chapter helps us assess that progress and gauge the distance to our ideal.

Three contextual points need explanation at the outset. First, by *professional citizens* we mean people who spend a significant part of their working lives in government, the nonprofit sector, or business developing solutions to public problems. Critics—some within the University itself—have argued that *professional citizenship* is an oxymoron, that true citizenship can only be practiced by amateurs. Our entering assumption is that these critics are wrong. The truth, we suspect, is that in modern industrial nation states, after centuries of intellectual specialization, professionals alone achieve that condition of sustained contemplation of the public good that Aristotle had in mind when he wrote (or spoke) into western political mythology the constitution of Athens.

Second, the course, which is largely a consideration of values, is embedded in a Master's program with a decidedly positive and practical bent. The bulk of the curriculum trains people in the skills of policy analysis and program evaluation. It teaches them about the policy process, about the economic foundations of public decision making, and about problems of implementation. The apparent clash of purpose and culture between our course and its pedagogical environment reverberates to some degree in class discussion and, more subtly, in students' study priorities. These effects, which are discussed at greater length below, may be mitigated—or aggravated—by the fact that "Citizenship" is a required course at IPS. In any case, we assert (and assert again) that the course is as relevant to practice as the rest of the curriculum.

Third, a particular research interest at IPS is the nature and role of private nonprofit institutions in society, and their relationships to both government and business. The teaching program likewise presents a multisectoral perspective on the policy process. This orientation shapes the Institute's corporate culture and the interests and expectations of its degree students. In contrast, the material and discussion in the citizenship course linger on conditions in large federal bureaucracies. This tendency, reflecting in part the accidents of our own experience, may lead some students to question the relevance of the whole endeavor.

The following sections of this chapter discuss objectives of the IPS citizenship course, the content of the course (as taught in 1994), problems we encountered, solutions we devised, and our ideas for defining and refining our product.

COURSE OBJECTIVES

The overarching purpose of the citizenship course is to encourage policy professionals-in-training to examine the premises of their enterprise at IPS and afterward: to reflect on values in public life and the value *of* public life; to look critically at institutions that train policy professionals; and to consider venues and conditions of the calling. The course is neither the beginning nor the end of such an examination. Rather, it is a structured opportunity in a demanding academic schedule for students to focus on their own objectives as well as the philosophical roots and institutional environments of their chosen profession.

Within this general framework, the readings, discussions, and writing projects planned for the course's 1994 incarnation had four particular purposes:

(1) To examine a central concept in the American political tradition, its European roots, and alternative ideas, and to deepen understanding of the democratic systems that, as professional citizens, most IPS students will ultimately serve.

(2) To explore the idea of professional citizenship and the development of institutions at American universities dedicated to the preparation of professional citizens. As we have suggested, there is debate within JHU about the value of this idea itself.

(3) To sample the character of the profession, that is, to consider aspects and venues of the bureaucratic condition. In this pursuit, as noted, we are somewhat limited by our own experience. One of us is a long-time student of the policy arts working in an academic setting, the other a senior career civil servant at the U.S. Department of Commerce. Together, our direct experience of professional citizenship and what we call "the bureaucratic condition" are restricted to the university and the federal government, and to our similar recollections of the radical politics of our aging generation. The lore brought to the classroom, gathered in these places and times, adds life to the discussions. Emphases implicit in the approach, however, do not always square with the experience and expectations of students.

(4) To exercise writing skills that are part of the foundation of personal and collective bureaucratic and political power. Good bureaucratic writing is clear and simple. In essence, it is good teaching. It makes complicated issues accessible to nonspecialists with short attention spans. Such writing may also persuade or arm a principal to defend established ground. It does its work quickly without intellectual hubris. And it is always delivered on time. The advantage it confers on the policy professional comes partly from the fact that in bureaucracy good writers are few.

In addition to these, the readings and discussions revealed at least two objectives that were not explicit in the original course plan. One, an examination of the value of a life involved with public issues, as opposed, for example, to a life involved with amassing wealth or making art, simply fell out of a comparative reading of Aristotle and Hobbes on the relation of the individual to the state. The second, a consideration of models of public life, was a by-product of our presentation of many readings by writers who were themselves professional citizens of an exceptional and diverse order—philosophers and scientists with political instincts and practical purposes.

Along the way, we were also obliged to lower at least one key expectation: that class discussions would produce a shared notion of the connotations and gradations of professional citizenship. On these points, despite our most emphatic efforts, divergence persists.

COURSE CONTENT

In the spring of 1994, "Citizenship and the Policy Professional" was offered as a weekly two-hour seminar to a dozen students: eight first-year Master's degree candidates, three one-year fellowship students from Eastern Europe, and a nondegree student working in the Baltimore City Government. Readings, though limited in length (on average, 100–150 pages a week), were substantively and at times stylistically demanding. Writing assignments included a term paper and five short exercises related to the readings and approximating formats that policy professionals use, such as issue briefs, talking points, policy guidance memoranda, and official correspondence.

The course was structured in three unequal parts, with what we hoped would be a rousing final session. The first eight weeks were devoted mainly to tracing the history of the classical idea of citizenship, from Aristotle to Jefferson to John Stuart Mill, and to the consideration of some critical perspectives on that idea (for example, Hobbes and Marx on the purposes of political action). In one session, however, we ventured outside this essentially western debate to examine some non European and premodern ideas, including Confucian, Iroquoian, and BaMbuti (Central African) concepts, about the relationship between individuals and society.

In weeks nine and ten, "training professional citizens" was a subject as well as an object of discussion. That is to say, we reviewed the origins and development of the idea that governance is a job for experts, and we examined intellectual and institutional factors at play in the emergence of public administration and public policy as distinct fields of study at American universities.

In weeks eleven and twelve, aspects of the bureaucratic condition were considered. In the first of these sessions, for reasons already explained, we focused on the work environment in the senior echelons of the federal civil service. However, the subjects discussed, including power, turf, institutional culture, tension between personal and organizational values, are common to government at every level and, in some degree, to all large organizations. Of these subjects, power is the most important. Access to power raises the contemplation of public issues to the level of citizenship. For policy professionals in government service, power is never exclusive and rarely direct. But the opportunity to influence events is real, and it is a primary appeal of the professional citizen's calling.

In the next session (week twelve), the global environment of the policy profession were examined. In the last two decades, institutions of multinational governance have gained new prominence because of several truly historic developments, such as integration of the global economy; the ending of the Cold War, which has opened the way for greater multinational cooperation in pursuit of collective security; a widening awareness that nations must work together to solve problems of environmental degradation, disease, poverty, population growth, and mass migration. These developments increase the likelihood that our students will practice professional citizenship on a global scale somewhere in the international civil service or in other contexts dealing with implications of the new realities.

For the thirteenth and final week we planned some intellectual fireworks and bought pizza for the class (offering circuses and bread before we distributed our course evaluation forms). We invited two senior Hopkins political scientists, one a leading exponent and the other an outspoken critic of the idea of professional citizenship, and we waited to see what would happen.

Of course, our subjects refused the bait. One proved sensible and conciliatory; the other developed a scheduling conflict at the eleventh hour. With only one side represented, conditions seemed ripe for reaching consensus. Alas, the effort foundered, not on the question of whether citizenship can be a profession, but on the issue of exclusivity, that is, whether the citizenship practiced by a policy professional (in government, a think tank, or an interest group) is distinguishable from the citizenship practiced by a corporate CEO who creates good jobs or a conscientious maintenance worker at the Capitol Building.

QUESTIONS AND ANSWERS

In a course that is nominally about values, are values taught? This is a particular case of the old chestnut in pedagogy: Should the teacher attempt to present a balanced survey of the range of major approaches to a given problem rather than focusing on the approach he or she endorses? There are at least three broad areas where values come into play for the policy professional:

(1)   The threshold choice between a life of constant and informed engagement with public issues and alternative career pursuits, such as the choice between Aristotle's and Hobbes's notions of the "good life," that is, between active engagement in democratic policymaking and the pursuit of a civilized and materially comfortable private life secured by sovereign power.

(2)   Ethics of the profession itself, for example, how to balance personal and organizational values; what to do if the boss says "cook the numbers."

(3)   Applications of general value systems, including views of social justice, ideas about the responsibilities of government, to problems of public life.

The first of these considerations became a major focus of discussion in the early weeks of the semester. Of course, most students, having decided to invest substantial time and money in graduate policy studies, had already examined threshold issues for themselves with varying degrees of self-awareness. The objective, therefore, was to reinvigorate that self-awareness and to enrich each student's reflection by placing it in the context of classical discussions of citizenship. We also suggested that the choice of lives is not completely rational. People find excitement and satisfaction in public life because of who they are. The policy profession is a calling. Not everyone receives the call.

We tended to treat the second area—professional ethics—as a corollary to individuals' development of their identities as professional citizens. This does not mean that responses to ethical challenges come automatically or easily to the self-conscious policy professional. Practical applications of professional principles can be as challenging as the application of physical theories to engineering problems. It is one thing to determine to organize your life around the solution of public problems; it is quite another to respond to conflicting interests among clients or constituents, and still another to know how to respond when your boss pressures you to "cook the numbers." In deciding what to cover, however, we favored the general over the particular. If we decide to expand examination of the bureaucratic condition in future editions of the course, we may spend more time on issues of professional ethics.

The third area—application of general value systems to issues of public life—seems to us the most challenging. The subject can be approached in at least two ways: by taking alternative value systems and their policy implications as a subject of study, like comparative religion, or by engaging explicitly or implicitly in the promotion of a particular philosophy or group perspective. In 1994, choosing either path was resisted. Part of our concern was practical. Along with other things we hoped to do, serious consideration of ideas of social justice and their applications to particular policy choices would have taken more than the allotted thirteen weeks. But the indecision also reflected a mutual reluctance to debate, between ourselves or with the class, the proper uses of a university, and a desire to avoid the risk of holding personal values too close to the light. It is acknowledged that some may see our hesitation on this question as a tacit defense of a broadly drawn status quo.

To be more precise, we presented Aristotle, Jefferson, Mill, and others as classic proponents of a set of democratic and humane values which seem to have inspired American policy development since the earliest years of the republic. We offered Marx and Alinsky as critics *within* that cultural heritage. And we sampled other interpretations of the relationship between individuals and society (such as Confucian ideas), given differences in technology, social scale, and environmental conditions.

The Euro-American democratic tradition is the ideological context of the JHU Policy Studies program and the citizenship course. In the 1994 course, therefore, we did not put on masks of false nonsectarianism and offer equal time to Confucius. We did, however, treat him and others with respect and encourage similar behavior from the students.

The aim for the class (including ourselves), after all, was to hone our conceptions of ourselves, our traditions, and the profession of citizenship. We (instructors) would hardly have expected to penalize students for disagreeing with us, but we did mean to challenge them to articulate their positions and purposes. And we agreed that the legitimacy of the challenge depended on our willingness and ability to do the same.

Is "professional citizenship" more than a slogan? The answer is "yes." As noted, however, we had considerable difficulty reaching agreement on what professional citizenship really means. The entering definition was Aristotle's own, transposed to an era of industrialized and democratic nation-states. Like Aristotle, it is meant to suggest that a life of continuous engagement with the common problems of society is a "good life"—a life that fulfills high human potential and, therefore, brings happiness to those able to live it.

Resistant to Aristotelian extremism, however, we noted that taste and talent for public life might not be defining human qualities, that other models of human potential and the good life were at least plausible. It is also argued that today, for most people, sustained and informed concern with public issues requires compensation; the purest citizenship *is* professional.

Needless to say, many students and even other IPS faculty had difficulty hearing this message. Some found it hard to divorce the Aristotelian ideal from its economic and social context and to apply it to their own experience. Others rejected the inherent elitism of an ideal of citizenship centered on the exercise of intellect. Some faculty suggested that too much specificity in the definition of professional citizenship could hinder vigorous program development.

It is not suggested that citizenship is or ought to be the exclusive domain of professionals. Moreover, given the depth and complexity of the troubles besetting society today, it is questionable whether any of us will find fulfillment (if that requires enduring social peace) without some level of active engagement with community problems. For the good of all, people who spend their lives mostly in other pursuits must also find time to cast informed votes and even to participate in neighborhood associations, political parties, and volunteer service organizations. To the extent that professional citizens do not share in such activities while accepting the burdens of private citizens in a democratic republic, they seem to invite questions about the practical relevance and emotional depth of their dedication to solving public problems. Professional citizens, to be complete, may need to be amateur citizens as well.

How do we convince students of the relevance of the course material? Most of the IPS core curriculum focuses on strengthening students' abilities in policy analysis, expanding their knowledge of analytic tools and the institutions and processes of policy making. A number of these courses are quantitative, courses in which answers, however well reasoned, can be wrong, and they impart a knowledge of technique that is widely valued by future employers. We have wondered more than once whether a course promising less clear-cut payback and less categorical performance measures could compete successfully with the rest of the IPS core program for the time, attention, and respect of veteran students.

One solution that was tried was to be engaging. We are uncertain whether we succeeded and, in any case, we are inclined with Machiavelli to conclude that for most purposes love is a less reliable motive than respect (or fear).

A second strategy was the design of the course itself. We attempted to make the material directly relevant to students' experience as students by examining citizenship as a professional identity and by considering the intellectual and organizational politics that have accompanied the creation of public policy programs at American universities. In addition, when the material lent itself to the purpose, the class was urged to consider authors' practical concerns and personal objectives. Finally, we offered academic and personal perspectives on the bureaucratic condition and augmented the presentation with short exercises in the kinds of writing that policy professionals are regularly asked to do.

CONCLUSION

We have continued to discuss issues that were only half understood, or understood but unresolved, in 1994. A semester of experience and the discipline of writing this chapter helped to see some things more clearly and to approach the course with more coherent purpose, especially with regard to the three questions discussed above.

On the most fundamental question, whether courses that address social values should also impart them, joint reflection has produced two conclusions. One of these is that the question is a trap, a debate always driven by moral passion and silenced by peer pressure, and for our purposes a place to visit perhaps, but not a place to stay. The other is that, implicitly at least, all courses impart values. Certainly ours does. The decision to focus on a political ideal of personal fulfillment is also a decision not to focus on other ideals, such as social struggle, economic justice, or the reaffirmation of community experience and values. The method of reasoned discourse itself is often offensive to zealots. We believe that our course would benefit from more transparency on these points.

In general, the answer is that we recognize a responsibility to put alternatives on the table, to acknowledge our orientation, and to make the best case we can for it, while referring to at least some alternatives. Also, it is likely that two instructors who are team-teaching will not be in perfect harmony on all points. Their interaction on disputed points may encourage general openness in the classroom and demonstrate the desirability of exploring reasoned alternatives on any given question.

On the definition of professional citizenship, we have resolved to live with ambiguity and let our students wrestle with the question themselves. We know what we think.

Capturing student energy and commitment is a continuing challenge. We have considered ways to tweak the syllabus, like spending more time on the practical aspects of professional citizenship and on nonwestern views of the relation between individuals and society; perhaps adding a session on the psychological roots of political behavior. And we have solemnly resolved to be even more engaging.

CHAPTER 6

Teaching Professional Ethics: Addressing the "Algorithmic Thinker"

JOHN G. POMERY

This chapter describes a teaching method developed to encourage moral sensitivity among students who exhibit a strong tendency to algorithmic thinking. In some areas of applied ethics, instructors experience great difficulty in presenting ethics to highly quantitative students from technically oriented disciplines.[1] These difficulties reflect the expectations of such learners that important questions necessarily have unambiguous answers, accessible to rational and logical persons through the application of well defined models. These students tend to be impatient with the perceived ambiguity and inconclusiveness of ethical theories and consequently are likely to reject or devalue ethics as a second-class conversation. In addition, where ethical theories implicitly conflict with received views about "invisible-hand" coordination of individual preferences (as in economics or finance) or with other discipline-specific presuppositions about the individual and society (such as notions of power in political science, self-concepts, locus of control, and theories of motivation in social psychology), the latter views are likely to be given absolute precedence.

Since algorithmic thinkers are prone to devalue any direct approach to moral reasoning, an indirect method may be more successful. To be successful, such an indirect method should: (a) initially be consistent with learners' heavy valuing of logical reasoning; (b) be able to generate, over time, some tolerance of ambiguity and of the presence of a human dimension in discussions; and (c) lead to acceptance of ethics as a valued topic, with a balanced position relative to the received perspectives of other academic disciplines. These requirements are quite demanding and suggest a need for a subtle line of attack. Such an approach tends to be time-consuming and to require a classroom environment that offers the opportunity for experiential learning where students feel comfortable exploring unfamiliar perspectives.

One premise underlying the author's method is that ambiguities inherent in moral conversation are not peculiar to the subject matter of ethics and morality. Rather, such ambiguities arise from structures of arguments found, but often ignored, in very mundane contexts. Moreover, these ambiguities frequently emerge in policy (or application) contexts, where debate can revolve around the appropriate way to frame a particular situation or about contentious definitional claims. Highly quantitative students in algorithm-oriented disciplines such as engineering or finance may encounter ethical difficulties because their technical focus excludes any room for relevant, but potentially dissonant, ethical sensitivity.

The teaching approach described here includes three key characteristics. First, students encounter undeniable examples of ambiguity and pluralism. These encounters are reinforced by presentation of logical and psychological theories which suggest the ubiquity of such ambiguity. Second, these encounters are carefully sequenced, from initial examples that are mundane, concrete, and impersonal, to later situations involving economic, political, and legal institutions. This sequencing is designed to minimize conflict with students' entrenched beliefs about the value of unambiguous conclusions and the power of technical perspectives. Third, the method uses devices, such as discussion topics and journal entries, to encourage reflection and a willingness to explore unfamiliar ways of thinking. In effect, the students are being invited to embark on a process of reconceptualizing their understanding of themselves, their discipline, their knowledge, and their role in society. Such a reconceptualization requires that students encounter new and plausible mental models. They make that encounter in a learning atmosphere that is open and affirming, and which supports voluntary experimentation with, and assimilation of, these mental models.

The next section of this chapter places aspects of this teaching approach and its presuppositions within the broader context of several literatures. The subsequent two sections describe in more detail some of the major features of the several courses taught by the author using this method. A concluding section discusses possible implications for the pedagogy of applied ethics, followed by an addendum reflecting on a problem-solving evaluation of the approach.

BACKGROUND

Algorithmic Thinkers

The term *algorithmic thinkers* is intended to overlap with a number of concepts (noted below), often better established or more familiar to many readers. Algorithmic thinkers are characterized as being committed to rational, unemotional, logic-based thinking; as valuing closure and lack of ambiguity; and as valuing their discipline-specific ways of thinking. As such, a stereotypical algorithmic thinker may well be a "linear" thinker, or in other terminology, one who learns and thinks sequentially as opposed to globally.[2] Yet the stereotypical algorithmic thinker has characteristics that may go beyond a narrow conception of linear thinking. Such thinkers are heavily committed to received ways of thinking, that is, to ways of thinking that have proved successful and have the authority of their academic discipline. They also have a presumption that important issues have clear-cut answers, once they are correctly presented and reasoned through with the appropriate algorithm.

The emphasis on closure and on reliance on logic, rather than on feelings or emotions, fits well with the distinction between so-called masculine-style thinking and feminine-style thinking. Masculine thinkers are characterized as focusing on outcomes, using competitive and confrontational methods to resolve disputes, and valuing logic and reason above all else. In contrast, so-called feminine-style thinkers pay much more attention to process and to relationships, allow more value to feelings, and prefer consensus building and conciliation in dispute resolution.[3]

In terms of the widely known Myers-Briggs personality typology, algorithmic thinkers are likely to be found amongst Ts rather than

Fs; that is, they tend to make decisions based on logical justification and reason ("Thinking") rather than on the basis of whether the decision feels right ("Feeling"). They are also likely to be found amongst Js rather than Ps; that is, they have a strong preference for closure and for absence of loose or dissonant ends ("Judgmental" in Myers-Briggs terminology), rather than tolerating loose ends, lack of closure, and ambiguity ("Perceptual"). More open to debate in terms of sources of information, they may be more likely to be Ss than Ns; that is, they rely more on concrete data ("Sensing") rather than patterns and analogies ("intuitive") in assimilating information. Also less clear-cut, Is ("Introverts") may be more self-sufficient in their reasoning and possibly more entrenched in their views than Es ("Extroverts").[4]

Another area of overlap is with creative thinking, as emphasized in the area of gifted education.[5] One of the prime concerns of educational practitioners in this area is to establish "avoidance of premature closure." Algorithmic thinking might be seen, in part, as obliviousness to—or, alternatively, a commitment to ignore—the dangers of premature closure. However, note that gifted education puts a major emphasis on (good) decisionmaking, whereas the author's teaching method tends to encourage learners to become comfortable with some absence of closure. In sum, algorithmic thinking is not intended to be a totally novel concept, but is to be thought of as closely related to a number of constructs found in social and educational psychology.[6]

Skirmishes in Academia and Beyond

The ideas underlying this teaching approach also reflect an attitude ("position" may be too strong a term) on a variety of wars and skirmishes that exist in contemporary society. Positions taken in these battles have major implications for how teachers and students situate ethics in relation to other areas of study. Put loosely but fairly succinctly, we (collectively) possess useful concepts such as *knowledge, objectivity, subjectivity, truth;* at the same time, what we understand by these terms is heavily dependent on positions taken, sometimes without conscious choice, about the nature, source, and reliability of what we know. Many battles rumble on, literally for millennia, based on intellectual commitments to different theories about the nature and sources of reliable knowledge.

For example, the editorial columns of *Science* and the editorial page of the *Wall Street Journal* have, on occasion, attacked such groups as postmodernists and social constructionists for their failures to appreciate the value of science, objectivity, and the like.[7] Yet one also can point to evidence suggesting that influential groups see a serious need for some movement in the direction apparently opposed by editorial writers of *Science* and of the *Wall Street Journal.*[8]

All this appears indicative of an important tension. Highly focused technical skills of engineers, managers, administrators, academics, and scientists are important, but they may not be adequate for dealing with broader issues in a rapidly changing and pluralistic world. The heated nature of this tension should be clear. Many individuals have much of their self-concepts linked to their technical skills, their standing within a profession, and—especially for many males—their ability to operate in a logical and rational fashion. To such individuals, the tendency to emphasize ambiguity, pluralism, social structuring of knowledge, and the like can easily be framed as arrant and dangerous nonsense. Yet many senior business executives and many government funding agencies, as well as some significant groups in academia, see things somewhat differently.

We end up with a challenge as to how to introduce aspects of ambiguity, pluralism, and what might be called "multi-perspectival" knowledge, so that students (and future employees, administrators, and educators) can make wiser decisions, while avoiding throwing the baby out with the bathwater. That is, we also need to avoid trivializing technical skills, scientific methods, and commitments to truth and integrity.

Behind this is a multifaceted problem of understanding our claims to understanding. In philosophy (and in rhetoric) we find competing theories about what is really important in order to see the true significance of this topic. In part, the problem arises from concerns over "foundations," that is, from the distrust of strong foundationalist claims, coupled with the apparent impossibility of any pure antifoundationalist credo. But here we are operating at a deeper level, in terms of beliefs about what to do about our (self-evident? tentative? fallible? pluralistic? power-driven?) foundational beliefs.[9]

In this context, algorithmic and highly quantitative thinkers are likely to place great value on what they perceive as objective, rational deduction; to place very little value on emotional, personal, subjective, or ambiguous topics; and to assume there is a clear-cut demarcation line between the two. If they are to be encouraged to take ethical conversation seriously, either ethics has to be moved into the realm of the purely objective and made accessible to algorithmic rule application, or the clear demarcation line has to be blurred between objective, technical, discipline-specific knowledge and the subjective world of opinions, tastes, and relativism. If the former is not a viable option, then the latter approach may be the only alternative.

Dealing with Ambiguity

It is no simple matter to blur the demarcation line between objective and subjective domains. For many academic disciplines, ethical perspectives may appear to conflict with basic presuppositions of that discipline; explanation and prediction are to some extent the enemy of moral conversation. Social sciences tend to shrink the perceived role of free choice by their causal and explanatory theories of human behavior; natural sciences and technological disciplines are likely to encourage a strongly demarcated view of "hard facts" and "soft opinions."[10]

What is needed is a way to bring learners to accept—that is, voluntarily to internalize the belief—that, while the objective-subjective dichotomy is useful, such a dichotomy also seriously constrains our thinking if taken as an absolute. At this point it would be nice to pick a philosophical position "off the shelf" which ties up all the loose ends, and offers the algorithmic thinker a level of closure. However any commitment to one specific "ism" risks leaving us with a seriously incomplete understanding of the nature of knowledge and of self-understanding. It would also lead to conflicts with those who are committed to other "isms."[11] A conjoining of all the various perspectives offers a much broader base from which to understand how we deal with foundational beliefs, and how that impinges on our perceptions of the nature and purpose of ethical conversation, but this inevitably introduces another layer of potential ambiguity.

Moral Imagination, Prototypes, and Internal Realism

There are major parallels between the ideas underlying the author's teaching approach and ideas found in the recent literature on "Moral Imagination." In a book by that name, Mark Johnson (1993) argues that ethical theory needs to get beyond (simply) a search for the right moral rule or a reduction of ethical discussion to matters of personal taste. Rather, there exists a key element of being moral which involves the ability to see things in a moral light. Moral training involves more than internalization and (algorithmic) application of rules, and morality clearly is more than a matter of personal taste. In an important sense there is a need for a "moral attitude" and a "moral sensitivity," even though such an attitude can be self-serving, self-deluding, or self-righteous.[12]

It may be no coincidence that Johnson owes much to a nexus of ideas found in authors such as George Lakoff (1987) and Hilary Putnam (1987).[13] Lakoff in particular puts a primary focus on a common source of potential ambiguity—the fact that we conceptualize objects, such as birds, not in terms of a list of necessary and sufficient characteristics, but in terms of prototypical (and "poorer") examples. While the notion of prototypical objects (and, by implication, of marginal or borderline cases) need not undercut much of traditional analytic philosophy, it (at minimum) draws attention away from seeking lists of necessary and sufficient properties and shifts it toward understanding the implications of the ambiguities in our lines of demarcation surrounding conceptual categories. "Who controls the definition?" becomes a very central, and often far from innocent, question.

Closed-Field Thinking

The teaching approach used here is also linked with the literature on dogmatism and with the concept of closed-belief systems; see, for example, Webster and Kruglanski (1994) for a study linking different perspectives on the need for closure. Such thinkers have a high commitment to specific ways of thinking and may use stereotypes and other devices to suppress any dissonance that might emerge. Put another way, "dogmatic" thinkers need, in addition to a strong control of definitions, very selective ways of admitting the presence of interdependence—or else such interdependence might undermine the legitimacy of their preferred ways of thinking. This limiting of the forms of admissible interdependence, both in terms of the volume and the nature of such links, may help explain the problems of teaching ethics to thinkers who place high value on technical and quantitative thinking. Such thinkers are likely to have strong demarcations between "precise" and "soft/sloppy" areas of thought and to see technical issues as largely divorced from ethics.

We can understand why there is increasing external pressure, from the business community and from government funding agencies, for example, for exposure to humanities and to ethics. The reluctance of closed-field thinkers to see the world in a highly interconnected form creates a compartmentalization of areas of discourse and a tendency to downplay indirect effects. At the same time, the increased interdependence and connectedness found in the world of commerce, in the complexity of policy issues, in the world of political decision making, and from a wide range of forms of cultural interpenetration all put an ever-growing premium on avoidance of premature closure.

This discussion points to the need for learners to be aware of how their thinking is structured by many forces. Personality type, learning type, educational experience, gendered thinking, and discipline-specific presuppositions all play a role. Commitments to theories of truth and to views of the nature of concepts or the value of an absolute objective-subjective dichotomy, often unexamined, feed through into attitudes toward ethics. As a result, algorithmic thinkers may lack the ability to deal with ambiguity and pluralism or even to take ethical conversation seriously.

A central belief underlying the author's teaching method is that, for algorithmic thinkers, serious consideration of ethical issues cannot get started until their love of compartmentalization and their aversion to ambiguity is displaced a little.[14] This is not an easy task, and it is not helped by a tendency in academia to force discussions into an "either/ or" mode. Moving away from the expectation of an unambiguous resolution of "either/or" choices, while preserving respect for the subject matter, requires a classroom environment which is accepting and forgiving, and one that allows for experiential learning, for collective discussion and affirmation, and for engaged, reflective, and internalized learning. In this environment there is a genuine hope that learners will become sensitive to the significance of ethical issues, comfortable with the presence of a certain level of ambiguity, and willing to accept a plurality of views with a role for considerations beyond the narrow scope of their own discipline. In other words, the learners develop some moral imagination and a deeper sense of their own humanity and of the nature of self-and-society.

TEACHING FEATURES

The author has taught, to date, seven courses based on the teaching method discussed here. The audiences vary from professional Master's-degree students in management to undergraduates in an economics elective. The exact structure of these classes has varied, partly as the result of an evolutionary learning process and partly as a reflection of the different goals of the courses or the different backgrounds of the participants. The prototypical offering was a required course for a fast-track group of professional Master's students in the Krannert Graduate School of Management. These students were very bright, highly motivated, with a predominance of engineering and other quantitative skills, and completely unprepared for the type of course they encountered. The structure of that course was based on some intuitive and unformalized views of the author about the problems of "reaching" such an audience. However, the impact, as recorded in self-reported "What I Have Learned" papers, suggests a significant, even dramatic, effect on the majority of participants.

Later courses have been electives in the regular-track professional Master's program or with undergraduates, and so have been subject to self-selection biases and have drawn from populations which are probably somewhat less "algorithmic" than for the prototype course.

Nonetheless, journal entries and standard course evaluations reflect a continued significant and even at times apparently life-changing impact for a high proportion of the learners.[15] This section will discuss briefly the role of three major features of the courses, namely discussion topics, journal entries, and class handouts.

Discussion Topics

One of the most important features of these courses is a series of (typically about 24) short discussion topics. Two or three students are assigned the responsibility of leading the discussion on a particular topic by giving some introductory comments and then moderating the ensuing discussion. The topics do not at first blush all seem to have much to do with ethics (see Figure 6.1 for The Vanishing Heap of Sand, an early topic). They differ dramatically from what might be called traditional case studies, and that is why the term *discussion topic* is used. In contrast to case studies, they are very brief (often between ten and twenty minutes), do not seek closure in any form, and are characterized by the almost total absence of participation by the instructor.[16]

Incomplete discussion stimulates continued thinking outside the classroom. "Unstructured" and open discussion allows students to experience the full diversity of views and to wrestle with the inevitable pluralism and ambiguity. Without fully realizing it, students are forced to adopt a more holistic approach, somehow reconciling technical expertise and professional mind-sets with values and perspectives formed by their family, religious, educational, and cultural backgrounds. Of course, they back into such a situation and are there before they realize it! The limited participation by the instructor creates a presumption that their views are respected and that they will be responsible for arriving at their own conclusions.

Journal Entries

A second key feature of the courses (added after the prototype course) is a series of journal entries. These writing tasks encourage the student

Background:	Suppose that we dumped a pile of ten million grains of sand on the sidewalk outside the Krannert building. This would be quite a significant heap of sand. Now use unemployed students, or underemployed faculty, to remove the sand one grain at a time.
	By the time we get down to no more than a handful of grains of sand, we clearly do not have a heap of sand; most of us would agree that four or five grains of sand do not comprise a *heap* (under usual terminology). When we started, we clearly did have a (substantial) heap of sand, and by the time we got almost to the completion of the task, we clearly did not; yet it is hard to find a point where, with n grains of sand remaining, we did still have a heap of sand, but with (n - 1) grains left, it was no longer a heap. At what point is a heap not a heap?
Questions:	(1) Is this example (generically known as the Sorites' Paradox) trivial, or does it have serious implications? (2) Is there indeed a correct value of n, or is there no satisfactory answer? (3) What, if anything, is the source of the apparent problem? What, if anything, does this example suggest about our ability to categorize, and to think, precisely? (4) Are there analogous problems facing managers, scientists, or others in society?

Figure 6.1. The Vanishing Heap of Sand

to be reflective in exploring the ideas encountered in the course from an individual perspective. The entries are deliberately left unstructured, and there is no explicit attempt to correct spelling, grammar, or logical argumentation. Instead the instructor responds to the *ideas* raised by the student—in part affirming and in part suggesting alternative ways of thinking or new dilemmas that might arise from the directions taken by the student. Good spelling, good grammar, and appropriate logical argumentation can be modeled within the instructor's response, but the purpose is not to judge the ability of students to "stay within the lines." These learners are encountering and exploring, sometimes for the first time in an academic setting, the presence and scope of ambiguity and the interaction between personal or family values and discipline-specific perspectives. As such, they need encouragement, and perhaps some gentle guidance, as they become engaged in the material.

Journal entries can vary from less than a page to seven or more pages, and are submitted four or five times in a semester. The length and the creativity grow dramatically as students realize that their ideas are responded to in depth and with empathy. Space constraints and privacy considerations preclude extensive quotations, but the remarks presented, as written, (in Figure 6.2) are representative.

One consequence of the journal technique is that the instructor not only creates a communal class experience during the discussion, but also has a highly individualized conversation with each learner through the sequence of journal entries and responses. The individualized response is quite time-consuming but appears to be essential to the nature of the course. Learners are typically challenged, intrigued, and sometimes intimidated by the ideas generated in the course; the individualized responses allow for affirmation, clarification of confusions, and freedom to develop ideas in directions that interest and make sense for each individual.[17]

Course Handouts

A third element of the courses consists of class handouts prepared by the instructor on a variety of topics from social psychology, aspects of philosophy and logic, areas of incentives, efficiency, ethical theories, and communities. These handouts are typically fifteen to twenty pages in length and are interspersed at carefully staged intervals within the sequence of discussion topics. The purpose of handouts is to provide some ways of making sense of the diverse perspectives and ambiguity encountered in the discussion topics, and to sort out the complexities of self-within-community. There is an inherent tension, in that any coverage of such a diverse, interdisciplinary range of topics is inevitably oversimplified, but still rather intense for students. For an instructor this creates concerns about the boundary between legitimate simplification and deliberate, or amateurish, bias; it also raises concerns among those students who have been accustomed to rely on memorization, or who expect a total understanding of everything on the first reading.[18]

"Every other course gives us finite information or tools that make the world seem very black and white. This course gave an opportunity to explore the world and realize that it is covered with gray. Ultimately that will make us better managers . . . "; "Your topics made me think, and thinking about topics like this changes my ethical behavior over time. . . . [I]t is good that this course was a required course. I would never have picked this course on the basis of the syllabus. . . . I am really glad that I took this course"; " . . . [I]f more people were exposed to the thinking in the manner that we were exposed to, the world might well be a better place"; "I think the most important concept, one that is not covered in any other class, is that there is no one right answer; the solution depends on how the question is framed. As a matter of fact I would like some of the other professors in the department to sit in on that lecture"; "This course, then serves to break students out of the mindset of assuming that there are easily derived answers to all of the business and policy problems with which the world is faced. The opposite may more often be the case, and the only easy derivations may result from oversimplification of complex problems"; " . . . [prior to this class I thought that] maybe I had chosen the wrong field of studies altogether, that I just did not fit into management studies. Although I have no problem with analytic skills and numbers, something was missing. Then I realized that management is all about this, making decisions without perfect information. There might not be a perfect or definitive answer, and that is just the way that management is"; "What we learn from this class is not whether we can influence the rest of the class to agree, but whether or not we will be willing to listen and appreciate other's opinions"; "Ethical issues are far more interesting than I thought they ever could be. I was one who always believe[d] that philosophy and ethics were dreamed up by those who could not come up with solutions in logical ways, and somehow did not feel smart because of it. . . . My evaluation of this course keeps changing for the better. As we further progress I can see my beliefs changing more and more. My girlfriend has even noticed the difference (she likes it)."

Figure 6.2. Selected Student Reactions

STAGING OF MATERIALS

An important aspect of the approach is found in the timing of materials. Recall that the target student population is assumed to be strongly algorithmic. Many of the brighter students just know that logic and rationality are the ultimate virtues, that all meaningful questions have unambiguous answers, and that discipline-specific approved ways of thinking are the only way to go. Not only does this often fit with personality type and learning style, but their educational experiences have consistently rewarded them for these beliefs. A head-on attempt to introduce ambiguity, or to give priority to ethical perspectives and theories, or to question the scope of entrenched discipline-specific presuppositions, all can lead to shutting out the entire course as a waste of time, or as an exercise in soft and fuzzy thinking. Tolerance for ambiguity has to be built up by starting from mundane, non-threatening examples and by giving theoretically plausible theoretical reasons for accepting that the world cannot always be forced into a single conceptual framework. The trick is to encourage the learners voluntarily to internalize the legitimacy of a certain amount of ambiguity before resistance can set in; then the scope of ambiguity can be extended and explained in areas that were previously inaccessible.

Note that the goal is not to create a bunch of naive relativists. After introducing a credible degree of ambiguity and pluralism, it is important to discuss and illustrate the value of personal integrity and common ground (through discussion of social contracts, the epistemology of game theory, traditional consequentialist or teleological ethics, or the ethics of discourse) and the value of a sense of community. The difference is that, by this point in the course, students understand the difficulties and the tensions involved in seeking some level of common ground and can see the need for constant attention and reflection.

The five stages in the presentation of materials are: (1) mundane examples of ambiguity; (2) introduction of human elements; (3) consideration of ethical topics; (4) coordination-conflict situations, such as markets, Prisoner's Dilemmas, social contracts, or a camping trip amongst friends; and (5) consideration of imperfect institutions, typically followed by (6) applications using examples appropriate to the purpose of the specific course.

Mundane Examples of Ambiguity

The first set of discussion topics involves objects such as Heaps of Sand, Table Tops, Chickens and Eggs, Counting Trees, and the like. None of these topics is particularly novel, and many revolve around prototypes, a choice of foundational beliefs, or competing conventions or perspectives.[19] While nonthreatening, concrete, and undeniably pluralistic in evoked responses, these topics provide a variety of new mental models. These models suggest a value in seeing a world-structuring element at play in any theory or observation. The traditional western and "masculine" desire to put an unambiguous truth value on any meaningful assertion begins to be experienced in its fullness both as a valuable contributor to scientific and technological advances and as a significant source of potential conflicts and misunderstandings.

Human Elements

These topics raise questions about the nature of individual choice and, for example, the boundaries between self-interest, heroism, and unconditional behavior. Such topics increase learner awareness of the diversity of views in the class but still do not build serious conflict with discipline-specific views; they bring an interplay between feelings and logic not found in the earlier discussions.

Ethical Topics

Stage three creates an interesting brew of ethical topics, mixing diversity, emotions, cultural and personal backgrounds, and intellectual and religious commitments. At this stage, ethics is often viewed as something totally distinct from quantitative disciplines, so there is limited dissonance experienced relative to discipline-specific beliefs and patterns of thinking. However, the depth of feelings, the diversity of views, and the significance of the topics penetrates the consciousness of all but the most resistant students.

Coordination-Conflict Situations

The course takes a crucial turn in a stage that was designed specifically for management and economics students, although its relevance is far broader. Situations of "coordination-conflict" are those in which coordination among participants can increase the benefits for all, but potential conflicts, over the sharing of costs and benefits or about implied joint goals, can arise and impede the realization of overall gains. Here many algorithmic students have a strong affinity for "invisible hand" arguments and tend to believe, based on the accompanying world-structuring for these arguments, that an unbridled, competitive and confrontational individualism is both necessary and sufficient for a "good (that is, productive and efficient) society."

By opening up discussions of a variety of coordination-conflict situations, such as camping trips among friends, the traditional Prisoner's Dilemma, market mechanisms, the course invites consideration of the roles of trust, incentives, private contracts, social contracts, and property rights. These issues frequently bring learners to a point of major dissonance. The earlier part of the course tends to lead them to internalize a strong belief in a ubiquitous ambiguity and pluralism that may now seem (suspiciously) suppressed in many of their other courses. Yet their algorithmic instincts and their professional training are likely to make them highly sympathetic to unambiguous conclusions about the efficacy of markets and competition. Since the instructor avoids telling them what to think, the tension is undeniable even when not explicitly articulated as the learners thoroughly process and reevaluate the alternative patterns.

Imperfect Institutions

The fifth stage, though significant, is briefer, and involves discussion of valuable and irreplaceable, but imperfect, institutions. The jury system is an excellent example, where the presence of known imperfections has to be balanced by a certain degree of loyalty to the institution and by recognition of the absence of obviously superior alternatives. This stage in the courses is significant for students because many thorny issues can be framed in terms of loyalty to imperfect institutions.[20]

Applications

Following the five stages of development, which seem to work well for current learner populations, it is useful to apply these ideas in a form akin to traditional case studies. These applications might be analysis of policy and regulatory issues (as in the prototype course), scenarios in international business ethics (as in the subsequent professional Master's courses), or consideration of different types of communities and national economies (as in the undergraduate courses). These applications provide a concrete experience of the tensions inherent in policy, ethical, and communal contexts where common ground is desirable, but multiple perspectives may be available or even unavoidable.[21]

In summary, this section points to the value of creating a sequenced introduction to ambiguity in connection with the nature of communities. This is done within an affirming environment that encourages student exploration of unfamiliar ideas and perspectives in a way that allows for reflection and application of ideas. This careful staging reduces students' resistance and increases their appreciation of the complexity and value of an "ethical balance" between monolithic standards and unlimited tolerance.[22]

CONCLUSION

The author's teaching approach is not offered as some "magic wand" for teaching ethics. It is an approach which takes time to develop and involves heavy instructor involvement, yet appears to have significant effects in learner populations encountered to date. It appears to be initially congruent with student algorithmic thinking patterns, it stimulates tolerance to human ambiguity, and it leads to an acceptance of ethics as a valued subject. The following represent the most central implications, conclusions, or areas of concern.

Domain of Applicability

There remain some open questions concerning the applicability of this approach. There is little doubt that many highly quantitative and technically oriented students from areas such as engineering, finance, and economics (as taught at some very quantitative departments) tend to overvalue deductive thinking, blissfully unaware of the element of world-structuring in their thinking. Such student populations have much to gain from exposure to at least one class that challenges their presuppositions in an engaged but rigorously grounded manner. Other populations, if they have a more limited capability for logical reasoning and a broader attachment to a form of cheap relativism, may need heavy exposure to logical analysis and the benefits of deductive reasoning. However, they, too, must learn to make sense of the balance between an open-ended relativism and the closed-field thinking which, at its worst, merges into dogmatism and prejudice.

The Public Administration Academy

The academy of public administration contains its share of students who are algorithmic thinkers. Compared to the public administration academy, one would expect learners in business schools to have a bias toward valuing self-interest or exclusive duties to shareholders. The danger for public administration, of assuming that one has the right way to see the world, may play out more in a lack of sensitivity to different cultures and socio-economic groups in the body politic, or in a failure to distinguish special interests from the broader good of the society.

The public administration academy is likely to embody a high level of awareness of issues and tensions relating to the grounding of societies in social contracts, constitutions, and the like. Nevertheless, disciplines such as political science have their own world-structuring views and their own blind spots, just as do economics and other business-related areas. Moreover, any professional program can encounter difficulties in the face of a culture of narcissism, hedonism, relativism, and cynicism found among many present-day students. Ironically, those same students exhibit a propensity to seek closure by appealing to discipline-specific "truths."

Instructor-Student Relations

This approach generally is predicated on the view that teaching moral sensitivity is not simply a matter of downloading ethical theories or sermons in a manner that is independent of the background and beliefs of the learner population. Rather it involves the instructor in joining the students in a life-long process of learning, reflecting and exploring that can only take root if grafted with the prior beliefs and presuppositions. The "relational" nature of this approach makes it an invigorating experience for the instructor in which each class brings different insights, challenges, and group dynamics.

Above all, this approach requires the instructor to be sensitive to his or her audience. It raises questions as to the adaptability of the course material to different audiences. Moreover, it offers an extra challenge when the class includes individuals with diverse backgrounds and beliefs. If such diversity can be channeled to increase students' appreciation of the variety of world-structuring possibilities in a pluralistic society, then it can be a major advantage; however, there is also a risk of having some subgroup(s) of learners tune out the entire process.

Academic Biases

In research-oriented universities in particular, there has been a strong tendency to focus on "internal," discipline-specific issues and expertise. At a deeper level, this alternative approach to ethics suggests that there is value in creating a breathing space in such institutions for an open conversation across disciplines by questioning (in a non-confrontational manner) the presuppositions of the various fields. Practitioners of the art of transdisciplinary thinking should be forewarned that their critiques will be exposed to the standard criticism of being "amateurs" from the perspective of each specific discipline, and the accusation of "not understanding" the esoterica of various disciplines.

Reconceptualization: A Therapeutic Dimension

This approach to ethics presupposes that education cannot avoid a holistic, experiential element. In many ways, the courses are a form of "therapy" in which algorithmic thinkers encounter—in an open, accepting environment—dissonance with their beliefs about the absence of ambiguity. The learners are invited to reconceptualize their perceptions of themselves, of their role in society, and of the nature of their technical knowledge and their background beliefs. Such an invitation has to be proffered sensitively and without giving the impression that the instructor has "the algorithm which is the key to all algorithms." In many research-oriented universities, some faculty are unfamiliar with this way of thinking about knowledge and this way of teaching, and some might become uncomfortable, if not hostile. Yet the increasing complexity of society is accompanied by pervasive spillovers from scientific, technological, and professional decisions and the rising expectations of institutions of higher education. Other institutions, such as the family, stable neighborhoods, primary and secondary schools, and the church appear to play a smaller role in communal awareness. All of these factors point to the likelihood that this type of integrative, holistic, experiential teaching will become an essential part of the university curriculum. The support of high-level business executives for this kind of approach, and the interest shown by U.S. federal funding agencies in encouraging genuine interaction between science and the humanities, are symptoms of a perceived need in higher education.

For ethics education, it might be argued that the presence of ambiguity, rather than being a mark of second-class conversation, is a signal of the central importance of the issues, by way of reflecting the confluence of multiple perspectives from technical disciplines, social sciences, ethical theorizing, and "deep" values of individuals and communities. The current chapter is offered as a piece of an ongoing, and probably never-ending, conversation about how to adapt education, and ethical teaching in particular, to a changing and increasingly interdependent and complex world.

Addendum: Solving the Problem?

It is natural to ask whether, and how, the author's teaching method solves the problem it addresses. Part of the response is that the conventional notion of problem solving may encounter its own ambiguities and could itself be part of "the problem."

As stated at the outset, a central goal of this approach is to induce "algorithmic thinkers" to take ethical reasoning and ethical issues seriously, despite their likely aversion to ambiguity and its dissonance with their discipline-specific ways of thinking. However, as one probes deeper there is a clear sense that what counts as a solution depends upon the way the problem has been framed, often implicitly biased by the vocabulary of the question. A widely used example refers to complaints about the slow service of elevators in a high-rise office building. Proposed solutions include faster elevators, more elevators, staggered starting and finishing times for office workers, and so forth. The users of this story then point out that each solution implies a restructuring of the nature of the problem. Thus the solution of faster elevators corresponds to the perceived problem that they are too slow; the solution of more elevators corresponds to the perception that the problem is too few elevators; the solution of staggered starting and finishing times corresponds to the perceived problem of peak-load constraints; and so on. The punch line is that the building owner installed large mirrors on each floor opposite the elevators, and this provided a distraction and thus eliminated complaints.

What are significant characterizations of "the problem" of teaching ethics to algorithmic learners? What are the insights and blindspots of each proposed characterization of the problem? To what extent could the author's teaching method (or alternative methods) solve such a problem? Obviously such a list of questions could be extended almost indefinitely. Here only a few alternatives are briefly considered.

Teaching Rigorous Ethical Reasoning

This is a legitimate goal for ethics instructors, and clearly it is a valuable part of ethical training. However, as mentioned earlier, exclusive emphasis on the rigor of ethics is likely to have limited impact on those students who are predisposed to reject ethics on account of its perceived ambiguity or its conflicts with discipline-specific thinking. Moreover, many highly quantitative learners are prone to be "bored" by the details of ethical theories and to possess strong logical skills anyway. The difficulty with this perspective is that it characterizes the problems of algorithmic thinkers as (a) lack of critical thinking skills, and (b) lack of exposure to basic ethical theories. It ignores the problem encountered if such learners simply decline to take ethical discussion seriously.

Teaching the Moral Absolutes

It is tempting to see society as drifting away from moral absolutes, and to see the solution to the problem as one of reminding learners of these absolutes. There are a number of difficulties here. Highly quantitative learners are unlikely to respect "moral piety" except from those they would consider to be exemplary role models, such as successful CEOs. In a pluralistic society, they are unlikely to accept a single source of "moral authority," and even if they did they are likely to differ in their interpretations of such sources in comparison to other patterns of thinking. In addition, anyone who has taught or discussed applied ethics is surely aware how quickly a near-consensus on broad principles tends to fragment into dissensus as specific examples and "borderline cases" are introduced.

   In general, the biggest weakness of both the first two characterizations of the problem to be solved is that they ignore the possibility that some (or many) learners will completely "disengage" from taking ethical discussions seriously. It is precisely this group that one would hope to reach and bring into the ethical conversation.

Teaching Learners to Get in Touch with Their Feelings

This way of characterizing the problem also may be a "straw person." It runs the danger of trivializing both the role of ethical reasoning and the importance of ethical behavior for individuals and for society. In isolation from other ethical considerations, it may invite either naive relativism or a skepticism about the importance of ethics as a subject for serious consideration—particularly if the learners are accustomed to highly reliable algorithms and are committed to discipline-specific patterns of thinking. At the same time, an effective approach to engagement in moral reasoning requires some linking up of professional dilemmas with values emerging in individual development, whether from family life, religious faith, or community culture. In addition, thinking about ethical dilemmas and recognizing a "moral dimension" in public and private life are likely to be facilitated by an ability to envisage the situation as it might appear to all those involved, not to mention as it might be portrayed by the media the next day!

Another Path (Less Travelled?)

The author's approach presupposes that the initial, unavoidable problem is to engage learners in taking ethical discussion seriously even when it is ambiguous, creates areas of dissensus, or conflicts with a simple-minded application of discipline-specific ways of thinking. The approach does involve some risk of short-changing rigorous ethical reasoning, and of encouraging naive relativism. However, if the learners become actively engaged in ethical conversations, even without technical rigor, then they are more likely to internalize the importance of ethics for self and for community and more likely to reflect on potential ethical dimensions of decisions before they act (less is undoubtedly more in this respect!). A balanced approach shows respect both for elements of decisiveness and for elements of openness; it makes connections with learners "where they are," and affirms the learners' own value as individuals. It also raises questions about the nature of self-and-community and provides frequent reminders and experiential demonstrations about the importance of personal integrity and of community values. The author's approach encourages "delaying" the act of decisionmaking in order to make room for listening to various perspectives and for reflection. Reflection without decision becomes pointless, but decision without appropriate reflection can be unethical and even dangerous. If we only had an algorithm for what counts as "adequate reflection," then there would be little need for this fourth kind of teaching approach.

NOTES

1. See, for example, the Wharton-Templeton Report (1993), especially the list of pedagogical problems reported there (p. 7). Note, in particular, the two items "student expectations of definitive answers" and "close-mindedness of technically trained students."

2. Even where the student is not strongly of the sequential-thinking type, he or she is likely to have been exposed to large doses of teaching in a linear, rational, deductive style.

3. See, for instance, Erez and Early (1993) for discussion of these cultural and other differences.

4. This is somewhat consistent with the observation that, among engineering students, Myers-Briggs' STJ's are over-represented relative to the general population; see Wankat and Oreovicz (1993), Chapter 13.

5. See Stein (1974), for example, who writes, "The adult in our society who complains about his own lack of creativity or who complains about the lack of creativity in others is often incapable of emptying his spirit of what he has learned. He is intolerant of ambiguities and doubts and fearful of the unknown. Rigidities, fears, and doubts are replaced by premature evaluations and parental 'don'ts' and 'shouldn'ts' that serve only to inhibit curiosity and exploration that might result in inspired and creative ideas."

6. None of what is said here should be interpreted as a blanket endorsement of any given theory; thus, for example, the Myers-Briggs Personality Typology has been criticized in the psychology literature, but in this chapter all such theories are used as suggestive (but presumptively imperfect). Moreover, the spirit of the teaching method is to encourage a sense of strengths and weaknesses in all types of learners and thinkers, rather than to define an ideal type.

7. See the fascinating editorial in *Science* (1993), or a recent example (less specifically directed) from the business press, Summers (1995).

8. Donaldson and Freeman (1994) with contributions by many prominent figures in business ethics, discusses the situating of "Business as a Humanity." Federal government funding agencies in the United States have been encouraging projects to cross-fertilize ideas between science and the humanities; examples include the program area *Science and Humanities: Integrating Undergraduate Education*, operated jointly by the National Endowment for the Humanities and the National Science Foundation, as in National Science Foundation (1994). (Clearly the cross-fertilization is intended to be a two-way street.) Recently, the Chief Executive Officer of a highly successful Fortune 500 company (see Bossidy 1995), addressing an academic audience with heavy engineering, science, and management representation, declared a strong preference for hiring professional workers who had exposure to the humanities, could work in a multicultural world, understood the importance of teamwork and of ethical behavior, and were not narrow technicians. (Of course, he added, the technical skills are still very important, but they need to come with well-rounded skills in interpersonal and self-awareness realms.)

9. Put another way, a claim to knowledge may mean quite different things to a scientific realist, a Putnam-style internal realist, a Habermasian or Popperian critical rationalist, a postmodern deconstructionist, or various (other) varieties of existentialists, pragmatists, relativists, inter alia. Baynes et al. (1987) is an excellent indicator of these tensions. Other references of possible value include Cherwitz (1990), McCarthy (1991), Bernstein (1983), Simpson (1987), and Hiley et al. (1991). Even disciplines that most directly address these tensions may have trouble finding a neutral stance. In order to survive as schol-

ars, academic philosophers, critical theorists, rhetoricians, and linguists are pushed to adopt and to some extent become committed to a specific position among the alternatives (varieties of realism, relativism, pragmatism, existentialism, deconstructionism, critical rationalism, etc.). Meanwhile, in "nonreflective disciplines," such as engineering, physics, or economics, academics may easily adopt a simple, often tacit, belief in a particular "ism" and find that belief reinforced with each increase in personal stature within the discipline.

10. The western world has a deep-seated tradition, partly exemplified by Kant, of dividing the world into an objective sphere (to be understood via scientific theorizing and testing) and a subjective sphere (relating to matters of taste); Putnam (1987) is very articulate on this point.

The position of ethics has always been somewhat problematic in the light of this inviting dichotomy; the (third) Kantian ethical sphere is both attracted and repulsed, on either side, by the objective scientific sphere and the subjective aesthetic sphere. (Kant also introduces a fourth, less-discussed, religious sphere, whose situation is even more problematic; see Schrag (1992) for an insightful discussion of many key issues from the perspective of Continental philosophy.) The key, in terms of differentiated spheres, is to try to wean the algorithmic thinker from using a simple meta-algorithm to categorize problems—namely the algorithm that says "unambiguous, discipline-approved, scientific, quantified" reasoning is objective, and all else is subjective, and hence viewed as second-class conversation.

11. For example, a postmodernist might insist that the primary focus be on the potential for deception or self-delusion (not to mention internal paradox) in any structured way of thinking. Certain brands of empiricists or scientific realists might want us to keep front-and-center the notion that an ideal, objective science is always the goal, even conceding the fallibility and imperfections of an actual scientific community.

12. There have been other attempts to flesh out missing dimensions of ethical theory (relative to the traditional focus on principles or consequences). Recent revival of interest in casuistry, which relies heavily on finding appropriate analogies, is one example. Even more visible is the (Aristotelian) focus on ethics-within-community, with a virtue theory that emphasizes growth of a virtuous individual as a dynamic, community-related process. These revived alternatives each have their own weaknesses but add to the tool kit of ways of thinking about ethics. Jonsen & Toulmin (1988) is a good starting point on casuistry; MacIntyre (1988) is a standard reference on contemporary virtue theory.

13. See Lakoff (1987) and Putnam (1987) for some antecedent references. Putnam's theory of "internal realism" resonates with, and is cited in, the work of Lakoff. Putnam is attempting to balance two important goals. First, the

validity of scientific knowledge is to be preserved by arguing for a form of realism, where the world as-it-is constrains and corrects our hypotheses. Second, room is made for multiple perspectives, and in particular for ethical conversations which are not totally subservient to the views of specific sciences, by arguing for realism and facticity in the context of particular ways of structuring the world. The purpose of this chapter is neither to defend nor to appeal to Putnam's theory in any absolute way. In fact, Putnam's own views are in a state of continual revision, and any adequate theory (assuming we had one and could recognize it as such) surely would have to find a way to balance "internal objectivity" with some breathing room for pluralism and multiple perspectives. (Moreover, even at this level, a Putnam-style theory is itself a mixture of world-structuring and world-discovery.)

14. In terms of James Rest's fourfold division of moral development into moral sensitivity, moral reasoning, moral motivation, and moral implementation (see Rest and Narvaez 1991, especially pp. 243–44), the emphasis in this teaching method is on the first stage, moral sensitivity, and in particular on removing possible barriers to allowing moral sensitivity and moral reasoning to enter into play. Perry (1970) suggests that the ability to deal with such ambiguity may have an age-related component.

15. A colleague in social psychology with expertise in detecting "self-serving" writings, has examined the "What I Have Learned" papers and journal entries and offered the opinion that the vast majority of the (extensive) strongly positive remarks appear to be very genuine.

16. There are dangers here, since little attempt is made to comment on the differences between reasoned arguments, opinions, and prejudice; some of these dangers can be mitigated by appropriate responses to journal entries, and most learners are not insensitive to these distinctions. However, there are also dangers in the case-study approach. Students in the prototypical course offered by the author emphasized that this was the first course where they did not feel they were trying to guess what the instructor wanted; where the true diversity of their cohort became apparent, and they felt they knew each other at a deeper level; and where they were free to offer ideas and to change their mind without risk of losing face.

17. Since students have varied backgrounds, the instructor has considerable responsibility to handle the interaction with care. Some groups who may need special sensitivity include: those whose religious faith can only be expressed in terms of claims to absolute, objective, and non-negotiable truths; those who have an equally fervent commitment to objectivity and rationality ("if only you'd look at it in the right way, there is only one objective, rational conclusion"); and those who are sufficiently inarticulate to be unable to start any sort of meaningful dialogue. In addition, Myers-Briggs STJ's may find the ambiguity, the implied questioning of received knowledge, and the personal dimensions of discussions and journals quite unsettling at first.

18. Other features have varied from course to course. With undergraduates, a portfolio seems to work well in encouraging ownership in the class and helping students to see how their ideas and understanding have evolved over the duration of the semester. Also with undergraduates, very simple start-of-class quizzes (from a precirculated list of questions) contribute to the incentive to read each handout before the corresponding class session. At either level, some midterm exams (again based on a list of precirculated questions) may be useful to encourage reflection and integration and to guide learners to identify key themes in the course. (One danger here is that exam scores may become too dominant either in the minds of the students or in the actual grading schema; the ones who do best in the exams are often the most dedicated but inflexible algorithmic thinkers.)

Particularly for Master's-level students, position papers are valuable as a form of application and integration of ideas. For undergraduates, a closing section on applied topics can be very effective in tying the ideas of the course together. The communal nature of the discussion experience makes attendance and participation crucial, although personality type and culture may lead to different modes of participation (including indirect participation via journal entries).

19. Thus the Chicken and the Egg were introduced as a very elementary example of a potential regress, although almost every class seems spontaneously to turn it into a science-religion confrontation; the Flat Table-Top contrasts the flatness from a "normal" perspective, the cratered nature under an electron-microscope, and the current inability in the original language of particle physics (that is, without resorting to approximation theory) even to describe macro objects such as table tops.

20. Science versus postmodernism, rules versus discretion, rule versus act utilitarianism, strengths and limitations of democratic systems, strengths and limitations of competitive economic systems, the difference between unambiguous truth values and the prototypical view of Lakoff, Johnson, and others, all find a common thread in this topic. Arrow (1974), Baynes et al. (1987), McCarthy (1991), Bernstein (1983), Simpson (1987), and Hiley et al. (1991) may be useful here.

21. An example of a policy issue might be evaluating the case for educational vouchers for primary and secondary schooling—a case which one group, despite its strong free-market preconceptions, found surprisingly complex and full of unexpected and troubling spillover effects. International business ethics cases often focus on conflicting norms between the source country and the host country of a multinational firm, with the scenario frequently complicated by an explicit ethical code within the firm itself; by the potential for (short-term) profits; and by possible adverse consequences for the individual decisionmaker. In the context of nations and communities, it is natural to look at political attitudes and behavior in the United States and at competing views of the social respon-

sibilities of the firm. This sets up comparisons with other countries, such as Japan, Korea, Chile, China, or the economies of Eastern Europe and of the former Soviet Union. One very effective unit compares dysfunctional or unfamiliar rural communities in Southern Italy or sub-Saharan Africa with the current situation of the Amish. In this context, Banfield (1958) can be a major revelation for those who believe that narrow self-interest guarantees efficient communities; for rural African villages, an in-house source, Lawrence (1993) is used for background.

22. This adjustment process is assisted by the presence of class handouts. A handout on social psychology introduces of personality types, learning styles, framing, moral development, and gender and cross-cultural differences. Two handouts spell out some themes in logic and philosophy, offering a sense of the drive for unquestionable foundations for ideal, value-free and complete knowledge, and how this affects our understanding of ambiguity. Godel's Theorems suggest the limits of foundationalism, even though pure antifoundationalism has little future. MacKay (1980), especially Chapter 7, is a good reference for the Infinite Regress Argument, which is at the heart of the tensions between decisiveness and openness; Boolos (1979) shows that the algebraic structure of the Infinite Regress Argument is a central feature of Godel's seminal (in)completeness and (in)consistency theorems. The latter theorems are closely related to the Loewenheim-Skolem theorems of model theory (see Enderton 1972), but learners do not need to be taken to the level of Loewenheim-Skolem theory. The very simple Infinite Regress Argument is perhaps the best single metaphor for tensions of the late twentieth century and an easy entry into disputes between science and humanities, different schools of philosophy, persons with different personality types, and those with differing views (and meta views) of applied ethics.

Later handouts focus on incentives, notions of efficiency, and a variety of ethical theories. They suggest potential distinctions between narrow notions of self-interest ("everyone cheats," "everyone is just out for themselves"), indirect reasons for cooperation (as in many repeated games), intrinsic motivation, and notions of principled or "unconditional" behavior, as well as reviewing traditional (economic) arguments of the efficiency of decentralized, individual choices through competitive markets, repeated games, bargaining games, or other mechanisms. The goal here is neither to create nor to reinforce a mindless faith in competitive forces, nor to argue that monetary and other extrinsic incentives and competitive opportunities are irrelevant. Rather, by exploring the strengths and weaknesses of each institution (seen as a way of treating coordination-conflict situations), by reframing (say) market mechanisms in terms of implicit assumptions about social contracts and common perceptions, and by exploring the interplay of trust, cultural expectations, and extrinsic contractual incentives, learners find their own balance between the roles of markets/contracts and of trust, norms, and ethical behavior.

The treatment of ethical theories exposes students to a wide variety of ethical views, focusing not only on traditional areas of consequentialism, principled behavior, and virtue theory, but also to (meta)-theories such as emotivism, prescriptivism, and moral realism. Learners see the application of ethical theories as involving—every bit as much as Heaps of Sand or economic theories of competitive markets—potential elements of framing and of social grounding. This approach assumes that, via the process of reflecting on ambiguities in discussion topics and of grappling with the strengths, limitations, and dissonances of perspectives from social psychology, logic, philosophy, economics, and elsewhere, the student-participants are now able to take moral conversation seriously without needing or expecting algorithmic guarantees.

The final handout, at the end of this period of discussion topics and handouts but prior to any applications, brings together a variety of perspectives on communities. These perspectives are drawn from organization theory, the economics of national and local jurisdictions, from modal logic, and elsewhere. Martin (1992) is an interesting exposition in organization theory. The ideas found in Boolos (1979) can be interpreted loosely in terms of communities of thought. Economic theories about sizes of firms, sizes of government jurisdictions, and the implications of "network externalities" are also grist for the mill. The emphasis of Smithson (1991) on the roles of taboo, suburbanization, and reductionism in warding off ignorance has some relevance. Communicative ethics, as for example in Benhabib (1992), also fits well. Casuistry and virtue theory can be re-integrated here. This provides a useful way for students to get a flavor of the ubiquity of situations where different perspectives, communities, or rules apply within groups, but where allowance has to be made to deal with intergroup transactions, to permit reasonable dissent within groups, and to leave open the possibility of revision of foundational group beliefs or norms in the face of changes in technology, knowledge, or other factors.

REFERENCES

Arrow, Kenneth J. 1974. *The Limits of Organization.* New York, NY: W. W. Norton.

Banfield, Edward C. 1958. *The Moral Basis of a Backward Society.* Chicago: The University of Chicago Press.

Baynes, Kenneth, James Bohman, and Thomas McCarthy, ed. 1987. *After Philosophy: End or Transformation?* Cambridge, MA: The MIT Press.

Benhabib, Seyla. 1992. *Situating the Self: Gender, Community, and Postmodernism in Contemporary Ethics.* New York: Routledge.

Bernstein, Richard J. 1993. *Beyond Objectivism and Relativism: Science, Hermeneutics, and Praxis.* Philadelphia: University of Pennsylvania Press.

Boolos, George. 1979. *The Unprovability of Consistency: An Essay in Modal Logic.* Cambridge: Cambridge University Press.

Bossidy, Lawrence A. 1995. "Whom to Hire: The Kind of College Graduate Business Will Need to Succeed in the Global Marketplace," Lecture. West Lafayette, IN: Purdue University, April 11.

Cherwitz, Richard A., ed. 1990. *Rhetoric and Philosophy*. Hillsdale, NJ: Lawrence Erlebaum Associates.

Donaldson, Thomas J., and R. Edward Freeman, ed. 1994. *Business as a Humanity*. New York: Oxford University Press.

Enderton, Herbert B. 1972. *A Mathematical Introduction to Logic*. San Diego: Academic Press.

Erez, Miriam, and Christopher Early. 1993. *Culture, Self-Identity, and Work*. New York: Oxford University Press.

Hiley, David. R., James F. Bohman, and Richard Schusterman, eds. 1991. *The Interpretive Turn: Philosophy, Science, Culture*. Ithaca: Cornell University Press.

Johnson, Mark. 1993. *Moral Imagination: Implications of Cognitive Sciences for Ethics*. Chicago: The University of Chicago Press.

Jonsen, Albert R., and Stephen Toulmin. 1988. *The Abuse of Casuistry: A History of Moral Reasoning*. Berkeley: University of California Press.

Lakoff, George. 1987. *Women, Fire, and Dangerous Things: What Categories Reveal About the Mind*. Chicago: The University of Chicago Press.

Lawrence, Pareena Gupta. 1993. *Household Decision-Making and Introduction of New Agricultural and Household Technologies in the Solenzo Region of Burkina Faso*. Ph.D. thesis. West Lafayette, IN: Purdue University.

MacIntyre, Alasdair. 1988. *Whose Justice? Which Rationality?* Notre Dame, IN: University of Notre Dame Press.

MacKay, Alfred F. 1980. *Arrow's Theorem: The Paradox of Social Choice*. New Haven: Yale University Press.

Martin, Joanne. 1992. *Cultures in Organizations: Three Perspectives*. New York: Oxford University Press.

McCarthy, Thomas. 1991. *Ideals and Illusions: On Reconstruction and Deconstruction in Contemporary Critical Theory*. Cambridge: The MIT Press.

National Science Foundation. 1994. *Undergraduate Education Brochure: Program Announcement and Guidelines*, document NSF 94–160. Arlington, VA: National Science Foundation.

Perry, William G. 1970. *Forms of Intellectual and Ethical Development in the College Years: A Scheme*. New York: Holt, Rinehart, and Winston.

Putnam, Hilary. 1987. *The Many Faces of Realism*. LaSalle, IL: Open Court.

Rest, James, and Darcia Narvaez. 1991. "The College Experience and Moral Development," Chapter 9 of *Handbook of Moral Behavior and Development*, Volume 2: Research, William M. Kurtines and Jacob L. Gewirtz, Hillsdale, NJ: ed. Lawrence Erlebaum Associates.

Schrag, Calvin O. 1992. *The Resources of Rationality: A Response to the Postmodern Challenge*. Bloomington, IN: Indiana University Press.

Science. 1993. "Postmodernism," Editorial, Vol. 261, page 143, July 9.

Simpson, Evan, ed. 1987. *Anti-Foundationalism and Practical Reasoning: Conversations Between Hermeneutics and Analysis*. Edmonton, AB: Academic Print. & Pub.

Smithson, Michael. 1989. *Ignorance and Uncertainty: Emerging Paradigms*. New York: Springer-Verlag.

Stein, Morris I. 1974. *Stimulating Creativity: Volume I: Individual Procedures*. New York: Academic Press.

Summers, Christina Hoffman. 1995. "The Flight from Science and Reason," *The Wall Street Journal*, Monday, July 10.

Wankat, Phillip C., and Frank S. Oreovicz. 1993. *Teaching Engineering*. New York: McGraw-Hill.

Webster, Donna M., and Arie W. Kruglanski. 1994. "Individual Differences in Need for Cognitive Closure," *Journal of Personality and Social Psychology*, vol. 67, No. 6, pp. 1049-62.

Wharton-Templeton Report. 1993. *Bringing a Global Perspective to Business Ethics*, a report for the James S. Kemper Foundation, and prepared by the Wharton School, University of Pennsylvania, with the participation of Templeton College, Oxford University, (Project Director: Thomas W. Dunfee).

CHAPTER 7

The Hyppolytus, *Public Administration, and the Need for Prudence*

HENRY T. EDMONDSON III

A common concern in the study and practice of public administration ethics has been the discovery and encouragement of principles, or at least ideals, that might guide administrative behavior. A related question receiving less attention is how skillfully administrators apply those principles to the specific challenges they encounter. That is to say, it is one thing to discover useful moral principles, but it is another challenge to implement those principles successfully.

In the Greek and Roman classical traditions and the Christian theological tradition, the specific moral quality that enables an individual to apply general principles to specific circumstances is called alternately moral judgment, practical wisdom,—or to use the classical terminology—prudence. For example, Aristotle teaches that the prudent individual is able not only to recognize a moral goal, but he or she also can calculate how best to achieve that goal.

In Euripides' play *The Hyppolytus*, the tragic playwright teaches that although someone may have high ideals, their activity may be destructive if they lack the flexibility and practical wisdom to integrate those ideals into their society. Such a person, represented by the protagonist Hyppolytus, is morally good but unable to fit his morality into everyday living. Consequently, Hyppolytus' arrogance and aloofness supersede any social benefit those around him might derive from his character.

Following an introduction, this chapter will offer a brief review of the classical background of prudence. Next is an acknowledgment of the contemporary interest in this virtue in public administration literature. The review of public administration literature focuses upon the attention given to the specific virtue of prudence, not the wider administrative interest in virtue in general. Following this illustration is a summary of the Greek tale of Hyppolytus. This tragedy is used as an illustration of the destructive effect of moral ideals when the virtue of prudence is absent. The chapter concludes with implications for public administration education, followed by several other remarks relevant to my argument.

THE CLASSICAL TEACHING ON PRUDENCE AND LATER REFLECTIONS IN PUBLIC ADMINISTRATION LITERATURE

An early description of prudence comes in Plato's *Republic*, where the philosopher identifies prudence as an essential virtue for the just individual and the just city. Discussion of the virtue surfaces in other Platonic dialogues such as the *Meno*, where Socrates leads an exploration of the best means to teach virtue. Aristotle provides the best and most widely accepted discussion of this virtue in his *Nicomachean Ethics*. Aristotle argues that prudence is the hinge upon which all the other virtues turn, noting that "some say that all the virtues are forms of practical wisdom." More specifically he designated prudence (*phronesis*) as an "intellectual virtue" that aids the expression of all of the virtues involved in day-to-day living, namely, the "moral virtues." On the other hand, prudence without the full complement of moral virtues is not prudence at all, but only shrewdness or cleverness. In this situation, the individual becomes skillful, but skillful only in the pursuit of narrowly conceived and self-serving objectives (1143b18–1145a11).

Prudence was absorbed into the theological tradition as SS. Ambrose, Jerome, Augustine, and Gregory the Great all recognized the preeminence of virtue among the cardinal virtues. Building upon Aristotle, St. Thomas Aquinas provided an even more thorough and systematic exposition of prudence explaining its operation and defining its manifestations as, for example, political (executive and legislative) prudence, domestic prudence, and military prudence (2a2ae, 47–50). Aquinas also warned of the vices contrary to prudence, such as carelessness in judgment, "ill-advisedness," and negligence. In the twentieth century, the Thomist scholar Josef Pieper has provided perhaps the best explications of the classical virtues in general and prudence in particular (1959, 1966).

Prudence, to take an example, guides a soldier faced with danger or hardship to avoid either cowardliness or foolhardiness in his actions. It enables him to exercise courage instead. Prudence is just as indispensable to the government contract manager faced with an opportunity for "whistle-blowing." Her prudence would be essential in weighing all the critical factors involved in her decision. These might include the personal consequences, the nature and degree of wrongdoing involved, the possibility of institutional reform, and the ratio of harm to good that might result from her actions.

Several discussions in public administration literature relate to this topic. Finer (1941) has noted, in his classic debate with Friedrich (1935), that "virtue itself hath need of limits." He warns that "we in public administration must beware of the too good man as well as the too bad." In his concern for the "imposition of zealotry" by public officials, he notes,

> A system which gives the "good" man freedom of action, in
> the expectation of benefiting from all the "good" he has in
> him, must sooner or later (since no man is without faults)
> cause his faults to be loaded on to the public also. (338)

By this Finer notes that idealism alone is not enough. Although he properly emphasizes the role of external controls over individual behavior, equally appropriate is the recognition that prudence provides the mechanism, so to speak, by which the public might benefit from the morality of the public official.[1]

In his tribute to Paul Appleby, Bailey (1965) advocates a trio of moral qualities and a trio of mental attitudes, all of which describe the character of the model public servant. The composite picture of integrity that Bailey proposes (which he claims also describes the late Appleby) captures handsomely the classical idea of practical wisdom.

Dobel (1990) is more explicit in his recommendation for prudence as the virtue that enables the administrator to achieve effective *and* moral results in administrative practice:

> I choose prudence, a traditional virtue, to give a stronger moral gloss to effectiveness. While effectiveness focuses exclusively on achieving postulated ends, prudence as a virtue adds moral constraints and aspects which broaden its domain and guard against abuses. (361)

Dobel further notes the need for prudence "because politics is not a frictionless plane for implementing clear goals"(362).

Prudence offers a means of coping with the political environment of "dirty hands" discussed by Walzer (1973), who in turn refers the phrase to Sartre's play *Dirty Hands*. Walzer aptly notes that public life involves compromises that cannot coexist with an unyielding position of moral absolutism. Cooper (1987) includes prudence as one of the requisite virtues for the public administrator. Such virtues provide strength of character and enable an administrator to adhere to ethical principles (321). A wider consideration of virtue in the context of the American heritage can be found in Rohr (1978), Hart (1984), and Richardson and Nigro (1987a, 1987b).

SUMMARY OF *THE HYPPOLYTUS* BY EURIPIDES

Hyppolytus is the devotee of the virgin goddess Artemis. As such he is privileged to hear her voice and feel her presence while he is hunting. Hyppolytus disdains Artemis' opposite and rival deity, the lascivious Aphrodite. Hyppolytus remarks, "I do not care for gods men worship in the night" (81) Aphrodite bitterly complains, "Hyppolytus . . . that saintly man, alone of all the people in this land . . . considers me the least important of the gods, spurns love making and will not join in an embrace" (78). His neglect provokes Aphrodite to seek vengeance against him by causing Hyppolytus' stepmother, Phaedra, to fall hopelessly in love with her puritanical stepson. Phaedra's servant naively tries to ease her mistress' pain by boldly confronting Hyppolytus with his stepmother's plight, hoping for his understanding and assistance. Instead, Hyppolytus, horrified, loudly denounces all women in general and Phaedra in particular. Phaedra, thus exposed, hangs herself.

In an attempt to preserve her reputation, Phaedra leaves a suicide note for Theseus, her husband, in which she falsely accuses Hyppolytus of sexual violation. As Theseus returns home from a religious pilgrimage, he discovers his wife's body and her note. He immediately confronts Hyppolytus and impulsively sentences him to exile, giving Hyppolytus no opportunity for a defense. Still worse, he uses one of his three curses, legacies of his father, the god Poseidon.

The curse proves most effective of all. A short way into his journey into exile, Hyppolytus' entourage meets the power of Theseus's curse. Traveling by the sea, his horses are frightened by a huge wave carrying an apparition of a monstrous, bellowing bull. The animals panic, and Hyppolytus becomes entangled in the reins and brutally dragged across the rocky earth by the terrified animals. He is returned to his father just as Theseus is told of his awful error and chastened by the goddess Artemis. In the final scene, an emotionally broken Theseus asks the forgiveness of the physically broken Hyppolytus, who freely grants it.

Throughout the play Hyppolytus asserts his own moral purity. The cumulative effect of these assertions is to highlight Hyppolytus' blind arrogance and lack of common sense, which gradually give a comical tone to his otherwise sterling character. In the opening scene he reminds the statue of Artemis, "For I alone among men am so distinguished as to be constantly with you and to speak and hear your words." When Hyppolytus learns of Phaedra's passion for him, he seizes the opportunity to condemn all women, and advises Zeus, ". . . if you wished to propagate the race of men, this should not have been brought about by women's means." The safest woman to have in one's house, Hyppolytus continues, is one "whose mind's a total blank, a simple useless thing." He explains, "I hate a clever woman, and in my house never would have one with more ideas than a woman ought to have" (99).

Hyppolytus then announces his solution to Phaedra's torment: "With running water I shall wash my ears and wipe away your words"

(100). When Theseus confronts Hyppolytus with his alleged incest, the young man exacerbates his father's anger when he contends, "Never will you behold a man more pure than I."

One view of *The Hyppolytus*[2] is as a series as imprudent acts cumulatively leading to the catastrophic consequences of the play. We have already noted Hyppolytus' own moral inflexibility. Phaedra's servant also naively acts as if the stark truth will magically resolve Phaedra's dilemma. Yet, because of her servant's clumsy attempt to ease Phaedra's emotional misery, Phaedra herself is plunged into abject humiliation and driven to suicide. Theseus, in his rage, precipitously condemns Hyppolytus to exile, preferring the guidance of anger to a reasonable investigation of his wife's accusations. He couples this pronouncement with a curse upon his son that is quickly meted out by the God of the Seas. One after another, the principal characters of Euripides' tragedy rush headlong into imprudent action. Although each seeks justice, their imprudence contributes directly or indirectly to injustice.

Hyppolytus is visited by his patron goddess Artemis in the last few minutes of his life. She mourns the loss of so devoted a mortal and denounces the jealousy of Aphrodite. In perhaps the most important line of the play, she reveals to Hyppolytus, "It was the goodness of your heart [that] destroyed your life." Artemis offers this startling analysis without commentary, so the audience is left to interpret its irony. An inference is not difficult, however. The Goddess seems to say that Hyppolytus was unable to manage his own moral purity. He lived by noble ideals but was unable to integrate those ideals into his own society. Early in the play, a nurse, in conversation with the ever-present chorus, accurately notes that men should not "try to be too strict about their lives. They cannot even make the roofs, with which their homes are covered, absolutely right" (93).

When Hyppolytus attempts to defend himself before Theseus against Phaedra's posthumous accusations, he confesses to a difficulty in articulation: "I have no skill at making speeches to a crowd"(111). As his frustration mounts, he complains,

> O gods, why then can I not loose my lips,
> I who by you am ruined, you whom I revere?
> . . . I know the truth, but do no know how I can speak. (112, 114)

Hyppolytus' deficiency in expressing his thoughts in speech is analogous to his deficiency in expressing his ideals in action. This defect symbolizes the fundamental moral flaw in Hyppolytus—his inability to convert his moral principles into acceptable behavior. It is important to recognize that Hyppolytus *is* morally good; his claims of personal rectitude, though distasteful, are valid. His problem is a kind of "moral muteness," or an ineptitude in translating his idealism into action. Hyppolytus acknowledges as much on his deathbed. Although he "surpassed all men" in his "purity," he recognizes with bitterness, "O useless the efforts I made out of kindness in service to men" (122).

RECOGNIZING THE NEED IN ADMINISTRATIVE PRACTICE

One might appropriately ask at this point whether we find public administrators today who share the moral deficiencies of Hyppolytus. Stated more broadly, is the discussion of the virtue of prudence and its corresponding vice, imprudence, relevant to public administrative practice and education?

The current approach toward handguns and other weapons in public schools provides one disturbing illustration of imprudence in public administration. The moral goal—the attenuation of violence in public education—is a worthy one. In the pursuit of this goal, however, we find gross injustices committed against high school students. For example, the *Atlanta Constitution*[3] reported that authorities expelled seventeen-year-old high school student Rose Marie Spearman and charged her feloniously for bringing African artifacts to class. Because these cultural objects from her primitive hometown in Africa included a knife, she fell victim to gun control measures. Although these measures were reversed several weeks later, Spearman suffered a great deal emotionally, academically, and socially. The actions taken against her represent an absurdly imprudent attempt to reach the moral goal of civil order in the high school.

In perhaps a more spectacular example of administrative imprudence, the Federal Aviation Administration (FAA) has conducted "diversity workshops" to teach male employees greater sensitivity to the special concerns of their female counterparts. Although many men no doubt need greater insight into the special concerns of women in the workplace, the means employed to achieve this goal were scandalous and bizarre. According to news reports, men were forced to walk through a gauntlet of women as the women were instructed to grope for the genitals of the men, ridiculing the sexual prowess of their male counterparts as they did so. "Women were also asked to look at photographs of male penises in various states of arousal and were told to use them to rate their male colleagues' sexual prowess." Department of Transportation Secretary Pena has asked the Department's Inspector General to investigate, stating that he is "deeply troubled" by the allegations. One of the male participants brought suit against the Department of Transportation; it was later announced that the DOT settled the suit out of court.[4]

The careers of two prominent Surgeons General of the United States, C. Everett Koop and Joycelyn Elders, provide a contemporary allegory of prudence and imprudence in the public service. Both hold strong, if not extreme, views, with Koop on the right and Elders on the left. Because of the intensity of their opinions, both individuals underwent controversial confirmation hearings before assuming office, Koop's being the more lengthy and difficult process.

Despite Koop's confirmation, Democratic Senators and Congressman predicted his rapid demise. To the surprise of many, Koop served seven successful years as President Reagan's Surgeon General. Once in office, Koop quickly won the support and admiration of his strongest critics, even powerful senators like Sen. Edward Kennedy (D-Mass.) and Sen. Howard Metzenbaum (D-Ohio). Koop demonstrated an appreciation of the principles of nonpartisanship inherent in his office, and he clearly announced his intention to serve *all* the American people, not just those on the religious right—to the disappointment of many conservatives, we might add! During his tenure, smoking declined dramatically, and AIDS education was promoted. His promotion of AIDS education for the general public was a principled decision on his part. Such education was not approved of by conservatives, nor was it politically supported by the Reagan administration. Koop's opinions on public health issues are still regularly sought by Presidents and by the media.[5]

Elders, President Clinton's appointee to the office of Surgeon General, on the other hand, was imprudence incarnate. Despite widespread support for her in a Democrat-controlled government and sympathy for her views in the media, she unrelentingly and unnecessarily offended her constituency. In the view of one observer, she acted "as though public opinion didn't matter," a terribly naive attitude in a republic. She showed an uncanny knack for saying the wrong thing in the wrong way at the wrong time. For example, her crass remarks about the conservative "love affair with the fetus" and her ill-conceived promotion of radical sex education rapidly undermined her political capital. Elders became not only ineffective but a glaring political liability for President Clinton, who ultimately was forced to ask for her resignation in December, 1994.

Koop's views were no less "extreme" than Elders'. In August, 1992, for example, Koop—the ex-Surgeon General—told a group of first-year medical students at Dartmouth College that for a physician to perform an abortion is a violation of the sacred Hippocratic Oath to which all physicians swear allegiance. One medical student said he was "really shocked by Dr. Koop's speech."

A fundamental difference between the two public administrators was that Koop was able to implement his moral views into public life, yet Elders was not. Koop had a firm grasp not only on his own moral views but on the principles that inhered in his office. He apparently knew when he must compromise and which of his views he had to balance with the democratic values that are inseparable from the office of Surgeon General. Elders' unchecked moral zeal wreaked such political havoc that at the time of this writing the future of the Surgeon General's office in question.[6]

IMPLICATIONS AND CONCLUSIONS

A concern for prudence is at the heart of administrative ethics, whether such a concern is explicitly recognized or not. As Denhardt notes, "Professional ethics can be understood as the rules of conduct that translate the profession's characteristic ideals, or ethos, into everyday practice" (1989, 187).

Recognizing the importance of moral excellence in general, and practical wisdom in particular will encourage their promotion in administrative ethics.[7] Case study materials are helpful in this regard. Their benefit lies not so much in developing the cleverness to untangle moral conundrums as in the opportunity for the vicarious exercise of prudence. Following the example of *The Hyppolytus*, we might use the creative or fine arts to illustrate and encourage this quality.[8]

In his *Ethics*, Aristotle begins the discussion of prudence, "Regarding practical wisdom, we shall get at the truth by considering who are the persons we credit with it" (142). Following this important insight, invitees to public administrative ethics classes might be asked beforehand to comment on the following work-related questions (or questions like them):

(1)   Do you find it difficult to put your moral ideals into administrative practice?

(2)   How do you compromise, when setting or implementing policies, without completely abandoning your values or values you consider essential for good governance?

(3)   Could you describe instances in which you had to accept or promote administrative solutions to questions which, although less than perfect, were the best that could be achieved?[9]

Prudence teaches tolerance for imperfection and for compromise. Administrators must accept that, in their role as public servants, the ideal is often unattainable. Compromise, though at times unpleasant, is the hallmark of democratic governance, whether the governing activity is executive, legislative, judicial, or bureaucratic. Compromise, however, does not mean abandoning one's principles. It means prudentially tailoring those principles in the pursuit of the public interest.

Anyone promoting tolerance and compromise, risks encouraging rank relativism, or a complete surrender of principles. At times, the step from compromise to capitulation may be a short one. Moreover, casting one's moral principles aside in the pursuit of a quick solution may be the easiest path. Prudence is needed to steer an ethical course between the Scilla of reckless idealism and the Charibdis of nihilism. Running aground on either hazard inevitably produces cynicism, which is the bane of ethics. For cynicism drowns hope, and without the hope of moral excellence, ethics is no more than abstract prattle.

As we have noted, prudence presupposes the existence of virtues and ideals ready and waiting for implementation. The debate continues, however, over which ideals are most suitable for the public administrator. This discussion of the ethos of public administration considers the following, sometimes competing, moral frameworks: bureaucratic professionalism, constitutional values, democratic values, and political values. As constructive as these discussions are, it will be unfortunate if scholars are paralyzed by this debate and thus unable to offer substantive values for practitioners to adopt.

Alasdair MacIntyre has suggested that we are becoming a generation of "moral stutterers" (Sommers 1993). Prudence can undoubtedly assist in reversing this trend and facilitating greater articulation in private and public life. We might note that a focus on excellence of character, represented in this paper by practical wisdom, puts administrative ethics on the "high road" rather than the "low road" of ethics. As Bowman (1990) notes, administrative agencies must have a vision for an ethic beyond "don't do wrong!" Since the emphasis of prudence is upon doing good rather than merely avoiding trouble, a renaissance of this traditional ideal brings a measure of nobility to the study and practice of public administrative ethics.

NOTES

1. This debate is of course much richer and fuller than this reference would indicate, and accordingly it deserves the full attention of public administration students at some point in their study.

2. A play such as *The Hyppolytus*, like other great works of literature, lends itself to various interpretations and applications. Many can be useful. I am not aware of an application such as mine that makes prudence the hinge on which the entire play turns. Sutherland suggests, in passing, that "we might interpret [*The Hyppolytus*] as a study in *sophrosyne*," or temperance (1960, 81). But he also notes the "layers of meaning" present in all of Euripides' dramas. Vellacott (1963), by contrast, sees in *The Hyppolytus* a story that contrasts unforgiveness and forgiveness. Although Aphrodite will not forgive Hyppolytus for spurning her, and Hyppolytus will not forgive Phaedra's weakness, Hyppolytus redeems himself as he dies by forgiving Theseus' rashness. According to Vellacot, *The Hyppolytus* is "the one extant Greek tragedy in which we see a wrong committed by one man against another issuing in true repentance and forgiveness" (xv).

3. Thursday, October 13, 1994.

4. *Washington Times*, September 12–18, 1994, pp. 1, 14. *The New York Times*, September 8, 1994.

5. Joan Beck, *Atlanta Journal and Constitution*, December 28, 1991, "Koop Rates AIDS Education His Top Success." *Atlanta Journal and Constitution*, February 19, 1995, "Ignore The Oscars—Here Are the Best Performances." *The Atlanta Journal and Constitution*, August 29, 1992, "Koop Says Abortion Violates Doctor's Oath," p. B-1.

6. For a fuller discussion of Koop's integrity in public office, see Bowman 1992.

7. We must acknowledge at this point the complete rejection of the classical tradition of prudence, first by the amorality of Machiavelli in the sixteenth century and later in the American tradition by the instrumentalism of William James and John Dewey. For Machiavelli (1950; Garver 1987), the volatility of fate, or "Fortune" as he personalizes it, demands that leaders substitute cunning and craftiness for prudence. For James (1907) and Dewey (1920, 1935, 1939), the classical ideals are defunct, most of all because they are nonutilitarian. Dewey went so far as to add the indictment that Greek philosophy and Christian theology were the tools used to preserve the socioeconomic "status quo." Obviously, I reject that view.

8. For more explicit ideas on using literature in teaching administrative ethics, see Edmondson, "Teaching Administrative Ethics With Help From Jefferson," *PS: Political Science and Politics*, June 1995, Volume XXVIII, Number 2, *The Teacher*, pp. 226–29. To see a recent discussion of the value of literature in conveying principles in general, see the symposium "Literature and Politics" in the same issue of *PS*. Also see Sommers (1993).

9. Instructors might also consider Cooper's (1992) recent compilation of biographical sketches of public administrators.

REFERENCES

Aquinas, Thomas. 1948. *Summa Theologica* (Fathers of the English Dominican Province, trans.). Wesminister, MD: Christian Classics.

Aristotle. 1984. *The Nicomachean Ethics* (David Ross, Trans.). Oxford: Oxford University Press.

Bailey, Stephen K. 1965. "Ethics and the Public Service," in Rosco Martin, ed., *Public Administration and Democracy: Essays in Honor of Paul H. Appleby*. Syracuse: Syracuse University Press.

Beck, Joan. 1992. "Ignore The Oscars—Here Are the Best Performances." *Atlanta Constitution*, August 29.

Bowman, James S. 1992. "C. Everett Koop: Integrity—No Matter What," in Cooper and Wright, eds., *Exemplary Public Administrators: Character and Leadership in Government*. San Francisco: Jossey-Bass Publishers.

Bowman, James S. 1990. "Ethics in Government: A National Survey of Public Administrators," *Public Administration Review*, 50, May/June, 345–53.

Cooper, Terry L. 1987. "Hierarchy, Virtue, and the Practice of Public Administration: A Perspective for Normative Ethics," *Public Administration Review*, 47, July/August, 320–28.

Cooper, Terry L., and N. Dale Wright, eds. 1992. *Exemplary Public Administration: Character and Leadership in Government*. San Francisco: Jossey-Bass Publishers.

Denhardt, Kathryn G. 1989. "The Management of Ideals: A Political Perspective on Ethics." *Public Administration Review*, 2, 187–93.

Dewey, John. 1920. *Reconstruction in Philosophy*. New York: Henry Holt and Company.

———. 1935. *Liberalism and Social Action*. New York: G. P. Putnam's Sons.

———. 1939. *Freedom and Culture*. New York: G. P. Putnam's Sons.

Dobel, J. Patrick. 1990. "Integrity in the Public Service." *Public Administration Review*, 50, May/June, 354–66.

Edmondson, Henry T. III. 1995. "Teaching Administrative Ethics with Help from Jefferson." *PS: Political Science and Politics*, 28, June, 226–29.

Euripides: Medea, Hyppolytus, The Bacchae (Phillip Vellacott, Trans.). New York: The Heritage Press.

"FAA Conducts Diversity Workshop." 1994. *Washington Times*, September 12, pp. 1, 14.

"FAA Settles Diversity Workshop Suit." 1994. *The New York Times*, September 8, p. 15A.

Finer, Herman. 1941. "Administrative Responsibility in Democratic Government." *Public Administration Review*, 1, 335–50.

Friedrich, Carl J. 1935. "Responsible Government Service Under the American Constitution," in *Problems of the American Public Service*. New York: McGraw-Hill.

Garver, Eugene. 1987. *Machiavelli and the History of Prudence*. Madison: University of Wisconsin Press.

Hart, David K. 1984. "The Virtuous Citizen, the Honorable Bureaucrat, and 'Public Administration.'" *Public Administration Review*, Special Issue, 44.

James, William. 1975. *Pragmatism*. Cambridge: Harvard University Press.

"Koop Rates AIDS Education His Top Success." 1991. *Atlanta Constitution*, December 28, p. 8A.

"Koop Says Abortion Violates Doctor's Oath." 1992. *Atlanta Constitution*, August 29, p. B1.

MacIntyre, Alasdair. 1984. *After Virtue* (2nd ed.). Notre Dame: University of Notre Dame Press.

Machiavelli, Niccoli. 1950. *The Prince and the Discourses*. New York: The Modern Library.

Pieper, Josef. 1966. *The Four Cardinal Virtues: Prudence, Justice, Fortitude, and Temperance*. Notre Dame: University of Notre Dame Press.

Pieper, Josef. 1959. *Prudence*. New York: Pantheon Books.

Plato. 1985. *The Memo* (R. W. Sharples, Trans.). Chicago: Bolchazy-Carducci.

Plato. 1968. *The Republic* (Allan Bloom, Trans.). New York: Basic Books.

Richardson, William D. and Lloyd G. Nigro. 1987. "Administrative Ethics and Founding Thought: Constitutional Correctives, Honor, and Education." *Public Administration Review*, 47, September/October, 367–75.

———. 1987. "Self-Interest Properly Understood: The American Character and Public Administration." *Administration and Society*, 19, August, 157–77.

Rohr, John A. 1978. *Ethics For Bureaucrats: An Essay On Law and Values*. New York: Marcel Dekker.

Sartre, Jean-Paul (1949). "Dirty Hands" (Lionel Abel, Trans.), in, *No Exit and Three Other Plays*. New York: Vintage Book.

Sommers, Christina Hoff. 1993. "Teaching the Virtues." *The Public Interest*, 11, 3–13.

"Student Expelled For Artifacts in Class." 1994. *Atlanta Constitution*, October 13, p. 4A.

Sutherland, Donald. 1960. *Hyppolytus in Drama and Myth*. Lincoln and London: University of Nebraska Press.

Euripedes. *Three Great Plays of Euripides* (Rex Warner, Trans.). 1958. New York: New American Library.

Walzer, Michael. 1973. "Political Action: The Problem of Dirty Hands." *Philosophy and Public Affairs*, 2, 160–80.

CHAPTER 8

Using Codes of Ethics in
Teaching Public Administration

JEREMY F. PLANT

Teaching ethics has become an accepted part of the curriculum of graduate programs in Public Administration (PA). Indeed, coverage of ethics is required for those seeking accreditation by the National Association of Schools of Public Affairs and Administration (NASPAA). Scholars have noted how the resurgence of interest in administrative ethics in the past twenty years, especially the concern for the role of government and discretionary administrative action in the name of the state, has returned to themes expressed in the formative decades of Public Administration (Catron and Denhardt 1994; Hejka-Ekins 1988). The common thread is stated by John Rohr: "the heart of the ethical issue for American bureaucrats is that through their administrative discretion they govern a democratic polity" (Rohr 1978, p. 49). How best to educate students around that issue has been less clear. Considerable diversity in approach, emphasis, rigor, and instructor qualifications persists, even in accredited programs. The situation is not likely to change in the foreseeable future (Catron and Denhardt 1994).

Increased interest in teaching administrative ethics has coincided with the ethics explosion in the United States (Lewis 1991; Cooper 1994). Questions of morality and right conduct in public affairs are now considered to be as significant as the traditional concerns of

* The author wishes to thank Professor Cynthia Massie and Mr. Richard White of the School of Public Affairs, Penn State Harrisburg, for their thoughtful criticisms of this essay.

Wilsonian Public Administration: efficiency, accountability, and the progressive introduction of rationality into public life. The burgeoning interest in ethics is reflected in the proliferation of what can be termed the "artifacts" of public ethics: codes of ethics, statements of organizational and professional goals and values, statutes (especially at the state level) identifying acceptable (or, more commonly, unacceptable) behavior enforced by law.

All ethics artifacts can be used in teaching ethics courses. This paper focuses exclusively on one type, codes of ethics. How can codes of ethics be used to assist in the ethics education of individuals pursuing careers in public service? How do they fit into the various educational strategies that are being used in PA programs around the country? What is the particular importance of the updated code of the American Society for Public Administration (ASPA)? This is the subject addressed in this chapter.

Three arguments are made in favor of broad utilization of codes in teaching administrative ethics. First, they are artifacts, and they are real; they can be used to bring *reality* to the discussion of moral principles, ethical dilemmas, and right conduct that otherwise may take on ephemeral or abstract qualities. Second, they link *professionalism* with ethics in a way that enables students and practitioners (often one and the same in MPA programs) to see the connection between work-related specifics and more generalized issues of public service in a democracy (Mosher 1968; Plant 1994). Third, despite the shortcomings of much actual codemaking, the *process* of creating codes is one way of linking moral discourse and moral deliberation to the day-to-day reality of associations and political institutions.

Nonetheless, codes of ethics have not been well loved among ethics scholars. Despite the adoption of a code by the American Society for Public Administration in 1984 and the reverence in which some codes of long duration, especially that of the International City/County Management Association, are held, codes are considered by many as either irrelevant to practitioners (Gortner 1991); overly legalistic and restrictive (Rohr 1978; Foster 1981); or statements based on professional credentialism and economic advancement rather than moral judgment (Plant 1994). They typify, in Rohr's well-known term, "the low road" of how to stay out of trouble (Rohr, 1978, pp. 51–2). The sense that codes are meaningless in inducing ethical conduct, or not based on strong and systematic moral reasoning, or grounded in adequate understanding of underlying ethical theory has no doubt limited their utilization in teaching administrative ethics.

This essay is intended in part to show how effective codes of ethics can be when combined with instruction in moral reasoning and the ethical dilemmas endemic to modern governance. I take it as a given that effective ethics education in a professional field such as PA requires attention both to underlying concepts and ethically charged situations likely to confront practicing professionals.

BACKGROUND

Before proceeding with strategies to use codes of ethics in teaching ethics in Public Administration, let us briefly review the background of ethics codes in the United States. It is important for instructors to understand that codes of public ethics are based on a variety of motives and intellectual traditions. Codes contain elements of three traditions: jurisprudence, normative political philosophy, and professionalism (Kernaghan 1974; Chandler 1983; Plant 1994). As products of legalism, codes attempt to specify right conduct and proscribe wrong conduct, often attaching procedures for identifying and verifying misconduct and pursuing disciplinary actions. Their intent, and often their impact, is to limit discretion and channel administrative activity into narrow bands of compliance. Even if worded in the language of philosophy or normative political theory, legalistic codes—especially those promulgated by levels of government—stress avoidance of wrongdoing, usually financial conflicts of interest, over positive moral reasoning (Plant and Gortner 1981; Lewis and Gilman 1991; Dobel 1991).

The legalistic approach to codes in the post-Watergate era has resulted in a burst of restrictive codes and ethics legislation. McCullough (1994) summarizes the legalistic approach to ethics in this way:

A good code of conduct establishes standards of behavior for public servants. It includes clear and strict regulations on conflicts of interest, acceptance of gifts and travel, post-employment restrictions, nepotism, and the improper use of public office. Limits on the financial interests of government officials and employees in government business are set. It is important that these codes not appeal to the lowest common denominator. In the "give and take" involved in getting legislation passed, it is important that high standards be maintained in the code of conduct. (pp. 247–78).

Before leaving our discussion of legal reasoning as the basis of ethics codes, it is important to raise the issue of real and perceived violations of proper conduct (Thompson 1985; 1992). Legalism complicates the democratic issue of perceived wrongdoing. Are codes intended to eliminate the perception as well as the actual incidence of wrongdoing? The notion that codes are a "low road" often comes from claims by individuals that conduct unbecoming a public official is protected by the specific caveats of a code. An example from contemporary public life might be Speaker Newt Gingrich's argument that his contract to write a book (and receive a large advance payment) does not fall into the category of proscribed activities for a congressman, despite the suggestion of potential conflicts of interest and the obvious similarities to similar problems that brought down Speaker Jim Wright, problems that were publicly noted by Gingrich himself. It is precisely this tendency for legally reasoned codes to be reduced to hair-splitting application that concerns ethicists in Public Administration who argue from the tradition of normative political discourse (Rohr 1978; Denhardt 1989).

Normative discourse in Public Administration focuses on inner controls rather than external management of conduct. It is a tradition that dates back to the 1930s in the writings of John Gaus, Marshall Dimock, and especially Carl Friedrich, whose ongoing debates with Herman Finer clarified the argument over internal and external means of creating ethical behavior (Cooper 1994). The tradition languished for decades until the identification in the late 1960s and early 1970s of bases of administrative behavior outside the traditional normative constructs of hierarchy, political control, and strict bureaucratic accountability (Appleby 1952; Bailey 1964).

Two somewhat distinct traditions of normative discourse evolved. The New Public Administration movement focused on social equity and positive notions of justice. Democratic constitutionalism, in the words of John Rohr, its leading proponent, "looks for practical ways in which civil servants might operationalize their oath to uphold the Constitution of the United States" (Rohr 1994, p. 505). Both have had little good to say about codifying ethical conduct, since their emphasis is on the moral reasoning of individuals. Only the base of reasoning varied, from philosophical constructs of justice to the meaning of democratic values in the contemporary context of action (Hart 1974, 1984, 1989). Words such as *virtue, benevolence,* and *honor* form the key to both these traditions. They are words far removed from either legalistic or positivistic justifications for codes.

The third basis of codes is the continuing professionalization of public affairs (Cigler 1990). Professionalism is an attempt to link values with expertise in the performance of specialized tasks. For the professional, each day brings the challenge of applying core knowledge and core values to unique events, each slightly different from what has gone before. Professionalism in government has been a major theme of the literature since Mosher (1968) pointed out how far Public Administration had moved from the strict organizationalism of traditional bureaucratic theory toward control by professionals. Professionalism in society had paralleled the rise of modern Public Administration and in many ways contributed to it. Professional associations have drawn membership from public officials for over a century (Arnold and Plant 1994) and have provided a number of codes of ethics that bind (sometimes through the individual, sometimes by official recognition of credentials by the state) individual practitioners.

Codification by professionals emphasizes internalization of norms by the individual, but asks the individual not to be a moral reasoner but a practitioner who needs the assistance provided by the code to understand accepted values in the world of practice. Codification as impacted by public professionalism leads to specificity, but unlike the legalistic tradition it puts the individual decision maker and not some enforcer in the central role. Enforcement, if it does occur, tends to be in the hands of peers.

Professionalism as a motive includes economic as well as moral reasoning as a justification for including provisions of codes. Economic reasoning identifies the ways in which favorable exchange of value, to the profession as a whole or to individual professionals, results from the adoption of codes and the enforcement of proper conduct. It assumes that society will find either the appearance or the enforcement of a professional code as a justification for restricting access, denying the need for public regulation, narrowing the bases of litigation for malfeasance, or other economic benefits that may be appropriate. The language of the code may be important, but it rarely is assessed using philosophical analysis.

The key to understanding ethics codes is in the language. Codes are collections of words. In the wording of codes is the key to their understanding and their use by teachers. It is to the wording of codes that we now direct our attention.

CODES OF ETHICS AS ARTIFACTS

Codes of ethics have one great advantage to the teacher of public ethics: they are *real*. They are groups of words, often printed in uniform manner for distribution to a set audience. They can be reproduced, gathered, compared, cut-and-pasted, used as course handouts or discussion items. To many students of PA, who are accustomed to dealing with the written word and sometimes prejudiced in favor of a supposed "real world" of practice, contrasted to a shadowy world of academic theory and jargon, codes help to demystify a course on ethics and add legitimacy to the undertaking.

A number of options are thus presented to the ethics instructor. One is to examine a number of codes, looking for the common threads or the unusual and particularistic. Immediately two approaches beckon. One is to look at the language of the codes and see it as a clue to the power they have in producing ethical action. As Chandler (1989) notes, the wording of codes embodies "the symbolic power of words. They inspire, they set a tone, and they create expectations" (p. 617). What makes the wording of one code inspiring and another pedantic or preachy? How does the specific wording of the code enable it to meet the expectations of different audiences?

One is reminded of the story concerning T. S. Eliot at a tea party. A distinguished matron approaches the famed poet and says, "Mr. Eliot, I have a wonderful idea for a poem." Eliot looks down at her through horn-rimmed glasses and says cruelly, "Madam, poems are made with *words*, not ideas." So too with codes. The wording is critical to their success. As Meier (1993, p. 194) points out, many writings on ethics, including the ASPA code, "have been criticized for using concepts (moral ambiguity, courage, optimism, and so on) so ambiguous [sic] as to defy definition."

Fortunately, examples abound whereby the actual language of codes can be compared. First, there are excellent examples of successful codes that have been reworded to reflect the changing conditions (or sometimes to word them more elegantly and effectively). Two that offer a number of opportunities to the instructor are the ICMA code, in place since 1924 and modified extensively in 1938, 1952, 1969, 1976, and 1987; and the ASPA code, reworded in 1994 after ten years of existence, and discussed in detail below.

One teaching approach is to take the older code (the one in use immediately before the most recent iteration) and ask students to assess the language critically and suggest revisions. This can be done either through in-class small-group sessions, allowing ample time for discussion; out-of-class group assignment; or individual reflection outside the class setting. However done, the objective is to compare what the students have produced with the actual revisions of the codes as a starting point for discussion. Is the purpose of the revision a clarification, simplification, or a continuing approximation of the core values of the group or society under changing conditions? Making the ICMA code gender unspecific is a good example of the latter. The ASPA code is an example of simplification both of language and of organization and presentation.

The role of the instructor at this point is to facilitate critical examination of the differences in wording in two respects: as an exercise in language and expression, and in terms of the moral values represented by the differences among the draft codes. This allows the instructor to move into a categorization of ethical approaches (such as, consequentialism, deontology, virtue ethics) or, if the course included discussion of ethical approaches beforehand, to clarify and make more substantial through the examples previous discussions of such approaches. It is also an opportunity to bring to the attention of the students the importance of law, normative political theory, and professionalism as motives for codification.

Focusing on the language of codes and the relationship of words to moral values has the effect of moving the discussion past literalism into process considerations as well. How different is the crafting of code language in a group setting, compared to the work of the individual working in isolation? How does codemaking stimulate discourse on morals and lead to better connections between moral reasoning and the ethical artifact?

A critical variable in the use of codes in teaching PA is the composition of the ethics class. Is it composed of inservice students, and if so, what is the range of occupational specialties (for example, health care, educational administration, criminal justice)? How many individuals are bound by codes of ethics promulgated by employers or professional associations? How many, through ASPA, have thought about codes of ethics prior to enrolling in the graduate program? Preservice students, by contrast, usually lack firsthand familiarity with codes, but may not suffer the cynicism about codes so common among public servants (Gortner 1991). A class mixing the two groups is the most challenging to the instructor, but the one that may yield the most interesting (and contentious) discourse about the proper wording of a code and its impact on behavior.

CODES AS MORAL REASONING AND POLITICAL PHILOSOPHY

Codes are artifacts constructed out of words. But they are also attempts to give expression to public values. As I have argued elsewhere (Plant 1994), codes of ethics for public administrators are necessary political statements to reinforce the idea that public officeholders must adhere to higher standards of conduct than others in society. They increase the legitimacy of public administration by extolling democratic values and public service as public trust.

The idea that codes are statements relating ethical conduct to democratic values enables analysis to move beyond language to the ideas behind them. Does the code encompass the universe of values and related behaviors that constitute ethical administration in a democracy? What trivial aspects of conduct are included, and what is left out? Are the provisions of the code based on moral reasoning, professional advantage, or normative political theory? Again, the first requirement for effective teaching is a supply of numerous codes and some explanation of what type of organization, profession, or government unit has developed the code.

The code of the American Society for Public Administration (ASPA) is particularly useful for teaching purposes. ASPA aspires to play a central role in the profession and discipline. Its code is a logical candidate to use, singly or by comparison with others, in sorting out the intellectual roots of the principles and canons included. ASPA's position as the generalist association representing the universe of Public Administrationists in the country—academics and students as well as public servants—makes its code the most widely disseminated and the most frequently cited (along with that of ICMA) in the literature. The revisions of 1994, in which the original twelve canons of the code as adopted in 1984 were grouped into five principles, are illustrated below (See Figure 8.1).

A careful reading of the preamble of the code is a first step. Advancing professionalism and public awareness of the importance of public service ethics are noted as the justification for promulgating the code. The code is designed for the professional public administrator or academic, not the citizen or the elected official, as close reading of the document reveals. A code proclaiming the need to "conduct official acts without partisanship" (III.6) or "be prepared to make decisions that may not be popular" (I.8) is not likely to be useful for elected officials or civic activists.

Looking at the list of five principles and determining what they as a set say about the definition of the ethical problem in the field is the next step. In a sense, the principles identify major streams of writing and research that have molded the ethics debate within ASPA and the field in general. Principle I, Serve the Public Interest, is an amalgam of the Appleby and Bailey mandarinism and the New Public Administration interest in citizen involvement and commitment to social

American Society for Public Administration
Code of Ethics

The American Society for Public Administration (ASPA) exists to advance the science, processes, and art of public administration. The Society affirms its responsibility to develop the spirit of professionalism within its membership, and to increase public awareness of ethical principles in public service by its example. To this end, we, the members of the Society, commit ourselves to the following principles:

I Serve the Public Interest

Serve the public, beyond serving oneself.
ASPA members are committed to:

1. Exercise discretionary authority to promote the public interest.
2. Oppose all forms of discrimination and harassment, and promote affirmative action.
3. Recognize and support the public's right to know the public's business.
4. Involve citizens in policy decision-making.
5. Exercise compassion, benevolence, fairness and optimism.
6. Respond to the public in ways that are complete, clear, and easy to understand.
7. Assist citizens in their dealings with government.
8. Be prepared to make decisions that may not be popular.

II Respect the Constitution and the Law

Respect, support, and study government constitutions and laws that define responsibilities of public agencies, employees, and all citizens.
ASPA members are committed to:

1. Understand and apply legislation and regulations relevant to their professional role.
2. Work to improve and change laws and policies that are counter-productive or obsolete.
3. Eliminate unlawful discrimination.
4. Prevent all forms of mismanagement of public funds by establishing and maintaining strong fiscal and management controls, and by supporting audits and investigative activities.
5. Respect and protect privileged information.
6. Encourage and facilitate legitimate dissent activities in government and protect the whistleblowing rights of public employees.
7. Promote constitutional principles of equality, fairness, representativeness, responsiveness and due process in protecting citizens' rights.

III Demonstrate Personal Integrity

Demonstrate the highest standards in all activities to inspire public confidence and trust in public service.
ASPA members are committed to:

1. Maintain truthfulness and honesty and to not compromise them for advancement, honor, or personal gain.
2. Ensure that others receive credit for their work and contributions.
3. Zealously guard against conflict of interest or its appearance: e.g., nepotism, improper outside employment, misuse of public resources or the acceptance of gifts.
4. Respect superiors, subordinates, colleagues and the public.
5. Take responsibility for their own errors.
6. Conduct official acts without partisanship.

IV Promote Ethical Organizations

Strengthen organizational capabilities to apply ethics, efficiency and effectiveness in serving the public.
ASPA members are committed to:

1. Enhance organizational capacity for open communication, creativity, and dedication.
2. Subordinate institutional loyalties to the public good.
3. Establish procedures that promote ethical behavior and hold individuals and organizations accountable for their conduct.
4. Provide organization members with an administrative means for dissent, assurance of due process and safeguards against reprisal.
5. Promote merit principles that protect against arbitrary and capricious actions.
6. Promote organizational accountability through appropriate controls and procedures.
7. Encourage organizations to adopt, distribute, and periodically review a code of ethics as a living document.

continued

V **Strive for Professional Excellence**

Strengthen individual capabilities and encourage the professional development of others.
ASPA members are committed to:

1. Provide support and encouragement to upgrade competence.
2. Accept as a personal duty the responsibility to keep up to date on emerging issues and potential problems.
3. Encourage others, throughout their careers, to participate in professional activities and associations.
4. Allocate time to meet with students and provide a bridge between classroom studies and the realities of public service.

Enforcement of the Code of Ethics shall be conducted in accordance with Article I, Section 4 of ASPA's Bylaws.
In 1981 the American Society for Public Administration's National Council adopted a set of moral principles. Three years later in 1984, the Council approved a Code of Ethics for ASPA members. In 1994 the Code was revised.

The American Society for Public Administration • 1120 G Street, NW Suite 700, Washington DC 20005 • 202/393-7878 • http://www.aspanet.org

Figure 8.1. Code of Ethics

equity. Perhaps the common ground is indicated by the placement of I.1, "Exercise discretionary authority to promote the public interest." Discretion as a good is the obvious shared value of the two schools. Principle II, Respect the Constitution and the Law, is a blend of the legalistic approach, on the one hand, and the constitutionalists who argue for the promotion of the values embedded in constitutions and the moral worth of swearing an oath to a higher law, on the other. Principle III illustrates the importance of the virtue approach to ethics, although most of Principle I and Canon II.7 fit with its emphasis on exemplary action and a focus on the individual (Cooper and Wright 1992). Principle IV, Promote Ethical Organizations, begins with a statement affirming organization humanism, but later canons balance this with a concern for formal structures and processes to promote accountability and due process. Principle V, Strive for Professional Excellence, illustrates the importance of codes for enhancing professionalism as well as the ability to engage in moral reasoning.

The instructor can develop class discussion in two ways. First, does the list of principles sum up the universe of ethical issues in the field? Second, looking at the principles separately, where do they come from in the literature on ethics, and how are they guides to ethical behavior?

The instructor can analyze the ASPA code for its choice of words as well as ideas. Does the ASPA code live up to its hopes of comprehensiveness, relevance, and clarity? Is it a statement based on ethics, a political document, or a basis of public professionalism? My own experience indicates that the ASPA code seems more comprehensive and much better organized in its 1994 wording than in its original language. So much so, in fact, that it seems to many students to have been transformed from the typical "statement of ideals" sort of code to one that really says something. The grouping of canons into the five categories is a key to making the new code seem so different. It provides the opportunity to assess the logic and internal consistency of the items within each category and to look at the array of principles to see how well they encompass the universe of ethical concerns in the public service.

One does not have to look far to find controversy in the ASPA code. Canon I.2 states unequivocally that ASPA members must "oppose all forms of discrimination and harassment, and promote affirmative action." Yet the current debate raging over affirmative action finds many believing that it is in fact a form of discrimination and a violation of the moral principle of equality before the law. Advocates of "color-blind equal opportunity" (CBEO) seek the moral high ground for their opposition to AA (Kinsley 1995). Any instructor using the ASPA code in the classroom had best be prepared for a rousing debate on the ethics of affirmative action and the representativeness norm in general. It is underscored by the apparent redundancy between Canons I.2 and II.3, which states that members should "eliminate unlawful discrimination." The difference, of course, is that principle I is concerned not with legal but with moral reasoning: affirmative action is not just law but an ethical imperative, a positive duty to advance and not simply a constraint to suffer.

The challenge to the instructor is to deal analytically with the issue of affirmative action (or similarly hot political issues). Is the argument for affirmative action simply a moral one? Certainly not. Economists have come out on both sides of the issue, meritocrats arguing against it on the basis of limiting opportunities for talented nonprotected-class individuals, and equalitarians in favor of it on the basis of enhancing the upward mobility of talented minority individuals (and perhaps legitimating the toil of other minorities who now feel that the system has treated them badly for reasons other than race, gender, or national origin). Is it hypocritical to be in favor of affirmative action in principle but fearful of its consequences in one's own career or the aspirations of one's children? Certainly. Here John Rohr's idea of the value of hypocrisy is relevant:

> It is hypocritical to urge others to adhere to norms we violate ourselves, but it is also profoundly civilized to do so. Civilizations demand the handing on from one generation to another of the standards that define a people. Thoughtful persons do not want their children's moral vision narrowed by their own moral failings and hence, wisely, they preach what they fail to practice. (Rohr 1995, p. 11)

The important point is that the code puts the ball in play; its language requires us to pay attention to the issue. Hypocrite or saint, AA protector or CBEO missionary, the issue is joined by the code, and it allows us in the classroom to enter into the debate with some practical consequences attached.

A second controversial area is the economic impact of codes, especially those promulgated by a professional association such as ASPA. Does the wording of the code limit access or competition, or otherwise add to the value of membership in an exclusive group of practitioners? If so, is it intentional or a by-product of the professionalization process of which it is a part? Or is the code a public relations tool to convince society of the need to revere and value public servants or a particular public profession? Few studies of codes have used economic motivation as a key to understanding behavior. Unfortunately for researchers, economic motives behind codes represent a category of Simon's decision premises that are almost impossible to identify with certainty as causation for action. But it may nonetheless be useful for the instructor to force discussion on codes to consider whether they are framed for the purpose of adding value to the work of ASPA members.

CONCLUSIONS

Codes have to be presented to students for what they are: efforts to use language to encourage ethical behavior. Codes are imperfect instruments to move us closer to whatever moral utopia we imagine human beings are capable of creating. They sometimes show a confusion of professional, legal, and moral reasoning. They often thinly disguise economic opportunity with the patina of moralizing. They collect dust on office walls. They may on occasion give comfort to the coward that the right words can substitute for right action. The empirically minded find little evidence that they are the basis of moral activity.

This essay has suggested that codes of ethics form a critical connection between language and the interest of Public Administration in ethics. The fact that they are manifestations of the desire of the state and of professional associations to elevate the work of the public service gives them a good deal of utility in teaching PA. The focus has been on analyzing them as exercises in language rather than as producers of behavior. We still know little about the premises of decisions, and the tradition of self-reporting through questionnaires and interviews does little to validate the movement of subjective data to the realm of objective knowledge. Case studies that purport to show the impact of codes, or that use codification or code enforcement to draw some conclusions in the classroom about ethics or professional standards, are useful and should be supplemented by the actual introduction of codes into the class setting.

Codes, like the stories told in organizations or the exemplary conduct of virtuous administrators, have the capacity to elevate the work of the public servant and link it to the higher vision of democracy. As Rohr points out, PA all too often is drudgery; "it deals with day-to-day problems that have lost their glamour" (Rohr 1995 p. 18). With this often comes cynicism, indifference, and defeatism—things that are truly bad for the soul of individuals and the future of democracy. Codes, to use the language of T. S. Eliot in *Four Quartets*, use affirmational language to create either attachment to practical affairs or detachment, but never indifference, "which resembles the others as death resembles life" (Eliot 1971, p. 142). In the final analysis, this is the task of teaching ethics in the Public Administration program: finding a way to inject a faith in the possibility of operant moral and democratic administration in the face of the intractibility of problems and the cynical manipulation of public opinion and symbols that now pass for politics and journalism. Few tasks in our society are harder, and few are more important. Codes help to lend an air of reality to the undertaking.

NOTES

1. "Code of ethics" is used as the generic name for a variety of terms in actual use: codes of behavior, statutory codes, and so on.

2. I use the term "canon" here without explicit language in the ASPA code using that term.

REFERENCES

Appleby, Paul H. 1952. *Morality and Administration in Democratic Government.* Baton Rouge: LSU Press.

Arnold, David S., and Jeremy F. Plant. 1994. *Public Official Associations and State and Local Government: A Bridge Across One Hundred Years.* Fairfax, VA: George Mason Press.

Bailey, Stephen K. 1964. "Ethics and the Public Service." *Public Administration Review,* 24, 234–43.

Catron, Bayard L., and Kathryn G. Denhardt. 1994. "Ethics Education in Public Administration." In Terry L. Cooper, ed., *Handbook of Administrative Ethics.* New York: Marcel Dekker.

Chandler, Ralph C. 1983. "The Problem of Moral Reasoning in American Public Administration: The Case for a Code of Ethics." *Public Administration Review,* 43, 32–39.

Cigler, Beverly A. 1990. "Public Administration and the Paradox of Professionalism." *Public Administration Review,* 50, 637–53.

Cooper, Terry L. 1994. "The Emergence of Administrative Ethics." In Terry L. Cooper, ed., *Handbook of Administrative Ethics.* New York: Marcel Dekker.

Cooper, Terry L., and N. Dale Wright. 1992. *Exemplary Public Administrators: Character and Leadership in Government.* San Francisco: Jossey-Bass.

Denhardt, Kathryn G. 1989. "The Management of Ideals: A Political Perspective on Ethics." *Public Administration Review,* 49, 187–93.

Dobel, J. Patrick. 1992. "The Realpolitik of Ethics Codes." Conference papers of the Conference on the Study of Government Ethics, Park City, UT.

Eliot, Thomas S. 1971. *The Complete Poems and Plays 1909–1950.* New York: Harcourt, Brace & World.

Foster, Gregory D. 1981. "Law, Morality and the Public Servant." *Public Administration Review,* 41, 29–33.

Gortner, Harold F. 1991. "How Public Managers View Their Environment: Balancing Organization Demands, Political Realities, and Personal Values." In James S. Bowman, ed., *Ethical Frontiers in Public Management.* San Francisco: Jossey-Bass.

Hart, David K. 1974. "Social Equity, Justice, and the Equitable Administrator." *Public Administration Review,* 34, 3–11.

Hart, David K. 1984. "The Virtuous Citizen, the Honorable Bureaucrat, and 'Public' Administration." *Public Administration Review,* 44, 111–20.

Hart, David K. 1989. "A Partnership in Virtue Among All Citizens: The Public Service and Civic Humanism." *Public Administration Review,* 49 101–5.

Hejka-Ekins, April. 1988. "Teaching Ethics in Public Administration." *Public Administration Review,* 48, 885–91.

Kernaghan, Kenneth. 1974. "Codes of Ethics and Administrative Responsibility." *Canadian Public Administration,* 17, 524–41.

Kinsley, Michael. 1995. "The Spoils of Victimhood." *The New Yorker,* March 27, 62–69.

Lewis, Carol W. 1991. *The Ethics Challenge in Public Service*. San Francisco: Jossey-Bass.

Lewis, Carol W., and Stuart C. Gilman. 1991. "Ethics Codes and Ethics Agencies: Emerging Trends." Conference papers of the Conference on the Study of Government Ethics, Park City, UT.

McCullough, Harriet. 1994. "Ethics Legislation." In Terry L. Cooper, ed., *Handbook of Administrative Ethics*. New York: Marcel Dekker, 243–65.

Meier, Kenneth J. 1993. *Politics and Bureaucracy* (3rd ed.). Pacific Grove, CA: Brooks/Cole.

Mosher, Frederick C. 1968. *Democracy and the Public Service*. New York: Oxford U. Press.

Plant, Jeremy F. 1994. "Codes of Ethics." In Terry L. Cooper, ed., *Handbook of Administrative Ethics*. New York: Marcel Dekker, 221–41.

Plant, Jeremy F., and Harold F. Gortner. 1981. "Ethics, Personnel Management, and Civil Service Reform." *Public Personnel Management Journal*, 10, 3–10.

Rohr, John A. 1978. *Ethics for Bureaucrats: An Essay on Law and Values*. New York: Marcel Dekker.

Rohr, John A. 1994. "Constitutionalism and Administrative Ethics: A Comparative Study of Canada, France, the United Kingdom, and the United States." In Terry L. Cooper, ed., *Handbook of Administrative Ethics*. New York: Marcel Dekker, 505–25.

Rohr, John A. 1995. Keynote Address to the National Symposium on Ethics and Values in the Public Administration Academy, Tampa, FL, February 2 (mimeo).

Thompson, Dennis F. 1985. "The Possibility of Administrative Ethics." *Public Administration Review*, 45, 555–69.

Thompson, Dennis F. 1992. "Paradoxes of Government Ethics." *Public Administration Review*, 52, 254–59.

CHAPTER 9

Teaching Public and Private Sector Ethics: Some Fundamental Differences and Surprising Similarities

ROBERT W. SMITH

As public administrators look to the twenty-first century, one of the significant trends they must grapple with is the increasing reliance on the private sector to provide a variety of public services. Hence, the greater the frequency of privatization and shared partnerships, the greater the need for public administrators at all levels to understand the nature of both business transactions and business ethics. Donald Kettl echoes the sentiment that "Government by proxy unquestionably produces a more complex policy system, characterized by more complex public-private relationships that threaten to attenuate the ties between government and citizens" (Kettl 1988, p. 26).[1]

Public administrators have responded by acknowledging both the theoretical and practical sides of privatization and shared partnerships (e.g., Kettl 1993; Osborne and Gaebler 1991; Perry and Rainey 1988; and Weinberg 1983). Yet as public administrators find themselves involved in more and more privatization scenarios, it is essential to take proactive steps toward better understanding ethics in the private sector. This can be accomplished by closely examining the ethical perspectives of business and by developing a fuller understanding of business ethics.

Given the broad scope of the topic, it is not possible to present an exhaustive treatise. Instead, a synopsis is provided of the major tenets that emerge when comparing public and private sector ethics curricula. The inquiry was prepared from a synthesis of course syllabi, textbook material, interviews with ethics instructors, and a survey of the relevant literatures.[2]

The chapter begins with a section on the treatment of business versus public ethics in the literature. The main body of the essay compares some major themes that emerge when examining course content in both fields. The discussion concludes by suggesting that the ethics curriculum in the public sector can be strengthened by drawing upon the differences *and* similarities with business ethics.

BACKGROUND

Although any systematic reduction of materials for comparative purposes is problematic, particularly in a diverse field such as "ethics in government," it is nonetheless appropriate to focus on a representative selection of the texts commonly used in ethics courses in public administration and widely cited in the ethics literature. Textbooks in this review include Bowman (1991), Cooper (1990), Denhardt (1988), Frederickson (1993), Lewis (1991), and Rohr (1989). Although widely acknowledged as hallmarks and frequently used in ethics courses, these works do not examine the role of private sector ethics; nor do they consider its relationship to ethics in the public service. Even research-oriented works such as Cooper's (1994) *Handbook of Administrative Ethics* do not focus on the role or influence of private sector business ethics.

This is not to say that the public-private ethics interface has not been examined by the field. One such study undertook an empirical comparison of public and private employee behavior in an effort to explore whether public employees were less ethical than private sector employees (Baldwin 1991). Berman, et al. (1994) examine differences between public and private ethics management in large cities and firms. Dennis Wittmer and David Coursey (1995) explore ethical work climates between government, nonprofit, and private sectors. These studies reveal interesting similarities and differences but do not systematically develop any thematic comparisons between fields.[3]

A view of texts widely used in business ethics curricula reveals a similar lack of consideration to, or acknowledgement of, public sector ethics (Beauchamp and Bowie 1988); DeGeorge 1986; Frederick, et al. 1992; Freeman 1991; and Jackall 1988).[4] These works summarily treat government as a stakeholder in the overall consideration of corporate social policy.

When examining the literature on pedagogical issues in each curriculum, there is a corresponding and somewhat surprising lack of interplay between public and private sector ethics. Catron and Denhardt (1988) examined seventy-four public sector ethics course outlines and identified four types of courses: (1) administrative ethics, (2) democratic/regime values, (3) philosophy or policy, and (4) "hard to classify." In another survey, some common curriculum components/topics were revealed such as the democratic ethos, ethical decision-making skills, and the influence of organizational norms (Hejka-Ekins 1988, p. 887). Cooper (1994) employs a similar overview of common themes, including citizenship and democratic theory, virtue, founding thought and constitutional tradition, the organizational context, ethics education, and philosophical theory and perspective.[5]

Surveys have also been used to investigate the teaching of business ethics (Paine 1988; Rozensher and Fergenson 1991; and Schoenfeldt, et al. 1991). However, much of the work focuses on issue areas that emerge in a review of business ethics courses (such as, "Wall Street ethics"). Other works consider only one element of ethics teaching, such as the use of decision-making models in business ethics classes (Mathison 1988). What is lacking in each academy is a systematic comparison of the themes used for teaching ethics in business and public administration programs. This chapter constructs such a thematic comparison. Moreover, it establishes a framework for examining the differences and similarities between fields with a view toward strengthening ethics education for the public service.

SELECTED THEMES

Public v. Private Sector Ethics Overview

Some public administration texts provide a summary overview such as a "Business Backdrop" (e.g., Lewis 1991, pp. 6–7). Such efforts acknowledge the management "roots" of public administration but advance the view that business considers ethics as only a secondary concern. First and foremost, public administration places primary emphasis on the democratic ethos. These texts emphasize that public and private sector ethics are different from each other.

Business ethics texts typically treat government as a stakeholder, or view government as a regulator, or address the business-government relation only to the extent that it supports a capitalist system (DeGeorge 1986, pp. 116–19 and Freeman 1984, p. 92). Many texts acknowledge the role of government as a moral arbitrator of sorts in a free enterprise economic system (DeGeorge 1986, p. 412). It accomplishes this mandate through the law and other enforcement mechanisms. There is no overt comparison between public and private sector ethics per se.[6] In fact, the presentation of government as an external stakeholder carries an adversarial connotation.

Business ethics is defined as the application of general ethical ideas to business behavior (Frederick, et al. 1992, p. 53). From this viewpoint ethics can be viewed as a division of applied philosophy (DeGeorge 1991, p. 45). Business ethics texts define ethics more broadly as a conception of right or wrong. Textbooks on public sector ethics also define ethics as judgments about what is right and what is wrong (Lewis 1991, p. 3). However, most also stress the fluid dimension of ethics as it evolved in the public service and do not necessarily focus on a single definition (e.g., Denhardt 1988, pp. 8–9).

Both fields move quickly from a philosophic foundation (in either deontology or teleology) and develop an applied perspective. This departure from the generic to the specific fuels the differences rather than the similarities. Clearly, when business ethics texts tackle issues of the corporation and its stockholders, the multinational corporation, or antitrust activity, the relevancy for public sector ethics is muted.

Texts on ethics in public administration articulate the need to serve the public interest or build an ethical public agency. This holds little relevance for business ethics, as is best illustrated when examining the treatment of conflicts of interest. The prohibition against public officials from being unduly influenced by private interests as they construct public policy is grounded in preservation of the public interest. This is very different from a conflict of interest based upon the economic concerns of a business firm that may be trying to prevent trade secrets from being divulged to competitors.

Scholars in both fields believe public and private sector ethics are fundamentally different. The distinction is drawn because of the differences between public and private morality (see Waldo 1994, p. 177). Waldo associates the terms of citizenship, security, justice, and liberty with the public interest. Therefore when actions are taken by government in the public interest, public morality involves actions directed towards the good of the collective body rather than a discrete entity such as the individual, the family, or the firm. His viewpoint emphasizes that the purpose of government is to make and enforce value judgments that determine social, political, and economic goals for society.

Few business ethics texts elaborate on the distinction between public and private sector ethics.[7] In contrast, they focus more on the interface between government and business as the basis for comparison. Business ethics texts define the role of the government as a system of allocation of power, where decisions are made on socio-political motivations and concern for the constituent citizen (e.g., Frederick, et al., 1992, pp. 219–20). An interesting viewpoint of the role of government is offered in some textbooks:

> . . . [government's] primary moral obligation is not to harm or cause harm to any of its citizens. This obligation is stronger and more important than the moral obligation to provide for the welfare of its citizens. The first is a demand of justice; the second a demand of welfare. (DeGeorge, 1986, p. 412)

Such descriptions of the role of government in society certainly reinforce the view that there are very real differences in how the public and private sectors define their roles and embrace different values. Further evidence emerges from a confidential, informal survey of business and public administration/political science faculties conducted as part of this inquiry:

It seems to me the primary differences between public and private sector ethics are in two areas: the different nature of their missions and objectives and the different stakeholders of these organizations, who may have different expectations. T. R.

The most glaring inconsistency between the fields of public and private ethics relates to public policy and the influence of the private sector in shaping laws, regulatory measures, . . . T. D.

One is a business/industrial system that values efficiency, innovation, . . . the other is a military/government system that values hierarchy, loyalty, . . . M. H.

. . . the biggest difference would lie in the perceived purpose of the professional organization. For instance, public organizations usually have as their guiding mission some understanding of service, while private institutions have as their guiding mission the creation of profit . . . The police don't try to operate on a profit margin, . . . while General Motors does not set out to serve people. R. H.

Although differences emerge in the articulation of basic values (such as, democratic ideals versus profit maximization), both fields, in an organizational setting, must deal with corruption, graft, bribery, fraud, conflict of interest, and notions of social or public responsibility.

SOME SIMILARITIES AND DIFFERENCES

In view of the lack of attention that each field devotes to the other, one method of analysis that is readily available is to compare the themes from major textbooks, representative syllabi, and available pedagogical studies in each field. While this approach lacks rigor (and recognizing the limitations imposed by a small sample of primary sources), such a review still affords an appropriate starting point to establish convergence and divergence of the fields.

Curricula Differences of Ethics Programs

Capitalism versus Democracy. The most fundamental distinction between teaching ethics in the public and private arenas is the primacy of the profit motive in the private sector and the lack of it in the public sphere. Profit maximization is considered to be a primary value in the system of free enterprise in a capitalist economic system. Values such as efficiency, competition, and individualism are also embraced by the business system.

In a democracy the core values associated with government are liberty, justice, and equality. These fundamental distinctions between the two systems tend to polarize the fields; profit is the objective for the private firm, while service is the objective of government. The best that both fields can do is to acknowledge the role of the other. For example, public administration acknowledges that the values associated with efficiency in the private sector represent an important characteristic worth replicating (for example, privatization). The private sector acknowledges the consistency between capitalism and the need for government to regulate certain aspects of business activity (for example, antitrust legislation).

Customer versus Citizen. In business, service to the customer is paramount. It is the embodiment of the firm's responsibility to fulfill the needs and desires of customers in order to maximize profits. Products should be safe, adequate information should be provided for their use, and there should be guarantees as to the durability or reliability of the product or service. Many of these "corporate responsibilities" are based upon laws that insure consumers are treated fairly, receive adequate information, are protected from potential hazards, and have legal recourse when problems develop. Most business ethics texts stress the moral obligation of a company to fulfill these responsibilities. They concede that past indiscretions have necessitated consumer laws and antitrust legislation.

Ethics in public administration is portrayed in a broader context where the focus of government is viewed as service to the citizen. The government mandate for ethics is far-reaching. The government holds a fiduciary responsibility not just to a segment of the population (customers) but to the entire citizenry. Public officials in the execution of their duties hold a public trust and confidence. As such, even an appearance of impropriety will come under increased scrutiny.

The customer is not the same as the citizen. All customers are citizens and are therefore afforded certain rights in a constitutional democracy, including protection from the private sector in the form of government regulation. Moreover, citizens carry an equal responsibility for preserving these same rights and guarantees for others in a democratic society. But citizens are consumers only part of the time. Consumers are afforded certain rights by the private sector, but only for the short-term duration of their interaction with the company. This usually corresponds to the length of the warranty or service contract. Government's interaction with its citizens is more of a long-term and reciprocal relationship bounded by its own "warranty"—the Constitution.[8]

Corporate Social Responsibility versus the Public Interest.   Corporate social responsibility can be portrayed in two ways: (1) abiding by the law and fulfilling legal obligations, or (2) fulfilling corporate societal obligations. Business ethics points to the stewardship principle as the basis for corporate responsibility. The actions of managers must not only achieve economic success but must also meet "societal expectations." Business ethics texts are quick to point out the limits of this type of social responsibility in terms of cost, efficiency, relevance, and scope. If corporate pursuit of a particular social policy proves too expensive, cannot be administered efficiently, is not the main purpose of the organization, or is too broad to reasonably undertake, the policy may be dropped. Government does not have the same luxury of ignoring the public interest if it happens to fall victim to one of these constraints.

The public interest in most public administration ethics texts does not come with such clear disclaimers. There are many definitions of the public interest. However, a common thread to all definitions is the obligation to future generations. The public sector also embraces the role of stewardship but in a more inclusive manner.

In teaching ethics, corporate social responsibility is more clearly articulated because of a rather specific agenda and overriding financial limits to meeting societal expectations. The broader mandate of public service requires consideration of each multi-faceted dimension of the public interest in constructing policies or administering government. It is necessarily a more difficult concept to clearly articulate, let alone fulfill.

Rule of Law versus Regulation. Public administration courses emphasize that ethics is grounded in a strong tradition of administrative legalism and notions about the rule of law, which binds public officials to higher standards that are rooted in the Constitution and woven into the very fabric of the American administrative state.[9]

In the teaching of business ethics, there is no such legal foundation. The law is treated as a minimum standard of social responsibility. Yet these same texts acknowledge that for businesses to be ethical (and meet societal expectations), they must do more than simply comply with the law. Moreover, business views the law as providing minimal standards that *constrain* business activities. This is clearly different from the public sector, where the law is a fundamental principle that *guides* the process of government.

Competitive Advantage versus Ethics as Good Government.—The underlying rationale for ethics in each field is clearly different. Business ethics courses stress the pursuit of ethical activity as being "good for business." When texts and instructors pose the question "why should business be ethical?" the following reasons are often given: (1) to meet public expectations about ethical performance and social responsibility; (2) to prevent harm to the general public or stockholders; (3) to protect business from unethical employees or competitors; and (4) to protect employees.[10]

In public administration, the reason to pursue ethics is presented as an end in itself. Ethics in the public service embodies broader notions that ethical behavior is a key ingredient to accountable, efficient, and responsive government. Integrity and trust are the foundations that serve as the basis for what government is all about. Government is built upon the idea of voluntary compliance, where citizens agree to give up some of their freedom and conversely agree to voluntarily comply with government edicts. However, the fundamental basis for this relationship is trust of government officials. The presumption is that ethical government is bound to produce a better government.

This comparison demonstrates that the differences in how ethics is taught by both academies is clearly linked to the fundamental differences between fields. However, by focusing on how ethics is taught in each field, there is an opportunity to move beyond these differences and explore the similarities.

Curricula Similarities

Individual Responsibility versus Organization Roles. Both fields struggle with the notions of individual responsibility within the framework of acceptable organizational culture, including norms and values that constitute the organization's ethical climate.

Clearly this theme has been much more developed in public administration. Ever since the Friedrich-Finer debates (circa 1935–41) the issue of individual responsibility versus organization role has been a primary concern in the public administration literature.[11] Democratic responsibility must be internalized by the public administrator in his/her dual role as citizen and bureaucrat as supported by the various trappings of government (rules and regulations). This helps to guide administrators toward ethical behavior in preserving a balance with their institutionally defined roles. This theme is reiterated in virtually all of the ethics textbooks in public administration.

For the private sector the quandary posed by individual ethical responsibility versus organizational loyalty is not clearly elaborated. This issue is dealt with more under the consideration of the ethical climate of the business. Indeed the ethical climate of business has received considerable attention (for example, Victor and Cullen 1988). Climate is important to the extent that it encourages employees to channel energies in a way that benefits the company. A widely cited study of private sector managers points out that four out of ten compromise personal integrity to meet corporate goals, and seven out of ten believed this to be wrong (Posner and Schmidt 1984, p. 211). This problem is equally evident in public administration as demonstrated by a survey that found 47 percent of public managers under pressure to compromise personal standards to fulfill organizational goals (Bowman 1990).

Most business courses stress the need to develop a sense of moral obligation and personal responsibility, but in careful balance with organizational mission and objectives. Discretion in public management and ethics has received critical attention in terms of the execution of public duties (Nigro and Richardson 1990; Dobel 1990). There is not a comparable examination of discretion in business management and ethics. However, in one study of employee discretion in seven countries, it was found that traditional hierarchical work relationships still prevail despite assertions in the literature that employee discretion and empowerment are the preferred models (Boreham 1992).

In addition, both fields address the problems encountered when employees follow their internal moral compass at the expense of the organization. The results can include dismissal or demotion in the worst scenario and severe damage to career opportunities in the best case.

Whistle Blowing.   Closely related to the notion of individual responsibility is the issue of whistle blowing. Both fields acknowledge that whistle blowing occurs and in certain circumstances is appropriate (for example, revealing safety hazards or bribery of government officials). Both fields acknowledge that whistle blowing carries great risks for both the organization and the individual, and that it should be used only as a last resort. Both underscore the necessity of protecting the accused and the accuser. Government whistle blowing carries more substantial protections for employees who blow the whistle (such as the 1978 Civil Service Reform Act, which greatly expanded these protections). There are fewer protections available to private sector employees (since information is considered proprietary). However, some states have extended protections to private sector employees who disclose information about the company.[12] Both fields recognize the role, if not the legitimacy, of whistle blowing as an effective mechanism to uncover fraud or abuse or unethical activity.

Training/Education.   Both spheres place an emphasis on the importance of education and training. There has been a proliferation of ethics training programs in both sectors over the past twenty years. Both fields tackle the utility of ethics education in the first instance. For example, Worthley and Grumet (1983) surveyed graduate schools of public administration to assess the effectiveness of teaching ethics in public administration programs. Jones (1991) conducted a similar survey of graduate business programs. The studies discussed the major problems encountered in trying to assess the "effectiveness" of ethics courses. They concluded that ethics can be taught but is effective only to the extent that the course preserves or enhances student awareness of ethical dilemmas or moral development and receives the support of top management.

Ethical Decision Making.   Each field articulates the need for improving ethical decision making in the organization and encourages the use of formal decision-making models. However, the models for business decision making emphasize the profit motive and assign extra consideration to attributes (and values) that strengthen the economic position of the firm. Hence, decision making proves to be more utilitarian for the private sector manager. Yet both fields utilize systems such as Kohlberg's stages of moral development or the Defining Issues Test to emphasize the necessity of moving to higher stages of reasoning.[13] They also stress the importance of leadership for inculcating ethics in the organization. Finally, there has been a renewed emphasis on incorporating practical "how to" guides to assist managers in formulating ethical decisions and behavior.

Standards and Codes.   Both fields promote the use of codes of conduct to guide ethical behavior in the organization. Public administration ethics emphasizes that codes can encourage high standards of behavior, increase public confidence, and assist in decision making. Effective codes stress simplicity and are based on a sense of administrative reality where the clients of such codes are the ethical members of the organization (Lewis 1991, p. 144). They typically include restrictions against conflict of interest and appearances of impropriety.

Codes in business revolve around criminal sanctions and procedural protections for employees and complainants. They are promoted as means for guiding managers and employees when confronting ethical dilemmas. Codes typically incorporate provisions addressing anti-trust, environmental, and consumer-sensitive activities. They also prohibit receiving gifts from contract vendees, promoting nepotism, or engaging in questionable relationships with competitors.

Business ethics concedes that codes provide more protection to the company than for employees or the general public. One reason may be that private sector ethics codes stress legal compliance rather than broader ethical perspectives. Nonetheless, 75 percent of all U.S companies have codes of ethics in place.[14] Overall, both fields conclude that it is probably useful to have a code, yet both question its utility as a means for enforcing or encouraging ethical behavior in the organization.

Role of the Professions. Both fields confront the role played by professionals who increasingly have come to dominate the rank and file of organizations. Historically professions have been seen as self-governing groups with sets of ethical standards that define the group as a profession. These standards are often at odds with the demands of the business organization. Are lawyers who work for a Fortune 1000 company bound by the codes of ethics promulgated by the American Bar Association or by the company? In contrast, is the city manager bound by the code of ethics of the International City/County Management Association or the public interest of the municipality? For teaching ethics in the public sector, how do professional norms and values conflict not only with organizational norms but with notions of democracy? (Denhardt 1988, p. 65)

Media/Public Image. The keen interest in the publicness of government activity has been heightened over the years with a seemingly endless series of scandals involving public officials. In government service a premium is placed on avoiding even the appearance of impropriety. All of these trends are linked to the notion of serving the public interest. However, business is equally concerned about its public image. The private sector has been beset by corruption and scandal throughout the twentieth century. Because unethical behavior negatively impacts business profits, there is a definite incentive for business to implement ethics programs—at least for public relations purposes.

In the public sphere it is easier to understand this ethical imperative, because it is part and parcel of the democratic tradition. In the
private sector, where the motivation of profit and competition are
premier values, the waters are a bit murkier. To the extent that ethics
can contribute to these ends or be utilized as part of a campaign to
foster a positive corporate image, there is an incentive to pursue a
comprehensive ethics program. Textbooks and courses in each field
pose the following question for determining the ethical basis for a
decision: "If the issue were to appear on the nightly news, would you
feel proud of your decision or would you be embarrassed by the
decision?"

Philosophy. Both fields provide a synopsis of the philosophic under-
pinnings of ethics. Yet both quickly depart from this foundation and
concede that ethics is really taught as applied ethics. What emerges
is perhaps one of the strongest similarities between business and
public administration ethics—the use of deontologically and teleo-
logically based philosophies to understand obligations to act ethically in both business and in government. Both fields invoke the
traditions of Plato, Kant, Bentham, and Mill in structuring their approaches to ethical reasoning. While business ethics places more
emphasis on a utilitarian view and on situational ethics, public administration follows more of an absolutist bent (typically around the
public interest).

Corruption/Fraud/Waste/Abuse. The most basic of comparisons to
be made between fields concerns the problems of corruption, fraud,
waste, and abuse in organizations. Ethics is concerned with limiting these transgressions against the organization. For the private
sector, ethics is viewed as a means to minimize or safeguard against
bribery, embezzlement, falsifying expense accounts, nepotism, and
conflicts of interest. The pursuit of ethical behavior (acting legally
and ethically) pay dividends to the corporation by avoiding penal-
ties or lawsuits. In the public sector, the goals of combatting corruption and waste are tied not only to notions of cost and economy,
but to the preservation of trust in the democratic institution of
government.

This comparison demonstrates that substantive issues associated with ethics, and the teaching of ethics, are similar in both fields. These similarities provide a rationale for utilizing a broader framework for the teaching of ethics in each academy.

Further Comparisons

Although differences exist between ethics in public administration and ethics in the business academy, similarities emerge in a review of ethics curricula. These similarities are also reflected in two other important areas in each academy.

Pedagogy. In both fields there is an increasing use of case studies to present ethical dilemmas which allow the student the opportunity to engage in role-playing or to systematically uncover ethical issues in certain situations.[15] Teaching utilizes small group discussion, intensive modules, and outside speakers. Both fields place increasing emphasis on a practitioner-focused approach to ethics, which incorporates some type of ethical decision-making guide which students can apply on the job when they leave the classroom.

Research Directions. Frederickson (1993, pp. 258–59) clearly articulates the research agenda for ethics in the public administration academy. He cites the need to use post-positivist methodologies in administrative ethics and argues for expanded use of case studies. He contends that research should focus on situational ethics, where ethical actions may vary according to the setting, the culture, and the profession. Another area for future research is to compare the impact of traditional hierarchically based approaches with newer organizational phenomena such as inspectors general and ethics officers. Frederickson argues for expanded efforts to evaluate the impact of ethics training on behavior. Finally, the academy needs to examine the effect of reduced administrative discretion on administrative ethics and on the operations of government.

In the private sector, Robertson (1993) provides a comprehensive outline of future research for the business ethics academy, which include better articulation of the normative foundations of empirical research (with behavior as a key dependent variable). She argues for efforts that focus on theory building. Future research should include the behavior of work groups, consumers, and shareholders. She calls for expanded use of other research methodologies—beyond case studies—with more emphasis on experimental designs. Finally, the research agenda should include making the research useful for application in public policy and management.

Although these themes vary, they are also similar. They argue for greater relevance in their respective fields and for greater variation in methodological techniques. They stress the importance of going beyond traditional units of analysis and point to the necessity of focusing on outcomes and behaviors.

Significance for Public Administration

This comparative inquiry does not set out to frame a paradigm shift for either curriculum. However, a curriculum which incorporates public and private ethics has benefits from at least two perspectives, which are shown below.

The Applied Perspective. A revamped curriculum would train public and private sector managers to view ethics through a broader lens. This approach would provide private sector managers with the training to understand the premium placed on ethical behavior and the democratic ethos in the public sector. When top corporate managers land appointments as high-level federal government officials, they will have a clearer idea of the ethical standards applied to them. This may, in turn, help them to avoid the ethical pitfalls many such officials have faced in past and current presidential administrations. On the other hand, whenever public sector managers enter into collaborative partnerships with business or run quasi-business entities, training in an interdisciplinarian curriculum will provide an ethic that helps managers to delineate the boundaries of what is acceptable in business versus what is permissible in government.

The Phenomenological Perspective. Studying the differences and similarities between public and private sector ethics in a revamped curriculum provides a frame of reference to evaluate how a concept called "ethics" is constructed by an organization to help meet its purposes and goals in relation to an external social and political environment. Examining ethics as a phenomenon of organizational life offers a unique vantage point from which to evaluate the influence of a variety of factors on ethical behavior or outcomes in the organization. These factors include the impact of corporate and government work climates on fostering ethics and the function of institutional mechanisms (such as ethics committees) in enforcing ethical behavior.

Ethics is viewed as an intuitive creation of the organization used to conceptualize reality or current practices.[16] This view cuts across both public and private sector organizations. It offers a method to critique what happens in theory versus practice, to contrast the role of the individual manager versus the organization and society at large, and to address the broader issues of what constitutes ethical or unethical behavior, who decides, and why.

CONCLUSION

This chapter offers a framework for understanding the overlap in how ethics is taught in the respective academies. Although the differences are fundamental in many respects, there are similarities lurking close below the surface. The goal for the public administration academy should be to not let the differences become blinders to the utilization of other strains of thought. To view ethics as an endeavor for only one field or one profession unnecessarily burdens the teaching of ethics. Government officials carry a special obligation as citizens and for citizens. They regulate commerce and participate in a capitalist society.

Indeed, this contention echoes the sentiments expressed by James Bowman twenty years ago when he argued for "an ethics of managerial action" that would cut across the boundaries between "free enterprise" and government (Bowman 1976, p. 54). In an era when the boundaries between the public and private sectors continue to blur, understanding business ethics and its limits and nuances may help public administrators to understand the ethical mazes that they must navigate as these boundaries continue to disappear into the twenty-first century.

NOTES

1. Kettl uses the phrase "government by proxy" to describe the provision of government goods and services through proxies such as contractors, grantees, and recipients of benefits (Kettl 1988, p. 9).

2. Materials and textbooks referenced in this chapter were solicited from syllabi from public administration and business ethics courses at the State University of New York at Albany, as well as extensive secondary sources from curriculum studies available in both fields. (These studies and the relevant literatures are cited in the accompanying bibliography.) To supplement these sources, informal interviews were conducted with a small sample of ethics instructors, including responses to a survey posted to the Internet on pertinent listservs.

3. The public-private distinction has been visited many times in the literature. Examples include Allison (1979), Emmert and Crow (1988), Kenney, et al. (1987), Murray (1975), Perry and Rainey (1988), Rainey, et al. (1976), and Weinberg (1983). However, none of these works examines the ethical dimensions of the public-private sector interface.

4. For a more inclusive list of the top ethics course texts compiled from a 1988 survey of 663 business schools, see Schoenfeldt, et al. (1991).

5. These themes were developed from a review of the literature (including major texts used in public administration ethics courses). This author used this work and the others cited in this chapter as a basis for extending this thematic review to include business ethics. See Cooper (1994, pp. 16–22).

6. Business ethics also makes a distinction between public and private (individual) morality. However, this is not the same distinction explored in this chapter.

7. The distinction between public and private sector ethics is not meant to overlook substantive work in both fields, perhaps the most notable being Bok (1978), that examine differences in public and private "morality." Also, both fields have certainly examined the distinctions between public and private values. See Nalbandian and Edwards (1983) and Baldwin (1991). The latter work suggests a similarity between public and private values, while the former suggests similarities across a wider range of variables.

8. This concept of a Constitutional "warranty" builds upon Rohr's (1989) work on the importance of the Constitution and subsequent Supreme Court decisions for providing an ethical compass for the public service.

9. For a thorough examination of the importance of the Constitution for articulating "regime values" that can serve as guideposts for administrators in pursuit of the public interest, see Rohr (1989, Chapter 2).

10. See Frederick, et al. (1992, pp. 39–42) for a more thorough treatment of the rationale for business ethics.

11. This debate is best illustrated by their respective works: Finer (1936) and Friedrich (1935).

12. From "GE Will Pay $3.5 Million To Settle Suits Brought By Whistle Blowers," as cited in Frederick, et al. (1992).

13. These tests are popular but are also criticized in some circles. See Kohlberg's chapter in Lickona (1976, pp. 31–53) and Rest (1979).

14. Frederick, et al. (1992) provide these data and cite other summary statistics on the proliferation of codes and institution-based approaches used by major corporations (for example, one in three Fortune 1000 companies have formally established ethics committees).

15. Two representative textbooks that illustrate this emphasis are Velasquez (1988) and Gutmann and Thompson (1991).

16. For a thorough discussion of phenomenology as a method of investigation, see Thevenaz (1962, pp. 37–67). Also see McCurdy (1973, pp. 52–53).

REFERENCES

Allison, Graham. 1994. "Public and Private Management: Are They Fundamentally Alike in All Important Respects," in *Current Issues in Public Administration* (5th ed.). New York: St. Martin's Press, pp. 16–32.

Baldwin, J. Norman. 1991. "Public Versus Private Employees: Debunking Stereotypes," in *Review of Public Personnel Administration*, Vol. 11., pp. 1–23.

Beauchamp, Tom L., and Norman E. Bowie, eds. 1988. *Ethical Theory and Busines* (3rd ed.). Engelwood Cliffs, NJ: Prentice Hall.

Berman, Evan, Jonathan West, and Anita Cava. 1994. "Ethics Management in Municipal Governments and Large Firms." *Administration and Society*, Vol. 26, No. 2, pp. 185–203.

Bok, Sissela. 1978. *Lying: Moral Choice in Public and Private Life.* New York: Pantheon Books.

Boreham, Paul. 1992. "The Myth of Post-Fordist Management: Work Organization and Employee Discretion of Seven Countries." *Management-Decision*, Vol. 30, No. 6, pp. 100–8.

Bowman, James S. 1976. "Managerial Ethics in Business and Government," in *Business Horizons*, Vol. 19, pp. 48–54.

Bowman, James S. 1990. "Ethics in Government: A National Survey of Public Administrators." *Public Administration Review*, Vol. 50, No. 3, pp. 345–53.

Bowman, James S., ed. 1991. *Ethical Frontiers in Public Management.* San Francisco: Jossey-Bass Publishers.

Catron, Bayard L., and Kathryn G. Denhardt. 1988. *Ethics Education in Public Administration and Affairs.* Washington, DC: American Society for Public Administration.

Cooper, Terry L. 1990. *The Responsible Administrator* (3rd ed.). San Francisco: Jossey-Bass Publishers.

Cooper, Terry L., ed. 1994. *Handbook of Administrative Ethics*. New York: Marcel Dekker, Inc.

DeGeorge, Richard T. 1986. *Business Ethics* (2nd. ed.). New York: Macmillan Publishing Co.

———. 1991. "Will Success Spoil Business Ethics?" in *Business Ethics: The State of the Art*, R. Edward Freeman, ed. New York: Oxford University Press, pp. 42–59.

Denhardt, Kathryn G. 1988. *The Ethics of Public Service*. New York: Greenwood Press.

Emmert, Mark A., and Michael M. Crow. 1988. "Public, Private, and Hybrid Organizations: An Empirical Examination of the Role of Publicness." *Administration and Society*, Vol, 20, pp. 216–44.

Finer, Herman. 1936. "Better Government Personnel." *Political Science Quarterly*, Vol. 51, pp. 569–99.

Frederick, William C., James E. Post, and Keith Davis. 1992. *Business and Society* (7th ed.). New York: McGraw-Hill.

Frederickson, H. George. 1993. *Ethics and Public Administration*. Armonk, NY: M. E. Sharpe, Inc.

Freeman, R. Edward. 1984. *Strategic Management: A Stakeholder Approach*. Marshfield, MA: Pitman Publishing Co.

Freeman, R. Edward, ed. 1991. *Business Ethics: The State of the Art*. New York: Oxford University Press.

Friedrich, Carl J. 1935. "Responsible Government Service Under the American Constitution." *Problems of the American Public Service*. New York: McGraw-Hill.

Gutmann, Amy and Dennis Thompson, eds. 1991. *Ethics and Politics: Cases and Comments* (2nd ed.). Chicago: Nelson-Hall Publishers.

Hejka-Ekins, April. 1988. "Teaching Ethics in Public Administration." *Public Administration Review*, Vol. 48, No. 5, pp. 885–91.

Jackall, Robert. 1988. *Moral Mazes*. New York: Oxford University Press.

Jones, Thomas M. 1991. "Can Business Ethics Be Taught? Empirical Evidence," in *Business and Professional Ethics Journal*, Vol. 8, No. 2, pp. 73–94.

Kenney, Graham K., Richard J. Butler, David J. Hickson, David Gray, Geoffrey Mallory, and David C. Wilson. 1987. "Strategic Decision Making: Influence Patterns in Public and Private Organizations." *Human Resources*, Vol. 40, pp. 613–32.

Kettl, Donald F. 1988. "Performance and Accountability: The Challenge of Government by Proxy for Public Administration." *American Review of Public Administration*, Vol. 18, No. 1, pp. 9–29.

Kettl, Donald F. 1993. *Sharing Power: Public Governance and Private Markets*. Washington, DC: The Brookings Institution.

Kohlberg, Lawrence. 1976. "Moral Stages and Moralization: The Cognitive Development Approach," in T. Lickona, ed. *Moral Development and Behavior: Theory, Research, and Social Issues*. New York: Holt, Rinehart, and Winston, pp. 31–53.

Lewis, Carol. 1991. *The Ethics Challenge in Public Service*. San Francisco: Jossey-Bass Publishers.

Mathison, David L. 1988. "Business Ethics Cases and Decision Models: A Call for Relevancy in the Classroom." *Journal of Business Ethics*, Vol. 7, pp. 777–82.

McCurdy, Howard E. 1973. "Fiction Phenomenology and Public Administration." *Public Administration Review*, Vol. 33, No. 1, pp. 52–58.

Murray, Michael A. 1975. "Comparing Public and Private Management." *Public Administration Review*, Vol. 35, pp. 364–71.

Nalbandian, John, and J. Terry Edwards. 1983. "The Values of Public Administrators: A Comparison with Lawyers, Social Workers, and Business Administration," in *Review of Public Personnel Administration*, Vol. 4, pp. 114–29.

Nigro, Lloyd G., and William D. Richardson. 1990. "Between Citizens and Administrator," *Public Administration Review*, Vol. 50, No. 6, pp. 623–35.

Osborne, David and Ted Gaebler. 1992. *Reinventing Government*. Reading, MA: Addison-Wesley.

Paine, L. S. 1990. *Ethics Policies and Programs in American Business*. Washington, DC: Ethics Resource Center.

Perry, James L. and Hal G. Rainey. 1988. "The Public-Private Distinction in Organization Theory: A Critique and Research Strategy." *Academy of Management Review*, Vol. 13, pp. 182–201.

Posner, Barry Z., and Warren H. Schmidt. 1984. "Values and the American Manager: An Update." *California Management Review*, Spring, pp. 206–12.

Rainey, Hal G., Robert W. Backoff, and Charles H. Levine. 1976. "Comparing Public and Private Organizations." *Public Administration Review*, Vol. 36, pp. 232–44.

Rest, James R. 1979. *Development in Judging Moral Issues*. Minneapolis: University of Minnesota Press.

Robertson, Diana C. 1993. "Empiricism in Business Ethics: Suggested Research Directions," in *Journal of Business Ethics*, Vol. 12, pp. 585–99.

Rohr, John A. *Ethics for Bureaucrats* (2nd ed.) 1989. New York: Marcel Dekker.

Rozensher, Susan G., and P. Everett Fergenson. 1994. "Business Faculty Perspectives on Ethics: A National Survey," *Business Horizons*, July-August, pp. 61–67.

Schoenfeldt, Lyle F., Don M. McDonald, and Stuart A. Youngblood 1991. "The Teaching of Business Ethics: A Survey of AACSB Member Schools." *Journal of Business Ethics*, Vol. 10, pp. 237–41.

Thevenaz, Pierre. 1962. *What is Phenomenology?* Chicago: Quadrangle Books, Inc.

Velasquez, Manuel G. 1988. *Business Ethics* (2nd ed.). Engelwood Cliffs, NJ: Prentice-Hall.

Victor, Bart and John Cullen. 1988. "The Organizational Bases of Ethical Work Climates," *Administrative Science Quarterly.* Vol. 33, pp. 101–25.

Waldo, Dwight. 1994. "Public Administration and Ethics," in Frederick S. Lane, ed. *Current Issues in Public Administration* (5th ed.). New York: St. Martin's Press, pp. 176–90.

Weinberg, Martha W. 1983. "Public Management and Private Management: A Diminishing Gap?" *Journal of Policy Analysis and Management*, Vol. 31, pp. 107–25.

Wittmer, Dennis, and David Coursey. 1995. "Ethical Work Climates: Comparing Top Managers in Public and Private Organizations," A Paper Delivered at the National Symposium on Ethics and Values in the Public Administration Academy.

Worthley, John A., and Barbara R. Grumet. 1983. "Ethics and Public Administration: `Teaching What Can't Be Taught'," in *American Review of Public Administration*, Vol. 17, No. 1, pp. 54–67.

PART III

Teaching Strategies:
Outside the Academy

CHAPTER 10

Ethics Workshops in State Government: Teaching Practitioners

WILLIAM D. RICHARDSON, LLOYD G. NIGRO,
AND RONALD L. MCNINCH

There is little question that interest in ethics education and training has been growing among both academics and practitioners. Even a cursory comparison of catalogs issued during the past decade by the average public university generally reveals a proliferation of courses on ethics offered at both the undergraduate and graduate levels.[1] Professional associations are increasingly adopting or modifying codes of ethics intended to guide the conduct of their members.[2] Governments have long been indirectly involved in the superintending of ethical conduct, especially on the state level through secretaries of state and the various commissions which issue licenses to certain practitioners.[3] They have also done so much more directly through the establishment of rules of appropriate conduct for public employees or elected officials and candidates.

Indeed, this last area has seen some of the more prominent reforms. These reforms consistently focused on the area with the most visible potential for abuse: financial conflicts of interest. (The Federal Election Commission's rigorous and long-standing financial disclosure requirements for candidates come immediately to mind.) On the federal level, one of the most important actors in this field is the appropriately named U.S. Office of Government Ethics (OGE), which arose from the 1978 Ethics in Government Act. Severed from the Office of Personnel Management in 1989 and made an independent agency, OGE issues *Standards of Ethical Conduct for Employees of the*

Executive Branch, an eighty-five page manual intended to guide the conduct of nearly three million executive branch employees. While a substantial majority of this manual is understandably concerned with financial impropriety, the OGE also has assumed broader responsibilities, such as that of coordinating and facilitating ethics education within the executive branch (U.S. Office of Government Ethics 1994, pp. 15, 36). State ethics commissions often assume some of these same responsibilities on a reduced scale.[4]

With all of this evident concern for ethics education and training for practitioners, one might expect that a fair amount of attention has been given to the content of such courses. In the case of the OGE, professional practice commissions, and the various professional associations that have explicit codes and standards of conduct, the answer is straightforward: they are first and foremost tasked with teaching those codes. However, what of those agencies or professional associations which have no such codes of their own but still desire that their employees or members have an "appropriate" education in ethics? While there has been some discussion of this issue in the literature of the various disciplines, there certainly is not anything approaching a consensus as to what should be taught (Catron and Denhardt 1994; Hejka-Ekins 1994, 1988; Kavathatzopoulos 1994; Marini 1992; Pratt 1993; Richardson and Nigro 1987; Rohr 1978; Torp 1994). And regardless of what is taught to practitioners under the guise of ethics education, there is surprisingly little literature evaluating the worth or practicality of such education to the future professional lives of those who receive it.[5]

When governments at all levels are being pushed and pulled in hopes of "reinventing" themselves, this seeming lack of evaluation of the effectiveness of ethics training is, at least on the surface, puzzling, since reinvention often requires confidence in the ethical virtues of public administrators who are given more discretion. If the citizens indeed are as dissatisfied with "big" government as contemporary polls indicate, it would seem that earnest and visible attempts at promoting more ethical behavior among those who comprise the greatest part of that government—the bureaucrats—should be encouraged.[6]

BACKGROUND

This essay describes our experiences in offering a series of "workshops on ethics" to practitioners employed by the Division of Family and Children Services (DFCS) of one large southeastern state. We designed a two-day session intended to be both thought-provoking and useful to the participants in their future professional careers. After lengthy meetings in which we came to general agreement with agency staff on the content of this workshop, all parties quickly concurred that it was very important to receive as much feedback as possible about the sessions from the participants.

We settled on a slightly modified version of an evaluation form that the agency's training staff had been using for some time to gather participant feedback on training sessions and instructors. At the end of each workshop, this evaluation was completed by every practitioner present. The responses in the immediate afterglow of the sessions clearly showed that a large majority thought the workshops were in some sense valuable and that they appreciated having had the opportunity to discuss the materials provided, especially the case studies.

However, there was no way for us reliably to ascertain the long-term effects the workshops might have on those who attended. Were the attendees going to return to their statewide field offices, bolstered and rejuvenated by the ethical seeds sown in the workshops and continue to flower? Was it possible that some of them would serve as models of appropriate habits and conduct for their coworkers? In the final analysis, we were not able to answer these questions. Applying lessons learned from this experience, this essay describes and discusses what we suspect are rather common reasons for the paucity of systematic evaluation research on the long-term results of ethics training in public agencies.

Bureaucratic Blockages and Managed Information

From the first session on, we tried to open channels of communication with the participants. The agency training staff, which handled all the arrangements for the workshops, declined to provide any information about the participants beyond their names. Trying to compensate for the lack of official information on the participants in the first workshop, in the next two we asked everyone to fill out brief information forms. However, this effort was not endorsed by the DFCS training staff member who diligently attended each workshop session, and the forms were not universally completed.

Workshop participants were encouraged to contact us directly if they had post-workshop questions or concerns. We noticed, however, that the training staff representative encouraged everyone to route questions through his office. This indirect line of communication between workshop participants and instructors effectively blocked efforts to contact participants with questions about the utility of the workshop they had attended.

Efforts to Conduct a Post-Workshop Survey Frustrated

When we were asked in September, 1994, to submit a proposal for another series of workshops, DFCS personnel raised a series of concerns about the sessions. First on their list was the issue of the long-term effectiveness of the workshops. We shared their concern and asked for permission to conduct a survey of all those who had participated in the previous workshops.

The survey was to be anonymous and run through the training staff office. This latter point was emphasized so that there would be no conflict of interest concerns and to ensure that the training staff had no reason to fear that we were trying to cut them out of the feedback loop. Additionally, the questions themselves would be developed in conjunction with the training staff and all associated mailing and distribution costs borne by us.

We stressed that the information obtained through such an instrument would enable us to gauge the strengths and weaknesses of past workshops and to put together more effective workshops in the future. After pondering the request for some five weeks, the head of the training staff rejected the idea of a formal survey as unnecessary. In his expressed opinion, the course was already well known through the grapevine and nothing further would be learned from such a survey. Instead he urged us just to submit the proposal for another series of workshops as soon as possible. Accordingly, no survey was done, and we were left with nothing more than a series of speculations and assumptions about the impact of our three ethics workshops on DFCS personnel.

Possible Sources of DFCS Resistance to Evaluation

While we may not be able to do more than note the scarcity of evaluations of ethics training, we are in a position to discuss the possible reasons this particular agency was reluctant to support a follow-up evaluation. Among these are the following:

(1) Because it has been the subject of many stories by the local media, DFCS is extremely wary of producing any document that might subsequently be reported in the media.

(2) While recognizing that ethics training is currently in vogue, DFCS's leadership may not be committed to ethics training. For the present it may simply be another box to be checked off as a required part of inservice training. The results of an evaluation survey, therefore, would be of little interest to higher management, since doing the training is essentially a shield against criticism of the agency.

(3) The agency is staffed by professionals, and professionals are likely to believe that they know how to do their jobs. They tend to be suspicious of outsiders who offer evaluations of their conduct and training.[7]

Media Coverage of the Agency and Its Effects

During the six years preceding our request to conduct a survey, the county or state offices of DFCS were the subject of at least forty-eight critical articles and editorials appearing in the daily newspaper of the state's largest city. For example, just before the initial workshop there were reports of its employees falsifying records after a baby's death; the resignation of its director; the ignoring of a reported child rape; the failure to investigate the abuse of a two year old because of an "address mix-up"; the failure to remove a two-year old boy from a home prior to his being beaten to death; the transfer of a county director under investigation for mismanagement to the state headquarters; the filing of sexual harassment complaints against various members of a county DFCS office; and the discovery of $164,000 in a secret account kept by one county DFCS office (*Atlanta Constitution* 1992).

In several instances, DFCS personnel fed the public outrage by refusing to release what they considered to be confidential information about how the agency had handled some of the cases. This posture only served to add to the perception of some observers that DFCS was more interested in hiding its mistakes than in correcting them.[8] Not surprisingly, the Lieutenant Governor spearheaded a successful effort to pass reform legislation which forced DFCS to reveal its confidential files to elected officials under certain circumstances. Given the public relations problems the agency was experiencing, workshops on ethical decision making for its managers and supervisors might have been considered attractive by management.[9]

AN ETHICS WORKSHOP FOR DFCS PRACTITIONERS

In January, 1993, we were contacted by DFCS, which was establishing a School of Management that was intended to graduate "Certified DFCS Manager(s)" (DFCS Catalog, 1993, p. 1). DFCS wanted to contract out the teaching of a required course on "Ethical Decision Making" that was already in the curriculum but had not yet been offered. An initial meeting with members of the Management Training Committee revealed that DFCS had not clearly identified either the purpose of such a course or its content. The only guidelines were that the course had to be taught on two consecutive weekdays at least three times a year and that it not require any preparatory reading by the students.

Because neither DFCS nor its parent, the State Department of Human Resources, had anything resembling a code of ethics, we suggested that such a document become a goal of the proposed course or workshop. As envisioned, the managers and supervisors attending each workshop would work to produce a working draft of a code of ethics for DFCS by the conclusion of the last session. It was hoped that this exercise would enable the participants to apply and better understand the various materials they would be exposed to during the workshop. Whether each succeeding session would build on the work of its predecessor or start anew was undecided before the start of the first workshop. This approach was accepted by the training staff, and we were given approval to develop the workshop around this goal.

The Evolution of Workshop Content

The first three hours of the initial workshop set forth explicit goals, ranging from "exploring what 'ethics' is" to "developing a code of ethics for DFCS." Various definitions of "ethics" were then presented and discussed from the perspective of democratic administration. Derivative issues of legitimacy and administrative discretion were treated before the participants engaged in a fairly structured self-evaluation of their own ethical principles. The morning closed with a presentation of the Athenian Oath and various federal and state codes of ethics.

The three hour afternoon session was devoted to case studies which illustrated or challenged the ethical principles explored in the morning. After reading each case, the eighteen participants were divided into four groups which discussed the facts and considered alternative courses of conduct.

Most of the next morning was given over to a detailed discussion of other codes of ethics, such as those of the American Society for Public Administration, the International City/County Management Association, and the National Association of Social Workers. The participants were divided into small groups for more intimate and, occasionally, detailed exploration of the strengths and weaknesses of the various codes. The period immediately preceding the lunch break was devoted to the presentation of two additional case studies which were to be topics for lunchtime discussion.

The final afternoon session started with a short follow-up discussion of the case studies. Nearly all of the remaining time was devoted to the group's efforts to devise the outline of a model code of ethics for DFCS. Working from flip charts, the efforts of the four groups were then presented, consolidated, and discussed.

Analysis of the evaluations completed by the participants in this first workshop, when combined with the comments of the DFCS training staff member who was to sit in on all of the workshops, led to certain conclusions about its structure and content. First, many of the participants disliked working in small groups. Second, there was general dissatisfaction with the attempt to formulate a model code of ethics for DFCS.

Part of the reason for this dissatisfaction was political. The participants were quite pleased with the idea of having a DFCS code but, given the turmoil in their agency, were perhaps justifiably skeptical about the prospects of such a code ever being adopted. Indeed, midway into our discussion, the observer from the training staff halted the workshop in order to insert the caveat that the devising of a code certainly did not have the endorsement of the agency's upper administration. Only the immediate promise by the authors that they would forward any code ultimately devised by this or subsequent workshops directly to the head of the agency prevented the rest of the session from being treated as an exercise in futility by the assembled managers and supervisors.

The presence of the observer was part of a troubling larger issue which was addressed in several of our early meetings with the training staff. We were concerned that the mixture of managers and supervisors could easily result in a group in which participants could find themselves taking the workshop with their administrative superiors. We asked if this would dampen free and open discussion. The training staff was aware of the possibility, but chose to deal with it by having the observer merely announce another caveat at the beginning of the first day's session: all discussions and comments within the workshop were to be considered confidential and were not to be repeated outside the confines of the workshop.

A third complaint was that there was insufficient time to analyze the various case studies. Fourth, and finally, the training staff especially wanted to see case studies which were more directly relevant to the day-to-day work of DFCS.[10]

As a consequence, the following two workshops abandoned the goal of establishing a code of ethics specifically for DFCS. Instead, the participants surveyed the established codes of six or seven social service agencies and professional associations. These sessions also emphasized case studies from the "helping professions." Occasionally, media accounts of local misdeeds were used to highlight common ethical problems, such as conflicts of interest. Group activities continued to be an integral part of the workshops, but on a reduced scale.

Evaluating the Workshop: The Participants' Perspective

The combined response rate for the evaluations from all three workshops was 95 percent, or forty-one out of forty-three participants. Since participants were required to complete the forms, the response rate was understandably high. The intended purpose of these evaluations was twofold: (1) to assist us in assessing what types of information or training the participants most benefitted from, and (2) to identify additional issues or problems that future workshop sessions might include. As we already mentioned, the goal of acquiring follow-up information on the long-term effects of the workshops on the professional lives of the participants was in effect blocked by the DFCS training staff.

Declining Workshop Evaluations

Participant evaluations for the second and third workshops were progressively less positive. Why did the evaluations show a persistent decline over the life of the workshops, despite efforts to make improvements based on available feedback? Among the possible reasons for the overall decline is that the workshop's initial success prompted agency leadership to strongly encourage "problem managers" to attend future workshops. Rather than attending the workshops for wholly voluntary reasons, at least five of the twenty participants in the final workshop were either very apathetic (one supervisor with twenty-three years of service openly read a newspaper throughout both days of his training session) or visibly resentful about having to be in attendance.[11]

On a more encouraging note, the responses to certain key questions were largely positive. Here, the workshops' content, the case study approach, and the delivery were generally well-received. With regard to the general desirability of and need for training in ethics, the participants were also quite supportive. Among the points consistently made by these managers and supervisors in their evaluations of the workshops were the following: (1) Ethics training is important; (2) Ethics training requires a considerable amount of introspection and assessment; (3) Many managers do not know how to determine (much less guide others toward) proper ethical behavior. Consequently, rigid standards or codes of ethics are preferable; (4) Nevertheless, ethical behavior needs to be leadership-driven; and (5) Ethics training should be directly linked to individual job tasks.

CONCLUSION

Our experiences with these three ethics-for-bureaucrats workshops provided several insights. First, from the standpoint of teaching ethical decision making to practitioners, both the written exit evaluations and the in-class responses showed that these practitioners preferred to learn from case studies directly related to their individual job tasks or work requirements. They were reluctant to extrapolate from the experiences and conditions of other agencies to those of their own. Second, it is helpful that a large number of negative stories about ethical problems in the public sector may be found in the popular news media, since they are a useful source of relevant case studies about the experiences of DFCS.

As we mentioned in the evaluation section, the higher administration of DFCS may be tempted to treat ethics training as a kind of panacea for problem managers. If so, the conveners of future workshops on ethics must be prepared to recommend (sometimes in rather strong terms) that additional types of training and support services be provided for these individuals. Third, therefore, is the importance of clearly specifying that ethics training of this kind is not intended as a remedy for ineffective management or inadequate supervisory skills.

Fourth, from a much broader perspective, there is an obvious need to develop an evaluation tradition for the growing area of inservice ethics education, especially one that goes beyond mere evaluations of participant satisfaction with the training experience. The whole premise behind ethics training is that it affects the outlook and, most importantly, the behavior of those who have received it.

Evaluations designed to track these kinds of outcomes may proceed along several lines. For example, individuals could be tracked over the course of several years to determine the impact of the training on their attitudes and choices through interviews, questionnaires, or reports by co-workers and supervisors. Another "macro" way of tackling the question might be to get longitudinal records of the frequency of "ethics problems" that show up in the media. In the case of an agency like DFCS, is there a decline in such reports over a period of time following the establishment of regularly offered workshops on ethics? Yet another possibility might be longitudinal tracking of the judgments of various key groups in the agency's environment, including interest groups, legislators, clients, and professional associations. The evaluation methods commonly used are largely restricted to exit questions and opinions solicited of those who went through the training often consisting of the "did you like it" kinds of questions.

Fifth, codes of ethics are political documents. It is entirely possible that the initial "develop a code" model we settled on with the training staff was threatening to key actors in the agency, or at least perceived as potentially controversial by the training staff. There was always the possibility that the street-level practitioners attending the training might come up with something that could be challenging to the agency's hierarchy and its well-known top-down approach to administration. For an agency experiencing the kinds of administrative change that DFCS was undergoing (during our two-year association with it, the agency had four different acting or "permanent" directors), anything that might fuel an already high state of internal and/or external turmoil was clearly threatening.

NOTES

1. For example, the six colleges of Georgia State University each list at least one course today. Ten years ago there were courses listed only in the colleges of Business Administration and Arts and Sciences. Not surprisingly, throughout the nation courses such as these frequently tend to be offered by the faculty of philosophy departments who may be well acquainted with the extensive philosophical literature of ethics. While courses on "ethics for nurses" and "ethics for business management" may entail a substantial intellectual leap from the more traditional scrutiny given to, for example, Aristotle's *Nicomachean Ethics*, they are nonetheless appreciated for the very positive effect they have on the enrollments of such departments.

2. Members of the American Society for Public Administration have numerous occasions to ponder that organization's code of ethics (first adopted in 1984), for it is frequently reprinted. The National Association of Social Workers recently revised its code, strengthening its "teeth." (Unlike some others, the ASW code has punitive provisions for wayward members.) The American Bar Association has made education in ethics a requirement of both law school programs and the in-service training that all practitioners are required to take on a regular basis. The American Medical Association has long had a similar (if even more rigorous) standard.

3. For example, states typically have professional practices commissions which may license professionals such as peace officers and even teachers. In the State of Georgia, a relatively ineffectual PPC was recently reinvigorated with an explicit *Code of Ethics/Standards of Conduct* containing punitive provisions. In a few short months of operation it has already lifted the licenses of a number of unfit teachers. Similarly, select committees of prominent professional associations whose members hold state licenses are generally tasked with investigating member misdeeds and then recommending appropriate state action. The ABA and AMA are among the more prominent associations which essentially police their own practitioners on behalf of the state government.

4. For example, the *Georgia Ethics in Government Act* (1994) established such a commission to serve as a watchdog over the financial dealings of candidates for elective office.

5. Among the more interesting works which do make some attempt to address the question of appropriate content, see Catron and Denhardt 1994, and Hejka-Ekins 1994.

In this context, it is important to distinguish between inservice and preservice education. As part of their degree programs, many undergraduate and graduate students may enroll in university courses on ethics which last ten to fifteen weeks. The amount and kind of material presented, as well as the depth in which it can be covered under these circumstances, is much different from the one- or two-day inservice training courses typically offered to practitioners. In this chapter, we are primarily concerned with the efficacy of the latter type of course.

There is a much more important issue which, unfortunately, cannot properly be addressed within the limitations of the present essay. If, as Aristotle contends, moral education is really about habituation or the gradual internalization of what is considered to be appropriate conduct, ethics is then really about character. From this perspective, there is reason to be skeptical about the prospects of positively affecting the future ethical behavior of young adults simply by exposing them to one or two university-level courses on the subject. Understandably, this leads to an even darker view when contemplating the likelihood of positively affecting the behavior of middle-aged inservice practitioners through occasional one- or two-day training sessions on ethics. In addition to Aristotle's *Nicomachean Ethics*, one should see Sir Henry Taylor's *The Statesman* for a treatment of ethics education understood as character formation.

6. In a curious way, the stress on ethics for public employees can be seen as a logical extension of the bureaucracy's historical search for a satisfactory basis of legitimacy within our democratic regime. The displacement of straight patronage by the late nineteenth century civil service reform effort saw the bureaucracy variously offer professional expertise or political neutrality as justifications for its clear exercise of that political power we call "administrative discretion." Placed alongside the unquestionable legitimacy of directly elected officials, these were admittedly not the most satisfactory explanations to the citizenry as to why bureaucrats should wield such power over their lives. From the standpoint of this lineage, the contemporary emphasis on ethics may be seen as a derivative attempt to fashion a justification based on a (mild) form of "moral soundness." (A stronger variant of this argument is found in Frederickson and Hart 1985).

7. This agency has been the subject of more than just media criticism. State officials at the highest levels have rammed through legislation forcing changes in the way the agency performs its mission as well as in the kinds of information it can withhold from the public.

8. In fairness, no accounting of the agency's difficulties would be complete without stressing the toll taken on those who must confront wrenching family situations day after day. Torn between the sometimes conflicting missions of preserving families and protecting children, caseworkers frequently have immensely difficult decisions to make. Not surprisingly, the supervisors and managers in our workshops consistently reported annual turnover rates of 25 percent among their caseworkers—in many circumstances, because of psychological and emotional "burnout."

9. In our early meetings with the DFCS training staff, the ultimate goal of enrolling all its managers and supervisors in the workshops was consistently stated.

10. The initial meeting with the training staff had established a consensus on one point, namely, the workshop was not to emphasize a "situational ethics" approach. The reactions to the first workshop, though, seemed to indicate that that was more precisely what the participants and the training staff really did want.

11. All three sessions of the workshop were deliberately scheduled on regular workdays so that the participants could receive full pay for attending. Additionally, the first session was held on a college campus in the largest city in the state. The second and third sessions were held in pleasant surroundings but progressively farther from urban settings. As a consequence, the final two sessions drew participants who were remarkable for both their long years of service and the rural locations of their home offices.

REFERENCES

Aristotle. *Nicomachean Ethics*. 1975. Translated by H. Rackham. Cambridge: Harvard University Press.

Atlanta Constitution. 1992a. June 9, Section XJ: 1.

———. 1992b. June 10, Section XJ: 1.

———. 1992c. June 23, Section D:3.

———. 1992d. June 27, Section D: 7.

———. 1992e. July 16, Section XJ: 1.

———. 1992f. September 4, Section XJ: 1.

———. 1992g. October 8, Section D: 3.

———. 1992h. October 9, Section C: 1.

———. 1992i. October 10, Section B: 3.

———. 1992j. October 15, Section A: 14.

———. 1992k. October 17, Section B: 5.

———. 1992l. October 18, Section D: 1.

———. 1993a. May 18, Section D: 1.

———. 1993b. May 28, Section XJ: 1.

———. 1993c. July 21, Section A: 10.

———. 1993d. July 23, Section F: 1.

———. 1994. May 25, Section B: 5.

Catron, Bayard L., and Kathryn G. Denhardt. 1994. "Ethics Education in Public Administration." In *Handbook of Administrative Ethics*, Terry L. Cooper, ed. New York: Marcel Dekker, pp. 49–61.

Cooper, Terry L., ed. 1994. *Handbook of Administrative Ethics*. New York: Marcel Dekker.

DFCS School of Management Catalog. 1993.

Frederickson, H. G., and David K. Hart. 1985. "The Public Service and the Patriotism of Benevolence." *Public Administration Review* 45 (September/October) pp. 547–53.

Hejka-Ekins, April. 1988. "Teaching Ethics in Public Administration." *Public Administration Review* 48 (September/October) pp. 885–91.

———. 1994. "Ethics in Inservice Training." In *Handbook of Administrative Ethics*, Terry L. Cooper, ed. New York: Marcel Dekker, pp. 63–80.

Kavathatzopoulos, Iordanis. 1994. "Training Professional Managers in Decision Making About Real Life Business Ethics Problems: The Acquisition of the Autonomous Problem-Solving Skill." *Journal of Business Ethics* 13 (May) pp. 379–86.

Marini, Frank. 1992. "The Uses of Literature in the Exploration of Public Administration Ethics: The Example of Antigone." *Public Administration Review* 52 (September/October) pp. 420–26.

Pratt, Cornelius B. 1993. "Critique of the Classical Theory of Situational Ethics in U.S. Public Relations." *Public Relations Review* 19 (Fall) pp. 219–34.

Richardson, William D., and Lloyd G. Nigro. 1987. "Administrative Ethics and Founding Thought: Constitutional Correctives, Honor, and Education." *Public Administration Review* 47 (September/October) pp. 367–76.

Rohr, John A. 1978. *Ethics for Bureaucrats: An Essay on Law and Values.* New York: Marcel Dekker.

Taylor, Sir Henry. 1992. *The Statesman.* Edited by David L. Schaefer and Roberta R. Schaefer. Westport: Praeger.

Torp, Kenneth H. 1994. "Ethics for Public Administrators." *National Civil Review* 83 (Winter) pp. 70–73.

U.S. Office of Government Ethics. 1994. *Third Biennial Report to Congress.* U.S. Government Printing Office.

CHAPTER 11

Ethics, The Academy, and Part-Time Civic Leaders

LOUIS C. ZUCCARELLO

A 1987 cartoon in the *New Yorker* magazine pictures the head of some mythical organization presiding over a meeting of his key executives. They are arranged around a large conference table, where he poses this question to them: "This might not be ethical. Is that a problem for anybody?" The cartoon leaves it at that. One wonders what the response will be from the lieutenants around the table, but if the concerns of this volume are as real as they seem to be, some of us would be worried that silence and tacit assent would be the sum total of the response.

The proliferation of articles in the professional literature, coupled with the increasing debate and discussion in the academy on the topic of ethics and public life, are testimony not only to the importance of the issue but also to an underlying discomfort with our capacity to address the issue.

H. George Frederickson (1993) reminds us that the increase in both the incidents and visibility of government corruption has alarmed the public and prompted calls to "do something." Very often doing something has meant setting up institutional safeguards and monitors to patrol the ethical frontier. Lewis Gawthrop (1993) reminds us of older and presumably better days when public service was based on "foundational" values, which, as he underscores, promoted the importance of purpose over process and which insisted on the pursuit of the good rather than on simply avoiding the bad. Richard Chapman (1993) writes, "Although the specific values of society may change, they are an important element in guiding discretionary power and influencing particular decisions in the public service" (p. 158). Chapman concludes by noting that the personal values of public servants are the most important element in public service ethics.

Acknowledging the importance of the issue and the fact that times have indeed changed, the public administration academy has engaged the issue of ethics in the public service and centered its attention on doing a better job in preparing public service professionals. There is debate on where, when, and how this should be done, but little doubt that it should be done as a part of professional development and of continuing education.

One may ask, however, if these efforts ever reach the large number of individuals who serve as part-time, paid leaders or as part-time volunteers in public service. Most have never studied public administration, and some may have little or no college training. It is also likely that this group has little familiarity with the literature of professional public service in general and with the work on ethics in particular. These men and women play important roles in the public service. It is thus essential that we include them in our discussions of ethics.

BACKGROUND

For the past five years, I have had the chance to work with relatively new public service participants in a leadership training program sponsored by the Southern Dutchess Chamber of Commerce in the mid-Hudson Valley of New York State. These men and women are nominated for participation by their corporations and agencies because they show the potential to be leaders in the public sector. Some are volunteers, and others serve in paid capacities. They represent a wide range of socio-economic, racial, and ethnic backgrounds and have various levels of experience with public service activities, ranging from none to highly involved. They meet for full-day workshops once a month and engage in one intensive weekend retreat during the year.

These individuals will serve as policymakers on local school boards, zoning boards, volunteer organizations, staff commissions, and on governing councils. They are clearly people who make a difference in public service. Nonetheless, they exist for the most part in isolation from the academy. Their approach to public service is largely one of common sense.

While they may ignore the academy, the academy has returned the favor by ignoring them. Yet we know that dramatic instances of corruption and unethical conduct have found their way into the arena populated by these public servants. We know that the ethical challenges faced by full-time professionals confront part-time citizen leaders as well. Part-time citizen leaders need our attention. However, efforts to define what we should be saying about ethics will be clouded by elements deeply rooted in American culture. Attempts to carve out an ethical core of basic values will be caught in the tension between an ever-growing individualism and a struggling attempt to maintain some sense of communal responsibility resting on shared values.

A MODERN PROBLEM WITH DEEP ROOTS

This tension was highlighted by Tocqueville, who noted that the thrust for equality produces an individualism that " . . . at first, only saps the virtues of public life, but in the long run it attacks and destroys all others and at length is absorbed in down right selfishness" (Bradley ed., 1945, p. 105). Tocqueville also highlighted civic associations and religion as key factors tempering the negative consequences of extreme individualism. Large, depersonalized population centers and living patterns, however, have shattered the supportive community that Tocqueville saw as a counterbalance to radical individualism. So while the tension between individualism and communal responsibility is an old one, the mitigating factors which tempered the effects of individualism have eroded.

Robert Bellah and his associates prove the accuracy of much of Tocqueville's vision: "It seems to us that it is individualism, and not equality, as Tocqueville thought, that has marched inexorably through our history. We are concerned that this individualism may have grown cancerous—that it may be destroying those social integuments that Tocqueville saw as moderating its more destructive potentialities, that it may be threatening the survival of freedom itself" (1985, p.vii). We have, in other words, reinforced the values of individualism, moral relativism, and ethical privatism to the point where we have dangerously wounded our ability to draw upon a shared ethic. It seems essential that there be some shared ethical consensus to provide the basis for dialogue about ethics. As we search for ways to develop "ethics for public servants," we must recognize the challenge that is fed by dangerous tendencies in American culture. Clearly my experience has been that the microcosm of civic leaders that I deal with has a view of the public order in which conflict over particularized interests reigns supreme.

Aware of the fragmented core of shared values, the academy seems anxious to get beyond minimalist laws and detailed bureaucratic regulations as the basis of public ethics. Yet, as Bellah describes, it is difficult to identify a shared basis for the ethical expectations we propose for public administrators and citizen leaders. Our attempts reflect the conflict within society at large. We debate not only the purposes of ethics education, but also the ground(s) that one might use as the basis for defining ethics in the public sector. We have debated the use of philosophical inquiry to identify principles and schools of thought which can guide us, and we have posited criteria which are generally accepted by the public and its leaders (for example, Anechiarico and Jacobs 1994; Rohr 1989; Callahan 1991).

Arguments for increased attention to discourse about moral values (see, however, Lee 1990) are quite sound when it comes to respect for the rights of the individual. They are persuasive in stating the need for an ethic that transcends an exaggerated individualism while still promoting the legitimacy of a lively marketplace of ideas. Note, for example, the judicious concern of Etzioni (1995). He agrees that free individuals need protection from government but maintains that they also need a community that sustains morality by drawing on the gentle prodding of family, friends, and neighbors. The socialization process is critical in shaping moral values and is indispensable for the moral community.

John Gardner's essay "Building a Responsive Community" cautions his readers, ". . . To require that a community agree on everything would be unrealistic and would violate our concern for diversity. But it has to agree on something. There has to be some core of shared values. Of all the ingredients of community, this is possibly the most important" (in Etzioni 1995, p. 170).

ORDINARY CITIZENS TALK ABOUT VALUES

My experience with civic leaders underscores much of what Tocqueville predicted and what Bellah and others (for example, Callahan 1981) later confirmed. Distinguished commentators approaching public sector ethics reinforce the Tocqueville-Bellah-Callahan thesis that our culture may have a distorted notion of the proper relationship between individual and community. While not wishing to suppress the free expression of ideas, one can still maintain that all expressions are not equally valuable, or more basically, equally true. Attempts to generate solutions to the problems of ethics in the public square are hurt by an inability to generate widespread, thoughtful discussion of the issues.

The people in the Leadership Seminar come with an assumption that they and their peers do in fact share a common set of values. They reveal this assumption in a general discussion about the meaning of ethics and the role of ethics in society. The discussion is experiential, without citation of philosophers or empirical studies. They tell each other what they think, and they frequently are surprised when they find that they do not all think the same way about issues which at this stage are purely abstract. Are there standards of right and wrong which all must observe all the time? Is the good what is best for most people at a particular time? Should each person follow his or her own standards of right and wrong and leave it at that, without outside discussion or comment? When the participants gradually gain the courage to speak about these issues, lively debates ensue with evidence drawn from newspaper headlines, TV shows, and personal experience.

Breaking the Ice

One of the first issues confronted is the legitimacy and propriety of discussing such matters as ethics and values in society. Serious discourse about ethical matters among a group of folks who are not quite strangers anymore, but still somewhat unknown to each other, is difficult to spark. The experience of the workshop has drawn me to appreciate even more the work of scholars concerned about the dwindling core of shared values in American society.

As we begin to explore different views on what should be the basis of ethics, there is often some embarrassment and reserve about saying anything at all. Eventually things get started; those who begin the discussion usually tend to express their views somewhat dogmatically. Among these opinions is the notion that ideas about right and wrong are personal and, in a sense, no one's business. There is a certain amount of discomfort in talking about values; there is a sense of invasion of privacy. However, once they have heard the ideas of their peers, most participants are provoked to counter the arguments with which they disagree. It is clear that most are not used to discussing ethics.

When it becomes evident that participants differ in their views about what ethics is, most are still hesitant to state their beliefs as any more than a personal opinion. Only the boldest will critique the views of others, and even they would ultimately agree that everyone is entitled to his or her opinion. Entangled in this log jam is the mutual understanding that each of their differing views is equally valid. The predominance of relativism is apparent, coupled with the discomfort participants experience in engaging people with different ideas. How does one disagree and still keep everyone happy, especially people one is just getting to know?

As concrete ethical problems are cited, a third element enters the discussion. A consensus may form around a particular value, such as honesty, and in the abstract it is generally agreed to be important. However, the consensus may shatter once confronted with a real-life dilemma where the issue is to act in accord with the principles that all had agreed upon earlier. A familiar refrain that enters the discussion is often something to the effect of "Be real. One can't always act ethically. To do so is to be naive." Echoing the words of Thrasymachus in Plato's *Republic* (yes, the discussion is that old), since justice and honesty do not produce the rewards that injustice and dishonesty produce, the street-smart thing to do "is to do what you gotta do." This particular brand of "realism" is another way of saying that you can't always be honest.

A related argument we usually hear involves the notion of a morality of scale: ethical norms seem to be more applicable to big issues than small ones, especially on means-ends issues. Thus Watergate was an ethical disaster, but the deception practiced by a school board to get greater taxpayer support is not so bad if it helps the children in the long run. ("We're doing it for the kids!")

Finally, one other initial outcome is the tendency of some participants to give up quickly. They confess to a lack of background experience for such discussions. We are a society whose discourse is increasingly framed in terms of sound bites. The participants are often satisfied with and limited to a quick, definitive answer, and many are surprised, if not threatened, by a follow-up question asking for clarification or elaboration.

Discussion Evolves

By this time the discussion has warmed up. When confronted with the relationship between law and morality, most participants quickly conclude that morality is broader than purely legal distinctions between right and wrong. During later discussions, however, when confronted with concrete situations, many quickly defend their positions exclusively with the argument that what they propose to do is not illegal and is therefore ethically acceptable.

We explored several other general questions. There tends to be an overwhelmingly positive response to the statement that in the past twenty years agreement in society on what constitutes proper ethical standards has declined significantly. However, a few begin to question the truth of the statement, and a small minority are drawn to the view that the agreed-upon standards are basically the same over time; no one argues that agreement has increased. The debate on this matter usually concludes that ethics and ethical standards are personal matters. Variation exists from individual to individual, and that's really no one's business. The same group is quick to conclude that society needs a system of shared values, but they are hard-pressed to describe what that system should be. The paramount barrier to doing so is the participants' inability to reconcile their emphasis on shared values with the prerogatives of individual autonomy.

By the time we get to the short concrete situations which ask for the exercise of ethical judgment, the group is getting more comfortable. People begin to question one another, and more frequently than before they openly challenge one another's views. They are becoming more aware of themselves and of the tensions and paradoxes within their ethical thinking. There is joking, and people let their guards down.

We ask questions such as, who do school board members represent? Might you be where you are because you represent a particular group and your presence helps to diversify the board? Do you then have a special obligation to represent that group in the deliberations and activities of the board, or is your primary responsibility to the greater community, or perhaps to yourself? The workshop also struggles with the question of sunshine laws. Is it appropriate, in order to get things done for the good of the public, to find ways of circumventing the law? Is it illegal or unethical, for example, to have informal coffee at the chairperson's house, just to straighten things out before the formal meeting of the board.

The simple question of on-the-job attendance likewise provokes a heated debate. One individual does not go to a number of meetings, does not get assignments done on time, but does show up for photo opportunities. All of this is related to the demands and expectations of his or her full-time job. Seems rather simple, some say. Resign. Not all agree that such action is in one's self-interest and recommend that one does the best he or she can and stick out the term.

Money and favors, of course, stimulate an interesting clash of views. Does one accept tickets to a hit musical from someone who benefitted from the action of the city council? The tickets are sent after the decision has been made as a gesture of thanks, and most of one's council colleagues are going to use the tickets and send a thank-you note to the donor. Does one take the tickets? Before the session is over, we explore whistle-blowing, how one would relate to the press, and what one thinks of the public's right to know.

Applying Principles

It is probably accurate to suggest that the vast majority of Americans know the "right" answers to many ethical questions posed in general and abstract form. It is quite another matter to ask them to apply those principles consistently in concrete situations. Recently, it surprised many observers to learn that Americans have little trouble identifying principles of civil liberties in the abstract, but that they differ significantly when asked to apply those principles in the concrete. McCloskey and Brill (1983) provided overwhelming evidence of the varied understanding and application of civil liberties among the public. The shocking part of the results was the number of citizens who were prepared to limit the speech and behavior of others on matters traditionally protected by the courts. Indeed, approximately 40 percent of the public favored suppressing expression of unpopular ideas.

Studies and my own experience with participants show that ethics in the abstract generates more consensus than ethics in the concrete. The privatism which increasingly surrounds ethics, joined with the exaggerated importance of individual self-interest, have drowned out concern for the common good. This poses a compelling challenge for those who believe that ethics in the public service should go beyond the promulgation of minimalist codes of conduct. There is no necessary conflict between the private values of citizen leaders and the public values which can stand as general principles for public servants. Under such principles, public servants would espouse values which promote the priority of personal integrity over personal gain. Acceptance of public service indicates a recognition of certain obligations as a member of the larger community. Ethical waffling by citizen leaders occurs when the values of public-spiritedness and the commonwealth are subsumed by the values and motives of the marketplace. The two are clearly different, but in practice their differences are often blurred by citizens who are asked to make quick transitions from their roles in the marketplace to newer roles in public service.

Discussion

When we finish with the workshop and written evaluations are collected and reviewed, the findings are enthusiastically favorable. The comment made most forcefully is that there is great need for this type of discussion. Many participants rate it as the most important workshop in the program because the topic is the most vital. Participants note that they rarely have the opportunity to discuss ethics in a systematic way, and the chance to speak about issues allowed them to see what they think about ethics. Some find that they are as surprised by their own answers as they are by the answers of others. One important outcome of the session is self-awareness.

Participants hear colleagues with differing views and realize that they must confront those opinions. The discussion process helps them to clarify their own views and to become more appreciative of the thinking of others. There is clearly value in hearing and saying things which in many instances were only thought about but never articulated before. At times, a discussion will lead one to reconsider and question views that had been energetically presented earlier. Under questioning, group members help each other to confront the longer-range implications of their short-range, quick and easy solutions. A variety of ends-means issues provoke substantial examination when concrete problems pose worthy ends with ethically questionable means. The results-oriented emphasis of modern society promotes a tendency to brush aside ethical questions about means in order to attain the desired results. It is an age-old issue, but one that bears frequent reconsideration.

Finally, there is the recognition at some point in the course that many of the ethical issues that public servants face are not clear-cut but are enmeshed in ambiguity. Yet the participants, who are at first put-off by ambiguity, come to recognize that all answers are not equal and that there are meaningful differences between varying approaches to difficult issues. It is quite natural to dismiss much of this emerging awareness as the standard set of issues which usually find their way into textbooks. Quite true. The fact of the matter is that this audience does not read those textbooks and has not been exposed to mainstream ethical analysis. Yet it is they who are called upon to resolve important ethical issues in a time of a dwindling public consensus on ethical values.

CONCLUSION

This chapter suggests that part-time citizen leaders constitute an important segment of the public sector. It is not a group that is likely to pursue higher education in public administration or in ethics. If the academy is to reach them, it must go out to them or make efforts to invite them into our conference rooms. Ideally, cooperation with private agencies who help to select these individuals should be encouraged. Programs which target newly elected or appointed officials can be established as part of an orientation to their responsibilities. Encouraging local governments to sponsor such programs in partnerships with area colleges and universities may also lead to reaching this group of civic leaders.

The programs in civic ethics should be relatively brief and allow for quick movement between the theoretical and the concrete. Long sessions on theory may discourage participants whose needs and questions seem more immediate. The academy has the challenge of translating the literature of research and scholarly studies into a language and substance that are meaningful to the lay person.

The need for public discussion about ethics, especially among citizen leaders, is not only desirable but anxiously sought by those who have been introduced to the issues. Often ethical questions address the very problems with which they have struggled in their roles as civic leaders, but which they have not confronted in a systematic and collegial way. The need and the audience are there.

Discussion on ethics in the public sector cannot proceed without recognition of the changing values within society and the present emphasis in the socialization process on the values of privatism, relativism, a distorted egalitarianism, and a radical individualism. We must heed the observations of those who warn of a dangerously "minimalist ethic" and of the "pacification of morals." While public administration academicians cannot solve the problem, we cannot ignore it. The academy has a particular responsibility to these public servants, not only to help sharpen administrative technique and process but to assist in sharpening their awareness of the higher purposes of their service. It must encourage and assist conduct befitting the dignity of this calling to public service.

REFERENCES

Anechiarico, Frank, and J. B. Jacobs. 1994. "Visions of Corruption Control and the Evolution of American Public Administration," *Public Administration Review*. 54, pp. 465–73.

Bellah, Robert N., et al. 1985. *Habits of the Heart*. New York: Harper and Row.

Callahan, Daniel. 1981. "Minimalist Ethics: On the Pacification of Morality." *Hastings Center Report*. 11, (5) pp. 19–25.

Chapman, Richard A. 1993. *Ethics in Public Service*. Edinburgh: University Press.

De Tocqueville, Alexis. 1945. *Democracy in America*. 2, Phillips Bradley ed. New York: Vintage Books.

Etzioni, Amitai. 1995. *Rights and the Common Good: The Communitarian Perspective*. New York: St. Martin's Press.

Frederickson, H. George, ed. 1993. *Ethics and Public Administration*. Armonk, NY: M. E. Sharpe.

Gawthrop, Lewis C. 1993. "The Ethical Foundations of American Public Administration," *International Journal of Public Administration*. 16, pp. 139–63.

Lee, Dalton S. 1990. " Moral Education and the Teaching of Public Administration Ethics," *International Journal of Public Administration*. 13, pp. 359–89.

———. "The Difficulty with Ethics Education in Public Administration." 1990. *International Journal of Public Administration*. 13, pp. 181–205.

Lewis, Carol W. 1992. "An Agency Ethics Audit," *International Journal of Public Administration*. 15, pp. 1619–32.

———. *The Ethics Challenge in Public Service*. 1991. San Francisco: Jossey-Bass.

McCloskey, Herbert, and A. Brill. 1983. *Dimensions of Tolerance*. New York: Russell Sage Foundation.

Rohr, John A. 1989. *Ethics for Bureaucrats*, 2ed. New York: Marcel Dekker Inc.

CHAPTER 12

Ethics Education in Municipal Government: It Does Make a Difference

WILLA MARIE BRUCE

This analysis is about ethics education received by municipal clerks and the extent to which that education influences their attitudes and perceptions on the job. The majority of research about ethical issues in municipal government has focused on political officials, whose antics create widespread public concern because of news media attention and other "watchdog" activities. What have less often attracted researchers' interests are those who occupy administrative and support positions in local government—those who are hired, rather than those who are elected. Little is known about the ethics education they receive. Less is known about the effects of that education on what they think about their work environment or about the performance of themselves and their co-workers.

This analysis contributes to empirically based knowledge about employee attitudes regarding ethics in local government by reporting the results of a study which included an effort to learn about the effects of ethics education on the attitudes of municipal clerks. Data reported here are from a survey of persons employed as municipal clerks who are also members of a professional association: The International Institute of Municipal Clerks (IIMC).

The more than seven thousand clerks who belong to the IIMC are encouraged to become a Certified Municipal Clerk (CMC). To achieve this designation, they earn points through formal college education, participation in professional conferences, and city-provided in-service training. In addition they must be employed as a clerk for at least three years and participate in an IIMC-recognized Certification Institute program which consists of a minimum of one hundred university-level student/instructor contact hours. Included in the requirements are fifty contact hours of public administration (PA), thirty hours of social and interpersonal issues (SII), and twenty hours of electives. Ethics education is a recommended, not a required, topic in the SII group (IIMC 1992). Certification Institutes are conducted in almost every state by a local university under the auspices of the IIMC. Certified clerks typically have completed thirty-five contact hours during one intensive week for three consecutive years.

The research reported here determined that a majority of respondents have received some form of ethics education, and found that education about ethics does make a difference in the way the clerks view and report handling difficult ethical decisions. The next section of this chapter offers background for the study. Following that are discussions of findings about education for ethics; what clerks believe constitutes an ethical work environment; the effects of ethics education upon their perceptions of corruption, and upon their attitudes about decision making and behaviors on the job. A summary and conclusions are then provided.

BACKGROUND

According to a recent technical bulletin (IIMC 1978), municipal clerks are the heart of city administration. The municipal clerk's job requires the traditional POSDCORB[1] duties of public administration and more. In many cases they are the embodiment of government for the citizen. They must be responsive to both elected officials and citizens, while maintaining political neutrality, and they serve as boundary spanners between the city and the citizen.

In terms of their job security, 86 percent of the clerks are appointed by an elected official in their municipality (IIMC 1978). In terms of the scope of their duties, "Technical Bulletin," Number 6 (IIMC 1978) indicates that over 90 percent of municipal clerks are responsible for the following functions: maintaining the official records and documents; answering inquiries from other departments and citizens; maintaining official council minutes book; maintaining official ordinance and resolution books; recording council minutes; arranging and preparing for meetings; administering oaths, and supervising clerical staff. More than 75 percent of the clerks administer elections; 66 percent issue business and nonbusiness licenses; 33 percent maintain vital statistics; and 31 percent manage municipal finances. Simply put, a county's municipal clerks conduct the everyday business of municipal government.

Clerks are encouraged to become members of IIMC, and that membership requires a signed commitment to a Code of Ethics (IIMC, not dated). That Code is shown in Figure 12.1. Clerks' professionalism is fostered through the IIMC-sponsored educational programs which lead first to certification and then to status in an Advanced Academy. Professionalism encourages ethical behavior (Gortner 1991). Yet the literature on political corruption suggests that realities may create pressures on administrative employees which could make ethical conduct difficult (Anechiarico and Jacobs 1994). Education is, of course, one way to encourage professionalism and to empower people to combat those pressures which can lead to corrupt behavior.

The ethics education received by municipal clerks occurs in three ways: (1) orientation to legislated city codes and practices, (2) in-service training about the value of ethical behavior provided by employing cities, and (3) workshops conducted to meet the SII requirement of the IIMC-sponsored certification education. In all instances, training models are typically what Hejka-Ekins (1994) calls "fusion" models. That is, they are directed toward teaching both compliance with legislation and personal integrity—in effect clerks are taught to do the right thing, as well as to do the thing right.[2]

The research reported here addressed the clerks' perceptions about the effect of that education by surveying a random sample of the more than seven thousand employed-as-a-clerk members of IIMC.[3] It answers the following questions:

(1) What effects does education in ethics have upon the perception of corruption in local government by municipal clerks?

International Institute of Municipal Clerks'
Professional, Personal Code of Ethics

Believing in Freedom throughout the World allowing increased cooperation between municipal clerks and other officials, locally, nationally, and internationally, I do hereby subscribe to the following principles and ethics which I affirm will govern my personal conduct as municipal clerk:

To uphold constitutional government and the laws of my community;

To so conduct my public and private life as to be an example to my fellow citizens;

To impart to my profession those standards of quality and integrity that the conduct of the affairs of my office shall be above reproach and to merit public confidence in our community;

To be ever mindful of my neutrality and impartiality, rendering equal service to all and to extend the same treatment I wish to receive myself;

To record that which is true and preserve that which is entrusted to me as if it were my own; and

To strive constantly to improve the administration of the affairs of my office consistent with applicable laws and through sound management practices to produce continued progress and so fulfill my responsibilities to my community and others.

These things, I, as a municipal clerk, do pledge to do in the interest and purposes for which our government has been established.

_____

Signature

Source: International Institute of Municipal Clerks
1206 North San Dimas Canyon Road
San Dimas, CA 91773

Figure 12.1. International Institute of Minicipal Clerks' Professional, Personal Code of Ethics

(2)   What effects does education in ethics have on attitudes about decision making by municipal clerks?

(3)   What effects does education in ethics have on attitudes about job-related behaviors of municipal clerks?

The typical respondent to this study lives in the United States, is female, age forty-one to fifty, white non-Hispanic, has completed some college, and is a Certified Municipal Clerk. She has completed some study of ethics, works full time, and has been in her position from one to five years. Analysis indicates some striking differences in attitude between those who have received education in ethics and those who have not, as well as differences in perception of the value of education between respondents who live in the United States and those who live in other countries.

Although 91.5 percent of the respondents believe that employees in their cities are generally ethical, 52.4 percent think that "Corruption probably occurs sometimes, but it's not evident." Indeed, 35 percent state that they "observed one unethical act in the past year," a finding consistent with Menzel's 1992 study of ethics in local government. Respondents believe themselves to be highly ethical, for 89.2 percent agree with the statement, "the way I live my personal life is as important as the way I perform my job."

In other words, most respondents view themselves as ethical persons working in cities where others are generally ethical. Whether their self-reports would represent the views of other city employees was not determined.

The next section discusses how ethics education takes place in the 522 cities represented in this study.

EDUCATION FOR ETHICS

Ethics education in some local governments occurs as a part of employee orientation as well as inservice training. As can be seen from Table 12.1, 52 percent of respondents report that their orientation includes instruction about what is legal and illegal, and 50 percent report that inservice education about the value of ethical behavior is conducted by their cities. An additional 15 percent report receiving education about ethics since becoming a clerk. Because of the phrasing and placement of the question, one might suspect that this occurs as a part of the specialized training required for clerks' professional certification.

While 50 percent of the cities represented in this study provide education as a means of preventing corruption, fewer communities in the United States do this than in the other countries in this study. The difference between the two groups is striking ($p < .01$), for 75.7 percent of respondents from "other countries" agree with the statement, "educating employees about the value of ethical behavior is one way my government prevents corruption," while only 47 percent from the United States agree with that statement.

ETHICAL ENVIRONMENT

Conditions which occur in cities which provide an ethical environment for employees were identified two ways. First, factor analysis, using varimax rotation, was performed. Second, contingency tables were constructed to determine the correlation between the educational variables listed in Table 12.1 and variables representing reported ethical conditions in the cities.

Factor analysis produced eighteen factors with Eigenvalues greater than 1.0000. These factors explain 61.7 percent of the variance in responses. One factor has relevance to this report. Factor 1, with an Eigenvalue of 6.29644, is the most powerful factor, explaining 12 percent of the variance, includes the statement "Educating employees about the value of ethical behavior is one way my city prevents corruption." Table 12.2 shows the specific questionnaire statements which cluster in Factor 1 and the correlation of each item with the factor itself. None of the other factors contains an education-related variable; rather they indicate how clerks think that ethical behavior is discouraged.[4]

The clustering in Factor 1 suggests that respondents believe that activities to promote ethical behavior must begin with the people who live in a community and who are committed to ethical government.

Table 12.1. Education in Ethics Variables (N = 522)

Variable	Percent Agreeing
All new employees in my city receive instructions about what is legal and illegal for them to do as a city employee.	52
Educating employees about the value of ethical behavior is one way my city prevents corruption.	50
Since becoming a Municipal Clerk, I have participated in educational sessions that addressed the issue of ethics.	65

Table 12.2. Top Ten Conditions in Ethical Municipalities

Condition	Correlation with Factor
Citizens in my city do not tolerate corruption.	.60112
People in my city must have high personal standards to be hired.	.58610
Educating employees about corruption is a way my city prevents it.	.55746
All new employees receive instruction about what is legal and illegal.	.55308
My supervisor encourages truth even if it could cost the city money.	.52129
Employees meet regularly to discuss ethical problems.	.51563
Laws in my city clearly define what is ethical and what is not.	.50426
The city attorney is a source of help.	.46570
A person would get fired for taking a bribe.	.45337
My City Code of Ethics is written so that violators will be fired.	.44703

They report that ethical behavior in city government is promoted by valuing high personal standards and educating employees about ethics, in a situation where supervisors encourage truth and where employees regularly come together to discuss ethical problems. These are statistically interrelated activities which characterize an ethical environment in a community.

Contingency tables demonstrate the strong relationship between community laws, codes of ethics, and education for ethics. Fifty percent of the cities represented in this study have laws which "clearly define what is ethical and what is not." In those cities, 68 percent also report that new employees receive instructions about what is legal and what is not. In cities that do not have ethics legislation, only 22 percent teach new employees about what is legal and what is not ($p < .001$).

A similar difference exists when cities have codes of ethics with sanctions. Although only 22 percent of the cities represented in this study have these formal codes, 83 percent of that group provide orientation about what is legal and what is not. Among cities with no ethics codes, only 43 percent give orientation. Not surprisingly, 63 percent of the cities which have codes of ethics also provide education about the value of ethical behavior, while only 46 percent of the cities without codes provide such education ($p < .01$).

Thus municipal ethics education does not occur in a vacuum. It is a part of an overall ethos of responsibility. When ethics education is provided, however, the differences in perceptions, reported decision-making processes, and respondents' views about their own and others' on-the-job provide evidence of its efficacy.

EFFECTS OF ETHICS EDUCATION
UPON PERCEPTIONS OF CORRUPTION

Corruption is a set of particularly insidious activities that undermine the very infrastructure of government. To assess how education is related to the perception of corruption in municipalities, the questionnaire asked respondents to consider the following statement before answering specific questions: Corruption is defined as "behavior which is illegal, or which advances personal benefit without regards to government benefit." The statements in which the presence of education makes a statistically significant difference in responses are discussed in the following sections.

An interesting and encouraging finding is the effect of education on perceptions about the ethical behavior of fellow workers. Fifty-two percent of the respondents from cities that provide ethics education believe that the employees in their city are "generally ethical." In those cities where ethics education is not provided, only 37 percent believe that employees are "generally ethical" ($p < .001$). Similar findings occur when the dependent variable is "During the past year, I have observed one unethical act by a city employee," confirming the validity of the responses.

Education also appears to foster a perception that reporting corruption is safe. In cities where respondents agree with the statement, "Educating employees about the value of ethical behavior is one way my city prevents corruption," 36 percent also agree that "Whistle blowing is a safe way to report corrupt behavior in my city." Only 20 percent in cities that do not provide ethics education feel safe about whistle blowing ($p < .001$). Education for ethics is not enough to encourage all to say they feel safe "blowing a whistle," however. As shown in Table 12.3, even in cities providing education, 32 percent of the respondents do not feel that this would be a "safe" way to address corruption.

Table 12.3. Whistle Blowing and Ethics Education*

Percent who believe Whistle Blowing is:			
	Safe	Don't Know	Not Safe
Cities with ethics education (N=261)	36	32	32
Cities without ethics education (N=261)	20	28	52

*$p < .001$

In cities where all employees receive instructions about what is legal and illegal for them to do as a part of orientation, similar statistically different perceptions exist (p < .01). As shown in Table 12.4, respondents from cities where new employees are taught what is legal and illegal are more likely to feel that whistle blowing will not adversely affect their own job situation, although it is not encouraging that 36 percent still say they don't feel safe about reporting what they think is corrupt behavior by another employee.

Orientation about legal issues also increases respondents' confidence that action will be taken if corruption is identified and reported. Eighty-four percent of the respondents from cities that provide orientation about what is legal and what is not believe that if corruption is reported corrective action will be taken, and only 9 percent don't know what will happen after a report (p < .001). Respondents from cities that do not provide such orientation, however, are not as confident (see Table 12.5). In other words, education about what is considered to be appropriate behavior encourages people to believe that it is safe to act responsibly when they see corruption occur.

Thus, to answer the first question asked in this research, education does affect perceptions about corruption. The more education about ethics respondents report receiving, the more likely they were to think themselves able to identify corruption, and to have the courage to report it.

Table 12.4. Whistle Blowing and Orientation*

Percent who believe Whistle Blowing is:

	Safe	Don't Know	Not safe
Cities with orientation about what is legal and illegal (N=271)	33	31	36
Cities with no orientation about what is legal and illegal (N=251)	25	31	44

*p < .01

Table 12.5. Confidence to Report Corruption and Orientation*

Percent who believe action will result from report:

	Action	Don't Know	No Action
Cities with orientation about what is legal and illegal (N=271)	84	9	7
Cities with no orientation about what is legal and illegal (N=251)	72	16	12

*p < .001

EDUCATION AND DECISION-MAKING PROCESSES

Education about laws and ethics shows a positive correlation with certain approaches to decision making that respondents report using in their jobs. While this research did not assess the outcomes of decision making, it does provide information on the processes respondents report using.

One way that clerks apparently are educated to make the "tough decisions" is to consult with others in their office. When the independent variable is "all new employees in my city receive instructions about what is legal and illegal," 72 percent of respondents from those cities providing such orientation report that "Whenever anyone in my office has a tough ethical decision to make, we discuss it and try to come to a group decision." Where orientation is not provided, 57 percent report that a group decision-making process is used (p < .001).

Clerks apparently are taught in both orientation and in-service education to utilize a consideration about "what is the greatest good for the greatest number?" as a guide for on-the-job decision making. Sixty-four percent of those in cities providing orientation about what is legal and not agree with the statement, "When making a difficult ethical decision, I do whatever will bring the greatest good to the greatest number of the city's residents," compared with 54 percent in cities that don't have such orientation (p < .05).

That difference is very similar to the responses of those who report that their city provides in-service education about the value of ethical behavior. Of that group, 63 percent of the respondents report using a "greatest good" calculus to make an ethical decision, while 49 percent of those whose cities do not provide in-service education report that method (p < .001).

Cities may be teaching ethical sensitivity and the importance of a "greatest good" approach to decisions, but the clerks' professional training seems to approach ethical education differently. Of the 66 percent of respondents who had participated in education beyond what their cities provide, only 57 percent report that they would ask, "What is the greatest good?" in making a job-related decision, as opposed to 62 percent of those who had not received such training (p < .001).

While this self-reported information is too brief to extrapolate overmuch, this leads to the speculation that professional associations may educate for a "low-road" approach to ethics which relies on adherence to a professional code rather than upon personal integrity or some decision-making calculus.

Education appears to empower respondents to use resources outside themselves to help with ethical decision making. Of those whose cities provide education about the value of ethical behavior, 53 percent find the advice of their city attorney helpful, yet only 36 percent in cities that don't provide education find the city attorney helpful (p < .01). It may be that education for ethics encourages people to seek outside advice before making tough decisions. This would be consistent with encouraging group decision making. Table 12.6 summarizes the ways that respondents report making ethical decisions.

Thus, to answer the second question asked in this research, education does affect the decision-making processes the respondents report using. Those who received ethics education were more likely to say they use a variety of decision-making techniques and to report involving others in exploring alternatives and deriving solutions to tough ethical dilemmas.

Table 12.6. Effects of City-Provided Ethics Education on Decision Making

Education about Ethics	Percent		Sig.
	Provided (N=261)	Not Provided (N=261)	
After group discussion	72	57	p < .001
Get help from city attorney	53	36	p < .01
Ask, "What is greatest good for greatest number?"	64	54	p < .01

ETHICS EDUCATION AND JOB-RELATED BEHAVIORS

Ethics education also appears to affect how respondents view their co-workers' behavior. Among respondents from cities that provide orientation about what is legal and what is not, only 30 percent report, "During the past year, I have observed one unethical act by a city employee." In cities that do not offer new employees information on what is legal and illegal, 43 percent of respondents say they observed an unethical act in the past year (p < .01). Thus orientation about legal and illegal behavior appears to shape perceptions about the behavior of others.

In cities that provide education about the value of ethical behavior, 48 percent report observing one unethical act in the past year, while 63 percent in cities that do not provide the education report observing one unethical act (p < .01). These responses indicate that education about ethics affects what one believes about the behavior of others.

One might speculate that increased education would lead to increased observations of unethical or illegal acts, as participants would learn what to look for and be more apt to recognize corruption when they see it. That simply was not the case. This study indicates that when people are educated about what is ethical and what is not, they are more likely to think that others are acting ethically.

Respondents are reporting that other city employees, and not just themselves, have received ethics education. That suggests that ethics education has also improved the behavior of those who participate in it. It makes no sense to conclude that ethics education increases one's tolerance for unethical behavior.

Data also indicate that, in cities which offer education about the value of ethical behavior, respondents have increased confidence that reporting corruption will bring corrective action. Eighty-six percent from those cities which do educate about ethics agree that "reporting corruption will get results," and only 7 percent don't know. Contrast that with cities which do not provide ethics education. In those cities, 72 percent agree that "reporting corruption will get results," and 18 percent don't know ($p < .001$). One might, therefore, speculate that education both decreases the incidence of unethical acts and increases the likelihood that people will feel it worthwhile to report observed improprieties.

Education even has an apparent effect on whether or not respondents say they would report unethical behavior by a friend! Of those who agree with the statement, "If I knew someone was acting in a corrupt manner, I would report that person even if he or she was a good friend," 53 percent live in cities providing education on the value of ethical behavior, and 38 percent live in cities where no such education is available ($p < .001$).

Clerks who have received education about the value of ethical behavior also are more likely to believe "I should try to influence city decisions when I know what decision would be best." Fifty-three percent of them think they should try to influence city decisions, while only 38 percent of those without ethics education would exert such influence ($p < .001$).

In addition, those in cities providing ethics education are more likely to believe that responsibility for ethical action is a part of their job. Of those respondents whose cities provide education in ethics, only 12 percent agree with the statement, "I'm not paid enough to make an ethical decision," while 20 percent from cities that don't provide ethics education say they aren't paid enough to make ethical decisions ($p < .01$). Thus education about ethics empowers clerks to participate in ethical decision making. It gives them confidence. It enhances personal integrity.

Table 12.7.   Effects of City-Provided Ethics Education on Job-Related Behaviors

Education about Ethics	Percent		
	Provided (N=261)	Not Provided (N=261)	Sig.
One unethical act observed in past year.	48	63	p < .001
Reporting corruption gets results.	86	72	p < .001
I would report a friend's unethical behavior.	53	38	p < .001
I'm not paid enough to try to influence decisions.	12	20	p < .01
I should try to influence decisions when I know what's best.	53	38	p <. 001

How city-provided education correlates with reported job-related behaviors is shown in Table 12.7.

Thus, to answer the third question asked in this research, education does affect attitudes about job-related behaviors. More of those who receive education about the value of ethical behavior than those who work in cities where no ethics education is provided think that what might be labeled "more ethical behavior" exists in their cities. Fewer respondents who have received ethics education report observing corruption; more respondents who have received ethics education say that if they observe corruption, they will report it in the confidence that reported improprieties will be addressed by city officials.

CONCLUSIONS

This study clearly indicates that orientation about behavioral governing laws and inservice education about the value of ethical behavior offered by municipal governments make a difference in the way respondents describe their on-the-job decision making and job-related behaviors. It does not seem too great a leap of faith to suggest that education about laws and ethics will positively affect the attitudes of all municipal employees, thus providing a means of decreasing corruption in municipal government.

Neither ethicists nor educators know much about the type of ethics training that is offered in municipalities (Hejka-Ekins 1994). Questions about who is providing the training and what ethics criteria are being taught are still to be conclusively answered. Yet this study sheds some light on what is taught.

This study indicates that about half of the cities which employ IIMC-member clerks offer either orientation or inservice training about laws and ethics. Within those cities, ethics education does not occur in a vacuum. It is a part of an overall ethos of responsibility that includes concern by citizens and commitment by both elected and appointed officials. When ethics education is provided, the differences in employees' perceptions, attitudes about decision-making processes, and how they report seeing the job-related behavior of others provide evidence of its efficacy.

Education increases the ability to define corrupt acts and the willingness to report them. It fosters the feeling that whistle blowing is safe and the belief that action will be taken when reports are made. The finding that acknowledged willingness to report corrupt behavior by a friend is greater among those who work in cities providing ethics education suggests that education affects values as well as attitudes.

With regard to what is being taught, one might suspect that there is a heavy emphasis on compliance with laws and policies. However, in this study, those who report receiving ethics education from their cities are more likely to agree that they try to influence city decisions when they believe they know what decision should be made. Those self-reports indicate that municipal ethics education fosters personal integrity as well as providing legal knowledge.

Decision-making skills apparently are a part of municipal ethics education as well. Those who receive ethics education are more likely to say they use a variety of decision making techniques on their job, and they are more likely to say they involve others in exploring alternatives and deriving solutions to tough ethical dilemmas. They also describe what might be labeled "more ethical behavior" than do those who work in cities where no ethics education is provided. They report less observed corruption and an expectation that improprieties will be reported and dealt with.

The research reported here is a step toward developing a body of knowledge about ethics education in municipal government. Conclusions are limited, because data were gathered from a survey which asked only for the perceptions of municipal clerks about the existence or nonexistence of certain personal attitudes and conditions in their cities, as they perceived them. Thus, it has produced a subjective picture of ethics education and ethical behavior in municipal government. The research did not verify that conditions in their municipalities were as reported. It did not include the attitudes of any fellow employees, and it did not contain any objective outcome measures. Many questions remain to be answered.

The issue of who provides the ethics training was not dealt with in this study, but it, too, is an important one for future research. While recognizing the uniqueness and community spirit of local governments, one has to wonder about the quality and content of ethics education when it is delivered without benefit of agreed-upon standards. Perhaps it is time for academicians to work more closely with professional associations and government entities to develop guidelines for ethics education in local governments. Clearly the development and delivery of ethics education is not limited to the academy. One wonders what role academic ethicists can and should play in fostering ethics in local government, and if, indeed, objective measures of the effects of education can be established. Future research should explore these issues.

NOTES

1. Planning, Organizing, Staffing, Directing, Coordinating, Reporting, and Budgeting.

2. The author's knowledge about clerks' education comes from ten years' experience as Director of the Nebraska Certification Institute, service on the Education Committee of the International Institute of Municipal Clerks, and from conversations with other directors and with Dr. Frank Adshead, Director of Education for the IIMC.

3. A stratified, systematic random sample of the employed-as-a-clerk membership in IIMC was surveyed. The membership includes clerks in eleven countries: Australia, Canada, Cyprus, Great Britain, Israel, Malaysia, Netherlands, New Zealand, Switzerland, South Africa, and the United States. Persons in eight of them responded to the survey. The mailing list, containing 7,335 names and addresses, was sorted by country and by zip code where these codes existed. Every sixth member in the United States and Canada received a questionnaire. Every second member in Australia and Great Britain was surveyed, as were 100 percent of the membership in the other countries Thus 1,129 questionnaires were mailed in the United States, and 157 questionnaires were mailed elsewhere.

To increase the likelihood that those surveyed would return completed questionnaires, a letter of support signed by the Executive Director and the Director of Education of IIMC was included in the mailing, as was a postage-paid envelope for the response. Surveys were mailed during the first two weeks of March, 1993. Usable responses were received from 522 clerks for a response rate of 41 percent.

The questionnaire was determined to be both reliable and valid. Reliability of results is assured by "size of population," and number of responses. When a population size of 7,335 yields a sample size of between 415 and 707, results have a reliability of + 4 percent. Validity is assured by inclusion in the survey of questions which were worded in a negative form, or which defined both corrupt and ethical behavior that might occur in a city. Responses to both kinds of questions addressing the same issue did indeed vary together.

The survey questionnaire was developed based upon a review of the literature on both administrative ethics and corruption in government. It contains seventy-five questions. The initial draft questionnaire was reviewed by two academic experts in local government. It was then revised and pre-tested on fifty practicing government managers. Responses were analyzed, and the questionnaire was again revised. The final questionnaire contains fifty-three items to be answered on a five-point Likert scale (strongly agree, agree, don't know, disagree, strongly disagree). Ten questions identify corruption controls which respondents were asked to rank order in terms of effectiveness, and eleven questions are about the respondents' background and other characteristics. The Statistical Package for the Social Sciences was used to analyze in question responses.

Data for this report on ethics education in municipal government were analyzed in three ways:

(a)   First, descriptive statistics were obtained about responses to each questionnaire item.

(b) Questionnaire items 1 through 53, which address ethical practices, were subjected to factor analysis based on a varimax procedure and a criterion of an Eigenvalue greater than 1.0. This determined which conditions exist together and produced a rotated factor matrix.

(c) Contingency tables were constructed to explore correlations of variables representing the conditions which can occur in cities with responses to the three variables which indicate that education for ethics takes place (see Table 1). Chi-Square was the test of statistical significance here, with $p < .10$ considered worth reporting.

4. For a discussion of these factors, see Bruce (1995).

REFERENCES

Anechiarico, Frank, and James Jacobs. 1994. "Visions of Corruption Control the Evolution of American Public Administration," *Public Administration Review* 54, no. 5 (September), pp. 465–73.

Bruce, Willa. 1995. "How Municipalities in Ten Countries Promote Administrative Ethics," *Hong Kong Public Administration*, 4, no. 1, pp. 55–75.

Gortner, Harold. 1991. "How Public Managers View Their Environment: Balancing Organizational Demands, Political Realities, and Personal Values," in J. Bowman, ed. *Ethical Frontiers in Public Management*. San Francisco: Jossey-Bass.

Hejka-Ekins, April. 1994. "Ethics in Inservice Training," in T. Cooper, ed. *Handbook of Administrative Ethics*. New York: Marcel Dekker, p. 70.

International Institute of Municipal Clerks (n.d.). "Application for Certification," Pasadena, CA.

International Institute of Municipal Clerks. 1992. *Certified Municipal Clerk Program: Minimum Requirements for IIMC Recognition.* Guide 2. Pasadena, CA.

International Institute of Municipal Clerks. 1978. *Clerks' Duties,* Technical Report No. 6. Pasadena, CA.

Menzel, Donald. 1992. "Ethics, Attitudes, and Behaviors in Local Governments: An Empirical Analysis," *State and Local Government Review* (Fall) pp. 94–102.

Nie, N. H., et al. 1975. *Statistical Package for the Social Sciences* 2nd ed. New York: McGraw-Hill.

Norusis, M. 1990. *SPSS: Statistical Data Analysis.* Chicago: SPSS, Inc.

Welch, Susan, and J. C. Comer. 1983. *Quantitative Methods for Public Administration.* Chicago: The Dorsey Press.

PART IV

Ethical Issues:
Programs, Students, Faculty

Postmodernity, Reform Fads, and Program Management: Presumptive Consequentialism vs. Discourse Ethics

CHARLES J. FOX

It has been often observed by public administrationists that organizational reform movements come in waves. I want to take that commonplace observation one step further and suggest that successive reform movements become increasingly symbolic and decreasingly substantive. They are, in other words, more and more signatures of what will be described as the postmodern condition: the loss of confidence in enlightenment and modern belief structures. The epiphenomenalism that is typical of the postmodern condition, in turn, entails a distancing of these symbolic reforms from the life-world experience of organizational life. This distancing, when repeated and increased over time, leads, it will be suggested, to cynicism and quietism among those toward whom the reforms are supposed to be directed. Cynicism and quietism, in turn, favor an ethics which will be called here *presumptive consequentialism*. Presumptive consequentialism is, furthermore, an inappropriate ethics for authentic academic pursuits. That is to say, mumbling the mantra of the latest wave of reform, as a convenient means to further even the most just and progressive programmatic ends, undermines the critical and intellectual independence of public administration as an academic enterprise. Especially in public administration should reform dogmas be bracketed and held up to scrutiny. They should not be cynically adopted for the imperatives of public relations. Discourse ethics, the essay concludes, is better suited than

presumptive consequentialism to the task of reconciling the conflicting imperatives of the academic enterprise and program protection.

BACKGROUND

I have, with Hugh Miller, argued elsewhere that fruitful insights about
contemporary public affairs follow from viewing policies as aspects of
the postmodern condition.[1] Doing so requires, at least for the sake of
argument, that one accept the proposition that we are undergoing a
fundamental sea change in advanced industrial societies. In other
words, the work and study of public policy formation and implementation now occur in a context so fundamentally different from the past
as to justify the judgment that we have crossed over from one era
(modernity) to another (postmodernity). As a word of warning/self-
defense, let it be quickly added that the epochal evolution did not
occur all at once. Modernism goes back to the Enlightenment rational-
ists of seventeenth century Europe. Postmodernism can be traced as
far back as Nietzsche while gathering momentum in the years after
World War II. A full-fledged explication of the transformation and its
implications is beyond the scope of this paper. Only the production-
symbol aspect of postmodernity can be sketched here.

In its production aspect the transformation from modernity to
postmodernity is associated with the widely noted movement from an
industrial to a postindustrial society, that is, from an economy based
primarily on the production of material goods to one based primarily
on information technologies, services, marketing, credit, and consumption. To be sure, this transformation, like the earlier movement from
agricultural production to industrial production, is one of dominant
tendencies or ideal-typical profiles. Of course we still produce agricultural and industrial commodities, but as the paradigm case of farm
labor was replaced by the paradigm case of the assembly line, the paradigm case of work today is an office where symbols are analyzed and
manipulated. This development has also been heralded as the advent of
the information age. Toffler (1980) and Gingrich make a similar point
about first, second, and third waves. As an aside, postmodernism (as a
theoretical orientation) adds that allied philosophical, epistemological,

ethical, political, cultural, and societal developments are of sufficient magnitude to warrant epochal differentiation.[2]

The main implication of the production metamorphosis to be teased out for the purpose of this argument is the theory of hyperreality, or what might be called *self-referential epiphenomenalism*. Again, only the surface of the argument can be expressed here. The postmodernist[3] analysis finds that words, symbols, and signs are increasingly divorced from direct life-world experience. Part of this split results from the switch from a society based primarily on production to one based primarily on consumption and information. Production requires group activity and communication based on the manipulation and processing of physical objects; there is a rootedness in production based on the direct interface between humans and material; symbolic meanings are similarly rooted.

Contrariwise in the consumptive economic mode of postmodernity, symbols float away, as it were, and procreate with other symbols, leading to what Jameson (1991) calls "the free play of signifiers." As the design of products to which symbols are attached becomes too complex for their consumers to master, symbols lose their mooring lines. Marketers take advantage of this detachment, manipulate the symbols, and attach them to other symbols. Thus do machines become sexy, cleaning fluids repair dysfunctional families, and the purchase of a particular brand of colored carbonated water signifies membership in a generation. Similarly in politics, symbols often purposefully mislead and replace deliberation over policy. "Willie Horton" becomes a logo for Massachusetts penal policy, "read my lips" is a fiscal policy, and "Clinton" becomes a modifier signifying "big-government-tax-and-spend" when attached to "health plan" or "welfare reform."

As exponentially more signs detach themselves from the life-world elements they were presumptively designed to denote, the signs are conceived as inhabiting a realm which postmodernists call *hyperreality*. Once a sign takes up permanent residence in hyperreality, any kind of reality which may be called empirical loses influence over it. Better yet, hyperreality attains a life of its own, outside and hovering above the experiential reality of day-to-day life. Celebrities, the O.J. Simpson case, sports, and much of electoral politics exist therein, with only the most tenuous relationship to the phenomenological reality of daily life. Moreover, hyperreality, or hyperspace, is extremely volatile and thin. A subjective expression of the same transformation is the popular lament about America's nano second attention span. It is also the case that exactly what gets paid such short attention to is random and arbitrary.

If the postmodern thesis is correct, the result of these events would be the loss of a certain shared and concretized rationality. Rational will-formation becomes increasingly difficult when language loses its ability to communicate the discrete workaday reality of public policy implementation and organizational life. Worse, symbols interacting in hyperspace without benefit of mooring in workaday reality can only come back around to distort any reform of that reality.

POSTMODERNISM AND ORGANIZATIONAL REFORMS

I want now to first suggest that recent organizational reform movements have actually participated in the postmodern condition, and that furthermore this mode of interpretation may at least add to the public discourse a layer of hermeneutic meaning.[4] So, in what ways can recent organizational reform movements be said to be postmodern?

One piece of evidence is the decreasing life span of reforms. The now-classical debates between generations of Taylorists and human relations advocates began in the thirties and continued to resonate through the sixties. Since then, in rapid succession, have come management by objectives (MBO), organizational development (OD), Theory Z, Japanese Management, Total Quality of Work Life (TQWL), In Search of Excellence, Quality Circles, total quality management (TQM), reengineering, and finally entrepreneurial, or reinventing government. The latter phrase is particularly postmodern in that the symbol "reinvention" subsumes three fundamentally contradictory public management theories: TQM, reengineering, and downsizing (Kettl 1995; Carroll 1995). It thus qualifies as a postmodern "conflated aggregation" (Fox and Miller 1995), which may be briefly defined as a number of contradictory concepts residing illicitly under the same symbol—a kind of exponential oxymoron.

A rough count finds that we have had ten major fads in twenty-five years, or roughly one every 2.5 years.[5] For any organizational reform movement to be substantively meaningful, one would expect longer periods of time to elapse from conception to implementation to evaluation to abandonment. Such short time spans suggest that the meticulous application of scientific findings to known problematics is not the dominant determinant of reform fads. If these conjectures have purchase, it suggests that the symbols of reform are more important than its accomplishment. To the extent that fads are more symbolic than substantive, they may be located in hyperreality more than substantive organizational reality. Hyperreality, in turn, is volatile, which helps account for the increasingly fleeting nature of the reform fads.

It is also important to point out that there is a kind of carnival clutter that surrounds these fads.[6] Most fads start with a best-selling book. These are followed by lucrative speaking tours by the authors. Then the business press picks it up, and it appears on the cover of *Business Week* and *Forbes*. Shortly thereafter consulting firms and training firms offer up newly minted "experts" on the subject and market these to organizations. Then academic conferences are organized around these themes, followed shortly by spates of tenure-driven "knowledge" creation, that is, journal articles. At the end of the three years, the business press surveys the organizations that have tried the fad only to find that the management person responsible for its implementation has either moved on or become disaffected with the reforms, often because of environmental turbulence. Throughout the process, savvy players learn to talk the talk, and when the next wave appears on the horizon, they quickly shift their vocabulary to accommodate the new buzz words; cheerleaders just learn new cheers. All of this occurs in rapidly metamorphosing hyperspace with scarcely a trace of it filtering down to the workaday life of organizations.

An incident illustrates these contentions. TQM was the major theme of the 1993 Orlando, Florida, annual meeting of the National Association of Schools of Public Affairs and Administration (NASPAA). NASPAA meetings are not so much academic ones as they are gatherings of program advisors and school deans—a meeting of academic management practitioners. The first plenary session of this meeting featured as speaker a young TQM "expert," perhaps in training as a motivational speaker. This speaker presumed to introduce this audience to the virtues of TQM. In a speech sprinkled with anecdotes from current events, selected for rhetorical not analytical effect, he then proceeded, with overheads, to present first an ordinary input-through-put-output-feedback-back to input systems circle. This model standing by itself was labeled, in ways too cute to capture in recount, as the old outmoded way.

Now instead, we were required by the imperatives of our times and by the protocols of TQM to add a new loop to the old loop; a new feedback loop was added parallel to the bottom of the old one (see Figure 13.1). Just after the output marker of the old loop would be grafted to the new loop, and shortly after the juncture appeared the marker "measurement of customer satisfaction" on this second trunk, with another marker "public perception of effectiveness" preceding the rejoining of the new loop to the old one just before input.

I do not know how universalizable this presentation was, but here it was clear that the TQM annex to the traditional systems loop was one entirely concerned with public relations and not with substantive performance. It was specifically emphasized that output measurements should be designed to affirm a positive interpretation of agency performance. Public relations, not scientific discovery of cor-

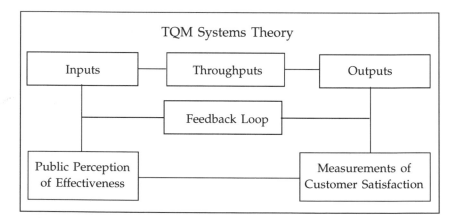

Figure 13.1. TQM Systems Theory

rectable program shortcomings, was the goal. Unethical, from the standpoint of the scientific canon, manipulation of the instruments by which "public perception of effectiveness" is measured was clearly O.K. Grafted on the normal systems effectiveness loop was a public relations loop pure and simple—a loop through hyperreality. Not effectiveness qua effectiveness was the goal, but the citizen perception of effectiveness, so that they would support whichever agency adopted the strategy.[7]

To put the polemic even more starkly: the management and chattering classes increasingly traffic in what I have elsewhere called "plastic disposable reifications" (*plastic* meaning multiple mold possibilities, *disposable* indicating inexpensive replaceability, *reification* meaning an epiphenomenal mental construction taken to be solid reality). International competition, the end of American financial hegemony, stagnating wages, eroding infrastructure, intractable social indicators, and deadlocked politics mean the end of substantive progress to which the culture became accustomed in the years after World War II. If positive change in a substantive sense is blocked, then let them eat symbols.

From the perspective of either intellectuals with memory or workers with declining purchasing power, the endless succession of reform fads turns skepticism about any one particular reform into cynicism.

There is a certain irony in the fact that most of the organizational reform fads share a commitment to involve, empower, and engage the wide range of organizational membership; all reform fads have elements of participatory management. Participation and the involvement of the whole human being in work tasks is universally celebrated as a way to motivate the work force to higher performance. The question which arises from the sequence of fads is why each successive one should be necessary, at least in relationship to this factor, when the previous one was so fervently articulated, embraced, and promoted. The answer must be that whatever amelioration of organizational structure occurred was either short-lived, incomplete, or both. Repeated rhetorical commitment by management without sufficiently significant reform falls victim to the "boy who called wolf" syndrome. The irony is that reforms ostensibly leading to enhanced motivation are actually demotivating. The work force becomes cynical and alienated from a management it does not trust who is seen primarily as manipulative.

It cannot be claimed that the above scenario has been played out in every worksite. There are, however, several municipal government organizations where the scenario does ring true. In these cases the reforms have usually been accompanied by budget cuts, reductions in force, and downsizing. Warm and fuzzy words about empowerment too often are accompanied by increased risk of traumatic career disjunctures. Although it is too early to tell, the Gore initiatives in the federal government seem to be similarly at risk, as spending reductions become more important than the substantive reforms that were supposed to have primacy (Kettl 1995; Carroll 1995). In any case it may be laid down as a general rule that scared workers do not make good reform partners. The widely reported tendency to use part-time "temps" without health and retirement benefits also belies the utopian claims of reform apologists.

I have suggested that reform fads like TQM may, at many worksites, be largely symbolic, and that the succession of them leads to workplace cynicism; this is at least a plausible interpretation of at least a portion of the problematic. This disconnection between promise and performance is sufficient at the very least to pose an ethical dilemma for public administrationists engaged in research and teaching.

PRESUMPTIVE CONSEQUENTIALISM

There are three identifiable aspects of programs in public administration: social scientific/critical, professional training, and program maintenance. Put another way, we have a research role, an educational role, and we must survive to do them. These three roles come in conflict when faced with reform fads. The social scientific/critical role would seem to require that a particular reform wave be thought of as problematic until its logic, environmental fit, and implementation protocols have been rigorously examined. The research/critical role is only somewhat compromised by professional training. Students need to graduate from programs knowing about past and current reforms.

The job interview or assessment center processes may require our graduates to show levels of enthusiasm for a particular reform that their academic courses may have dampened by criticism. Still, we have to trust our students to deal with the contradictions in their own work lives; the alternative of propagandizing students is unthinkable. The more striking contradiction occurs when programs are asked to uncritically apply a reform fad to their own operations. The most predictable response of program leadership is what I will call *presumptive consequentialism*, when the ethics of program survival take precedence. Response to the current TQM rage exemplifies this theme.

After having swept through the private sector, TQM is now enjoying a second life in the public sector. A cursory review of program bulletins at public administration conferences is enough to establish the premise. The TQM aspects of the "reinventing government" tendency and Gore's National Performance Review (NPR) are equally self-evident. Soon we will all have learned to call citizens and students "customers," signed on to "mission statements," and imploded in on ourselves in strategic planning group-think. A little over three years ago NASPAA incorporated TQM into its accreditation process following a similar move by the body that accredits business schools. At my university a program called "service-plus" has been implemented, accompanied by an inspirational session with cheerleaders, songs, and testimonials rivaling Mary Kay conventions, fundamentalist revivals, and the Nurnberg rallies. A similar enthusiasm seems to be the goal of the Gore reforms:

> After his talk, the Vice President turned the meeting over to a *motivational* consultant, John Daly, who told the assembly that optimism and effective communication were the keys to the success of NPR. *"It doesn't matter how good you really are, but how you communicate how good you are."* As a reporter present noted: "[Daly] ended his remarks by discussing customer strategies used by the Disney [the epitome of postmodern logo producers] company and led the group in a refrain from Snow White and the Seven Dwarfs' and off to work they went" (Moe 1994; emphasis mine).

Presumptive consequentialism is what happens when the program you lead is subjected to the reform fad you criticize. Consequentialism, in the jargon of ethicists, is the position that an act or a conscious sequence of actions is ethically justified by the good that is the anticipated consequence of those actions (Frankena, 1973). Utilitarianism is the best known variant of consequentialism and generally holds that an ethical act is one which increases the greatest good for the greatest number. The trouble with consequentialism has been summed up by the phrase "the ends justify the means." Some distant end that can be positively portrayed, such as a strong race, can justify despicable means, such as eugenics. Moreover, calculating the relationship between a particular means and more generalized ends is often thought to be beyond the capacity of even the most rational of humans. The main alternatives to consequentialist (or teleological) positions are deontological ones. A deontological stance admonishes humans to act, or refrain from acting, if it is immediately right or wrong regardless of the presumed consequences. It seems to me that deontological positions have moral weight that trumps consequentialist ones if one is forced to choose between these binary opposites.[8] But that is only true if one actually takes time to think about it. "Presumptive" as modifier to "consequentialism" means that the level of ethical self-examination required to bring this to analytical cognition does not happen.[9]

In the public administration academy, the conflict between our social scientific/critical role and the need for program survival breeds an ethics of presumptive consequentialism which entails deep cynicism. The new rules for National Association of Schools Public Administration and Affairs (NASPAA) accreditation is the case in point. In 1992 at the Cleveland meeting of NASPAA, mission-driven accreditation was adopted on a vote of a substantial majority of principal representatives of programs. The adoption was, admittedly, democratic. Mission-driven accreditation was sold, if memory serves, as a progressive move away from rigid and picayune rule compliance as proof of accreditation worthiness. Instead of "one size fits all," or "one best curriculum," now programs would be able to justify deviations from the rules (called standards) based on the uniqueness of mission.

But the devil is in the implementation details. I can testify, as last year was the actual result site visitation year for the program for which I am responsible, that has been the one-way command imposition on programs of the dogmas of TQM. The Committee on Program Review and Accreditation (COPRA) has promulgated a detailed set of additional standards requiring programs which hope for accreditation to, in a participatory way, develop and articulate a mission statement, translate the mission into specific goals and objectives, and develop specific performance measurements relating to the goals and objectives (Backoff 1993; Williams 1994). The result has been a 25 percent increase in the length of self-study reports and the recommendation from COPRA to begin ones self-study a full year in advance of its due date. Compliance with particular, specific standards seems to be in no way diminished.

It is not claimed that the process is all bad or that TQM principles are evil. However, the imposition of such principles from above, as it were, is not only a violation of authentic TQM principles themselves, but results in the cynical and unauthentic ethics of presumptive consequentialism. By such top-down processes TQM becomes the-one-size-fits-all one-best-way. And because we are generally committed to the good that our programs bring about (consequences), we have little choice but to cynically pretend to enthusiastically embrace its principles in the interest of program survival.

Otherwise dignified programs fulfilling an educational and research function are thereby coerced into the realm of public relations. Obligatory mission statements and performance measurements are examples. To ask for mission statements is to invite hyperbole. Can anyone write a mission statement without the word *excellence* in it? Can anyone admit that the law of averages will render, through no real fault of their own, some programs mediocre, perhaps even one's own? (I have read mission statements of junior colleges and Mexican diploma mills that make their institutions sound like Harvard.) Can anyone write that their mission is to get paid for credentialing in-service executives who know more about their tasks than the faculty putatively in charge of the courses? Can anyone write that their mission is to employ professionals as adjunct faculty to trade war stories with other professionals for a fee?

Performance measurements are similarly prone to public relations hyperbole. Suppose you have a student attrition rate that regularly runs 33 percent. Suppose there are multiple real reasons for it: (1) one of your core faculty members with tenure browbeats students and is a bad teacher; (2) after mature contemplation some students decide that public service is not for them; (3) the work load is greater than the students had anticipated; (4) students run out of money; (5) spouses put their foot down about being alone at night; and so on. Presumptive consequentialism tempts the poor program administrator, frantically trying to come up with what might look like an objective performance measurement, to state, at least partly disingenuously, that high attrition is proof of program rigor and product quality control. Lower attrition rates, on the other hand, can be cited to prove how nurturing and customer oriented ones program is. This is, of course, like many exercises in reverse program evaluation: get a numerical measurement of something and work your way back to some set of goals and objectives with which the measures comport. Again, just as our TQM "experts" cited above have baldly stated, the perception is more important than the reality. In postmodern terms, the perception becomes the reality. Public relations skills come to outweigh other more substantive competencies.

DISCOURSE ETHICS

I want to recommend that we guard against presumptive consequentialism. I truly mean "we" because the author also "goes along to get along" and claims no moral high ground from which to preach. Indeed, presumptive consequentialism is almost inevitable, given the usual limits of energy, imagination, and time. Presumptive consequentialism is a Simonian "satisficing" path. Fighting it at every turn would be quixotic. It is, nonetheless, too easy to fall into the habit; after all the ends are always good. But going along quietly is destructive of *authentic discourse*.[10] And, authentic discourse, as Hugh Miller and I have argued, is a process by which the postmodern condition can be ameliorated. It is a position with implications for ethics in that it adduces statements of "ought" and "should" from a phenomenology of authentic communication.

Three aspects of discourse are important for this analysis. First, following Habermas' theory of authentic communication or communicative competence, an authentic conversation requires a rough equality of chances to influence it. This protocol would militate against the exercise of hierarchical power. Since the consequences in presumptive consequentialism regrettably are set elsewhere, this ought to be resisted. In the case at hand, TQM supporters in the NASPAA Committee on Program Review and Accreditation (COPRA), should ensure that TQM critics are included in their deliberations. Group-think and the stampeding of plenary audiences should be avoided. More interactive sessions which promote rigorous queries about the issues should be scheduled. The presumption should not be, as it has been, that the truth of the matter is self-evident, and the only remaining task is to sell it. Especially members of the public administration academy should not, and should not have to, unquestionably acquiesce to the latest organizational fad to protect the very programs that are dedicated to knowledge of them.

I hasten to blunt the potential impression that some kind of conspiracy of a "them" is what prevents the application of discursive ethics; it is us. Even when there is the opportunity to speak up in a critical or questioning spirit, too few of us take advantage of it too seldom. NASPAA, for instance is not some impermeable monolithic institution. It is, I would affirm, well designed to allow and encourage discursive will formation. This evokes a second aspect of authentic discourse: willing attention (Fox and Miller 1995, p. 125). Vigorous agonistic discourse requires engagement and involvement of participants. On the other hand, this aspect of discourse militates against the imposition of mission-development retreats on those who, for whatever reason, do not wish to participate. Hence, at the program level, professors should not be forced to participate in mission and goal development retreats and sessions if they do not want to do so. Some people just want to be left alone to quietly and efficiently perform their functions. This is especially true of those made cynical by the succession of reforms.

A third and overlapping warrant for authentic discourse is the sincerity of the participants. Presumptive consequentialism is by definition an ethics of insincerity. Insincerity, in turn, reproduces itself and spreads. When public relations efforts are forced on participants, or participation itself is required, demarcation lines between sincere and insincere speech acts become blurred. Not even a consensual truth can be discerned or won, as no stable points of agonistic tension can be established from which it might be developed.

SUMMARY AND RECOMMENDATIONS

The title of this chapter is also the skeleton of its summary and conclusion. The essay begins by accepting the commonplace fact that organizational reform proposals succeed each other with such rapidity as to earn the label "fads." A conjecture is then offered that fadishness of organizational reforms is consistent with observations by those philosophers who have argued that we are in transition from one age (modernity) to another (postmodernity). Whether or not the postmodernist analysis is compelling, at least some real workers in at least some workaday organizational life situations become cynical when subjected to rapidly succeeding fads. This is especially true when the warm and fuzzy words of the fad act as smoke cover for RIFs and eliciting more work from fewer people at less pay.

The first three moments of this essay are intended to establish the problematic nature of organizational reform fads. Note that it does not attack the internal veracity or theoretical cogency of any particular reform quest. The analysis is more macro than micro. Actually, I am favorably inclined to some aspects of almost every reform fad. The purpose of this explanation is simply to establish that the research/ critical aspects of the craft of public administrationists can, and perhaps ought to, lead to a critical stance toward any particular fad or to fads in general. Thus brought to light is the first horn of a virtually intractable dilemma for the public administration academy. The opposing horn appears when a fad is applied to the academy itself.

Public administration programs are uniquely faced with a contradiction. We are caught between our knowledge-production function and the need to comply in order to survive in our particular organizational settings. There are many examples of public administrationists armed with sophisticated understandings of organizational dynamics who are forced to sublimate that knowledge in the face of their academic superiors not so sufficiently armed. Professional administrationists are too often under the organizational thumb of amateur academic administrators operating with idiosyncratic theories; power trumps knowledge. This essay has pressed that case through the prism of the NASPAA accreditation process.

The conflict between the academic guild, with its commitment to the canon of truth, and program maintenance within organizational environments, as illustrated by the case of NASPAA accreditation protocols, invariably leads to a resolution in favor of acquiescence to the latter at the expense of the former. I have called this the ethics of presumptive consequentialism. Under such an ethic public administrationists become schizoid. One virtue, the critical/academic aspect of their persona, is suppressed to conform to imperatives imposed from outside for another virtue, the survival of the very programs which undergird the accomplishment of their research/critical function. The modifier "presumptive" to consequentialist ethics entails a judgment that we of the public administration academy do not try hard enough to go against the flow. Discourse ethics is a corrective.

Discourse ethics requires commitment to a conversation in which all participants have an equal chance to influence the outcome. It also requires the willing attention and sincerity of participants. Presumptive consequentialism fails this test because, first, it is a response to power exerted from outside. Second, in the case of externally imposed TQM protocols, organizational members are forced to participate in mission development whether or not they are willing. Third, participants in the conversations described do not feel that they have the luxury of sincerity.

CONCLUSION

What can be done? Here are three suggestions: first, at the level of individual behavior, public administration scholars should be more forthcoming during the opportunities provided them. We should not tolerate intellectual incompetence with as much grace as we do. Of the options loyalty, exit, and voice, we should more vigorously pursue the last. The public administration community should adjust its culture away from quietism. When subjected to a vacuous motivational speaker, for instance, we should challenge the bromides. Discursive ethics requires the forthright and agonistic taking of stances and positions with, at the same time, a spirit of comity and a willingness to give way to the better argument. The peer review process for journal publication proves that the academy is capable of vigorous critical discourse.

Second, at the level of guild organizations, organizers of conferences and meetings (I have in mind especially NASPAA and ASPA) should work even harder than they now do to provide opportunities for dialogue and diminish the current commitment to one-way monologues. It is at conferences that we can meet with peers and discuss new research and ideas. More discursive sessions would mitigate against false impressions of consensus on issues where principled disagreements actually obtain. Specifically, reduce the number of presenters on panels, and expand the time for audience participation. Reduce the use of discussants, and allow the audience to be its own discussant. Use small-group breakout techniques so that public administrationists can get to know each other better and can feel more comfortable competing for enhanced word-space.

Finally, it continues to be important to develop the critical faculties in our students. As many classes as possible should be conducted as interactive seminars. Promote Socratic and organizational development and learning processes whereby students reach their own conclusions rather than being spoon fed predeveloped ones. As few classes as possible should be monologic lectures of received wisdom. The principles of discursive ethics are best taught by practicing them in graduate programs. Professors should be less the fount of expert knowledge and more the facilitator of authentic discourse.

NOTES

1. The more robust and careful explication of postmodernism occurs in Fox and Miller 1995, esp. Ch. 3.

2. Whether events and tendencies are regarded as continuations or shifts is a judgment call perhaps better left to future historians. One need not

accept the rupture theory of postmodernism, as, for instance, Anthony Giddens (1990) does not, to use nonetheless the analytical tools of postmodern theory.

3. The terms *postmodernism* and *postmodernists* are used to signify the theory, as opposed to *postmodern* and *postmodernity* to signify the era.

4. Having personally invested considerable time and effort outside my purely public administration pursuits to grasp, however haltingly, the language of postmodernism, I may, I admit, have become the proverbial child with a hammer to whom all things look like nails. Worse, the conceptual tools of postmodernism are so malleable as to violate the criterion of falsifiability. This admission is the best I can do to warn readers to use their own judgments as to the cogency of these claims.

5. Painting with a broad brush ignores the fact that reforms can easily exist side by side in the more substantive realm. I do not wish to demean the quiet organization-by-organization improvements that may have resulted from, for instance, sensitive OD practitioners.

6. These observations have an experiential base of eighteen years in the field, adding up to more than fifty-six academic, thirteen city management, and six NASPAA conferences.

7. As a member of the Arts and Sciences curriculum committee at my university, I am concerned that the most popular major is public relations, which has as its subject matter precisely the manipulation of public opinion along these lines. Have others in this readership had similar experiences?

8. I do not think we are limited to this binary or Hobson's choice (see Fox 1994; Fox 1989).

9. For levels of ethical scrutiny, see Cooper (1990).

10. Again, the full explication of authentic discourse cannot be made here, since it is a somewhat complicated argument. Please see Fox and Miller (1995).

REFERENCES

Backoff, Robert W. 1993. "Mission Driven Accreditation: An Approach to Strategic Quality Management," Paper presented at the 1993 NASPAA Conference, Orlando, Fla., October.

Carroll, James D. 1995. "The Rhetoric of Reform and Political Reality in the National Performance Review," *Public Administration Review.* Vol. 55. No. 3. May/June 1995, pp. 302–11.

Cooper, Terry L. 1990. *The Responsible Administrator* (3d. ed.). San Francisco: Jossey Bass.

Fox, Charles J., and Hugh T. Miller. 1995. *Postmodern Public Administration: Toward Discourse.* Thousand Oaks, CA: Sage Publications.

Fox, Charles J. 1994. "The Use of Philosophy in Administrative Ethics," Ch. 5, pp. 83–105, in Terry L. Cooper, ed., *Handbook of Administrative Ethics.* New York: Marcel Dekker.

Fox, Charles J. 1989. "Free to Choose, Free to Win, Free to Lose: The Phenomenology of Ethical Space," *International Journal of Public Administration,* 12: pp. 913–30.

Frankena, William K. 1973. *Ethics* (2d. ed.). Englewood Cliffs NJ: Prentice-Hall.

Giddens, Anthony. 1990. *The Consequences of Modernity.* Stanford: Stanford University Press.

Jameson, Frederick. 1991. *Postmodernism or the Cultural Logic of Late Capitalism.* Durham: Duke University Press.

Kettl, Donald F. 1995. "Building Lasting Reform: Enduring Questions, Missing Reforms," pp. 9–86 in Kettl, Donald F. and John J. Dilulio Jr., eds., *Inside the Reinvention Machine: Appraising Governmental Reform.* Washington: Brookings.

Moe, Ronald C. 1994. "The 'Reinventing Government' Exercise: Misinterpreting the Problem, Misjudging the Consequences." *Public Administration Review,* Vol 54, No. 2 (March/April) pp. 111–22.

Toffler, Alvin. 1980. *The Third Wave.* New York: Morrow.

Williams, David G. 1994. "Applying Public Management Concepts to Ourselves: Accreditation Under the New Master Degree Mission Standards," Letter to NASPAA Programs. Washington, DC: NASPAA.

CHAPTER 14

The Ethics of Faculty-Student Relations: Identifying Boundaries

MARCIA LYNN WHICKER

This chapter explores the boundary between ethical and unethical behavior in faculty-student relationships, a divide that is fuzzy, murky, and meandering. In addressing this boundary, the chapter is divided into three sections. The first section explores how generic notions of ethics are applied in the academic sphere, particular in the behavior of faculty toward students. Two standards—competence and fairness—are delineated as key. The second section examines two institutional challenges to monitoring ethics—the professionalism of faculty and the pressure to use an industrial rather than a medical model in dealing with students. In the third section, the ethical challenges presented by two structural features—legislative-like departmental decision-making and academic tenure—are explored.

WHAT IS ETHICAL BEHAVIOR
FOR PROFESSORS TOWARD STUDENTS?

Abstract ethical principles can be applied in an academic setting to professors and faculty-student relations. Various authors have different but frequently complementary suggestions regarding how this application should occur. Most suggestions for ethical behavior in faculty-student relationships may be grouped or regrouped around the two basic concepts of competence and fairness (Audi 1990).

(1)   The Competence Principle: Professors should be competent in their subjects. Competence implies that professors are capable with native capacity to master both the basics and subtleties of their fields. They should be well trained and current in knowledge of the field and trends, and they should know the tasks involved in successful teaching. Competence also means that professors have a clear sense of their role expectations, including the duties and limits of the professorial role, and that they perform with diligence, energy, and preparation.

(2)   The Fairness Principle: Professors should be fair to their students and colleagues. This implies a lack of bias on the basis of friendship or background characteristics, such as race, religion, gender, or political philosophy, toward any student. The unbiased professor engages in neither discrimination, that is, unwarranted negative judgments and actions toward an individual based on personal characteristics and the student's group membership, cronyism due to similar personal characteristics, nor partiality due to friendship, that is, unfounded positive judgments and actions due to personal traits, linkages and relationships.

Cody and Lynn (1992, pp. 8–9) discuss behavioral prescriptions of ethical professorial behavior which can be classified in terms of the competence and fairness standards. They argue that ethical behavior includes rendering honest judgment (fairness), working hard and efficiently (competence), maximizing the benefits of the educational institution to all students, and upholding the appearance as well as the actuality of propriety. Ethical behavior avoids lying, cheating, stealing, disobeying the law, conflicts of interest, and inefficient use of funds all potential violations of competence, as well as rudeness and unresponsiveness, cronyism and the advancing of the interests of particular colleagues or coalition of parties over the benefit of the whole, and pressure on students for actions solely beneficial to the professor (all potential violations of fairness).

How compatible are the broad standards of competence and fairness with specific models of teaching? Audi (1990, pp. 122–30) identifies four models of graduate teaching: the didactic, apprentice, collegial, and friendship models. While Audi does not exclude any model, he argues that no single one should dominate, and each may be inappropriately applied, particularly the friendship model. One might argue that each has potential weaknesses in meeting the ethical standards of competence and fairness.

(1)   The Didactic Model: This model uses the principle of the priority of the student's point of view, assuming that the student's view is the relevant one while imparting knowledge within a pedagogical framework. A potential weakness is a tendency toward tailoring the subject matter so greatly to the student's view to demonstrate relevance that key concepts are downplayed. This tendency challenges the standard of competence, where the competence of the professor as a professional is not communicated to the student.

(2)   The Apprentice Model: In this model, the professor may identify with the apprentice but employs professional closeness combined with emotional distance. Perhaps among the strongest of the current models, the potential danger is not present so much for students who are incorporated into an apprenticeship relationship, but to those who are not and are therefore excluded from its benefits while others are benefiting. The greatest challenge, then, is to the standard of fairness. The more selectively the model is applied, and the less strong the institutional structure is to assure its consistent application, the greater the threat.

(3)   The Collegial Model: In the collegial model, the professor approaches students as junior colleagues with a sense of shared role. This approach has advantages, but it incorporates a potential threat to the standard of competence, since professorial colleagues have different needs and concerns than do students. The closer students are to assuming a professorial role themselves, the closer the needs and concerns are of the professor and the students, but some gaps still remain. For colleagues, the primary goals are publishing, research, teaching, service, and performing administrative tasks. For students, the primary goals are mastery of the body of expert knowledge. While these goals may have

much in common, they are not identical, and the possibility remains that the goals of the professor could supplant the mastery goals of the students.

(4) The Friendship Model. This approach combines professional with emotional closeness and thus runs the risk of undercutting fairness in grading and assessment; bias in opportunities may also emerge. The model has the potential for conflict between the support required of friendship and the requirements of professorial duty. It may also allow friendship needs to supplant academic work and may lead to different assessments of students who are not widely different in overall merit. (see Table 14.1.)

Cahn (1994, pp. 9–44) examines how competence and fairness are applied by the ethical professor to teach with motivation, organization, clarification, and generalization. The professor carefully plans the course materials and schedule, is conscientious in setting and adhering to class rules and requirements, comes to all classes on time except for extreme circumstances, is available to and meets with students for consultation outside of class, and shows appreciation for the individuality of students by at least learning their names. The professor also differentiates between personal opinions about the subject taught, majority opinion, and established fact. Furthermore, the ethical professor returns assignments in a timely manner with detailed comments and tests student competence in a fair manner.

Table 14.1. Teaching Models and Potential Threats to Ethical Standards

Model	Ethical Standard with Greatest Potential Threat	
Didactic	Competence:	Too much student relevance undermines thorough training
Apprentice	Fairness:	Through inconsistent application and exclusion of some students
Collegial	Competence:	Professor's career goals may supplant students' goals of mastery of expert knowledge
Friendship	Fairness:	Personal loyalty of friendship may inject bias in professor's judgments

Testing is key to the educational process and greatly impacts faculty-student relations. Cahn (1994, pp. 9–44) concludes that ethical testing involves developing and using examinations that are representative of the course material, posing questions that require detailed answers, employing different testing formats, allowing adequate time, using clear instructions, and informing students of the relative weight of questions. Ideally, tests may be graded one question at a time for all students in order to reduce bias and minimize the influence of past student performance. In evaluating results, professors should employ a standard grading system in an unbiased manner where standards are clearly identified. The professor should lay out at the beginning of the course how the final grade will be determined and the weight of each component. The professor should grade on whether or not the student meets reasonable expectations rather than on a curve, should not refuse to give high grades if students earn them, and should avoid grade inflation so that highly achieving students are not deprived of distinction. Cahn concludes that ethical testing should seek to educate rather than to indoctrinate by demanding acquiescence through intimidation.

Testing involves both the ethical standards of competence and fairness. If tests are poorly designed, the standard of competence is undermined. If they are improperly administered or biased, the standard of fairness is undermined. Rich (1984, pp. 66–69) also discusses the role that ethics should play in testing. Testing has three purposes, according to Rich. The first is the selection, clarification, and appraisal of educational and instructional objectives, thus requiring professors to develop a system of evaluation for each course, to consult evaluation experts when they encounter significant problems or suspect their evaluation plan is inadequate to meet course objectives, and to make modifications as a result of test findings to fit the need and level of the students. The second purpose is the determination and reporting of achievement, requiring professors to respect students as persons, to provide valid tests for handicapped and foreign students, to handle tests in such a way as to not pejoratively label students, and to avoid invidious comparisons among students. Professors should also safeguard tests from violations of integrity, discourage student dishonesty, ensure privacy in reporting student grades and student papers, and follow institutional grading policies. The third purpose of testing is the planning, directing, and improving of learning experiences. Therefore ethical professors do not use tests as punishment or to exert authority over the class; they do use tests as a learning tool, to help them see where teaching has been ineffective, and maintain regular office hours to help students with questions. They do not use tests to indoctrinate or proselytize for personal religious, political, racial, economic, or other beliefs.

If ethical problems in faculty performance and faculty-student relations develop, those involved may not initially recognize the problems as such. Cahn (1994, p. 33) contends that professors often think they are better and more ethical than they really are in terms of the standards of competence and fairness. In part, this occurs because the classroom setting and faculty-student relations in general do not usually present controls on or challenges to the professor's professional behavior and personal preconceptions.

There are several reasons for this "unequal playing field" between faculty and students. The classroom rarely presents the professor with an opportunity for serious intellectual challenge, as students are beginners in the mastery of a subject of which the professors are supposedly masters. In the classroom, students often struggle to understand complexities long familiar to the professor. Students are concerned about gaining favor and a good grade; fearing repercussions, students may politically choose not to challenge or question professors even if they could. Finally, professors often deal condescendingly with younger people who have limited experience and accomplishments.

Competence and fairness, then, are widely recognized criteria for judging whether or not professors treat students and behave ethically. These standards permeate all aspects of faculty-student relationships.

INSTITUTIONAL CHALLENGES TO
IMPLEMENTING ETHICS STANDARDS

Two institutional features of universities and colleges tend to undermine the capacity of administrators to monitor and enforce ethical standards in faculty-student relations: professionalism of faculty and the fiscal and resource pressures to use an industrial model rather than a medical model for dealing with students.

The Professionalism of Professors

Critics often contend that professors are unaccountable for both their time and their actions. Thus professors can squander their time on personal activities that do not benefit students, and they can exhibit arbitrary behavior in faculty-student interactions. Yet professors are considered by society, institutional administrators, parents, and students to be professionals. The professionalism of the professorate presents challenges in the implementation of the standards of competence and fairness in two ways. First, professionals are typically granted greater individual autonomy than are other employees because of their particularized expertise. Second, few external controls exist to measure whether or not the standards of competence and fairness have been typically applied to professionals. (see Table 14.2.)

Table 14.2. Institutional, Structural, and Relational Threats to Ethical Standards

Feature	Threat to Ethical Standard
Institutional	
Professionalism of the Faculty	Professional autonomy reduces monitoring and enforcement of ethical standards.
Pressure to Use the Industrial Model	Creates undifferentiated treatment of most students and favoritism for those who receive attention.
Structural	
Legislative Decision Making in Departments	Peer consensus and the need to build political coalitions erode monitoring and enforcement of ethical standards.
Academic Tenure	Increases faculty autonomy and diminishes effective controls for monitoring and enforcing competence and fairness.
Relational	
Faculty-Student Friendships	Present potential for threats to fairness that are greater, the greater the power of the professor vis-á-vis the student friend.

The status of individuals within a profession is closely related to the degree of their mastery of the specialized knowledge (Piper 1994, pp. 2–3). Professorial prestige, and sometimes salary, parallel national and international recognition for scholarly contributions, and this perception of high status is likely to diminish the ability of students or administrators to question professorial decisions. Further, a professional's primary identity is with the profession rather than the employer; such an identity remains throughout the professor's working life despite changes in employment conditions. Professors who identify with their academic disciplines rather than their universities or colleges are less likely to be amenable to controls imposed by the latter to enforce competence and fairness.

Viewing professors as professionals reinforces their resistance to institutional evaluations of competence and fairness. Professionals are committed to "a calling" which often implies a degree of altruism; the professional's first obligation to the client takes precedence over self-interest. How, then, can university and collegiate hierarchies question the actions of a professor without impugning their own professionalism? A professional works directly with a client, sometimes on a confidential basis and often in private. Thus, how could universities monitor key aspects of faculty-student interactions even if they wanted to?

An essential factor in the definition of a professional is the gap between the client's and the professional's knowledge, based on the specialized body of knowledge the professional has acquired. This knowledge base constitutes the unlevel playing field discussed above which makes students often reluctant to challenge the competence and fairness of their professors. There is an equally large gap of knowledge between the professional and the senior management staff of the employing organization, unless that management is from the same profession. A professor may be from one discipline and any administrator or person in higher authority may be from a different discipline. These gaps make it difficult for administrators to judge a professional's competence and to control or supervise their methods or outcomes.

Given the autonomy that professionals enjoy, what controls are they subject to? Usually the experts themselves monitor the ethics of fellow professionals through often feeble efforts at self-regulation. In universities, self-regulation may take the form of peer evaluation and committee structures to evaluate records, performance, and problems. Yet other professions, such as law and medicine, have had difficulties exposing any but the most egregious violations. McDowell (1991, p. 1) discusses a conflict those who uncover wrong-doing face—between the duty of loyalty to a fellow professional and the duty to inform—a conflict that inhibits colleagues from monitoring and reporting violations by their peers. Unlike peer review of research, regulation of faculty-student relations is often of a personal nature, which may further inhibit any impulse by faculty to closely monitor each other.

For most professionals, *professionalism* presents an ethical conflict between two roles: the role of advisor to a client who asks whether certain services are necessary, and the role of provider of services that the client may need (McDowell 1991, p. 1). Professionals are frequently in the position of having the authority to create demand through their recommendations, for services which they personally can supply and financially benefit. To some extent, university structures mitigate this conflict by reducing the pressure upon individual professors to be "fiscally accountable," for example, by generating from student teaching and services sufficient dollars to cover faculty salaries. Typically, universities hold organizational units such as programs, departments, and colleges, not individual faculty, fiscally accountability. Universities and colleges also extend the time frame for applying financial accountability well beyond the fiscal year, even at the program and departmental level.

The absence of externally-imposed administrative safeguards for enforcing competence and fairness does not imply that strong internal safeguards generated by students will exist. Students may be inhibited from reporting violations, by virtue of the professor's authority to pass judgment on their performance in ways that have bearing upon the student's future. In recent years, the growing litigiousness of society in general and students in particular has partially offset these inhibitions. The increase in student litigation, however, has entailed a loss of trust and a diversion of professors' time and energy from meeting the standard of competence. Ultimately, excessive litigation may also erode fairness by making professors unwilling to pass negative judgments for fear of repercussions.

The characteristics of professions present, then, special challenges in implementing the standards of competence and fairness in faculty-student relations. The challenges come from the autonomy faculty have in deciding how to implement these standards, and from the weakness of external and internal controls and monitors on their implementation. When universities serviced a small portion of the total population and higher education was not crucial to financial and social success, less attention was placed on these challenges. But as the proportion of the population attending colleges and universities has grown, and the role of education in financial and social success has increased, legislators and the public have begun to scrutinize the operation of universities more closely. Part of this scrutiny involves pressure to reduce professorial autonomy and increase accountability, in theory to assure that ethical standards are met. But such pressure necessarily entails a simultaneous erosion of the professional character of being a faculty member. Dressel and Faricy (1972, pp. 1–5) argue that the autonomy granted universities as employers of professionals must be constantly guarded and protected against forces that would erode it.

The Industrial v. the Medical Model to Faculty-Student Relations

The way universities and colleges are organized further complicates the monitoring and enforcement of ethics in faculty-student relationships. Two models of higher education have been employed (Astin 1933, pp. 16–18). The first, the industrial model, is less appropriate, as it often is based on an assembly-line approach to creating outputs. Yet the press of large numbers of students, large classes especially at the undergraduate level, budgetary cutbacks, loss of faculty lines through attrition and retirement, and general austerity that has plagued academic institutions in the 1990s have all combined to lead to the adoption of this model in many settings. The ethical standard of competence may be challenged as it becomes increasingly difficult to adjust material to students, to give individual feedback, and to make exams that are appropriate. Fairness may be challenged as an assembly-line approach implies most students will not get individual attention, so those who do are seen as favorably treated. Providing fair feedback in such a setting is also difficult (see Table 14.2).

The second, the medical model, is more appropriate for higher education. As hospitals and clinics strive to improve the condition of patients, so do colleges strive to improve the condition of students. Medical treatment is based on a diagnosis of specific patient needs; similarly, educational programs are based on a diagnosis of student needs. Changes in patient condition through medical treatment are predicted in the form of a prognosis that assesses the level and type of illness. In higher education when this approach is used, student performance may be similarly predicted in order to fine-tune programs.

Two institutional challenges to ethical faculty-student relations, then, are the professionalism of professors and attempts by colleges to apply the industrial rather than the medical model. The first challenge, professionalism, grants professors autonomy in establishing boundaries in their relations with students. The second challenge, the application of the industrial model, often undermines competence.

THE CHALLENGE OF HIGHER EDUCATION STRUCTURE TO IMPLEMENTING ETHICS STANDARDS

In addition to the complications for implementing ethical standards that faculty professionalism and the industrial model generate, two structural features of universities have a significant impact on competence and fairness in faculty-student relations: legislative-style decision making at the department level and academic tenure.

Legislative Departmental Decision Making

The process of making decisions by majority vote on important departmental issues politicizes academic decision making and makes departmental structure resemble a legislature rather than a bureaucracy. This politicization increases the need for deal making within department's in order to build coalitions and further diminishes incentives for professors to monitor each other's adherence to the standards of competence and fairness.

In contrast to traditional bureaucracies, the organizational structures in universities and colleges are hierarchical at the top, with clear chains of command, but frequently operate by consensus and majority rule at the department level. This quasi-democratic character makes the basic operational processes of departments resemble a legislature more than a merit-driven bureaucracy (Whicker, Kronenfeld, and Strickland 1993, pp. 19–35). In making decisions, bureaucracies employ prespeci-fied standards, strive toward optimization, and employ technical analysis. Legislatures use peer consensus, coalition building, and deal making. The dominant value in bureaucracy is productivity. The dominant value in legislatures is political loyalty.

Through bureaucratic regulations and merit norms, bureaucracies are predisposed to emphasizing competence and fairness. Through peer-based processes, legislatures are predisposed to emphasize inclusion and democratic processes. Bureaucracies have the potential for becoming rigid and applying standards inflexibly. Legislatures have weak incentives to monitor the ethics of its members, for doing so undermines consensus, imposes ethical standards above the values of political loyalty, and undercuts coalition building and deal making. Legislatively generated decisions may not be incompatible with ethical standards and merit norms, but they also may be. A legislative organizational structure does not reinforce these norms if they are not present in the faculty members themselves.

The unique organizational structure of universities and colleges, where they are legislative at the bottom and hierarchial at the top, holds the possibility of gaining the best of both structures. But the potential for reaping the worst of both structures is also present. One consequence of legislative-style decision making at the bottom (department level) is to politicize more decisions, elevating the political aspects of decisions over the importance of monitoring and enforcing the ethical standards of competence and fairness.

Academic Tenure

Academic tenure enhances the autonomy of individual professors and reduces the ability and willingness of administrators to intervene in legislatively generated departmental decisions. Tenure also has the consequence of increasing the politicization of decision making and heightening the importance of peer consensus.

At the department level, the costs of challenging peers for minor ethics issues in areas where boundaries are already fuzzy is juxtaposed with the benefits, and rarely do the benefits win. Students who cannot arouse faculty support in a coalition-driven process have few attractive options. Tenure ensures that department members who have it will likely work closely together for numerous years in a quasi-legislative peer relationship, thus raising the potential costs of challenging a colleague even for major ethical violations.

One solution is to disperse the responsibility for monitoring ethics violations from the department itself to another group, usually the ethics, grievance, or investigatory committees. This strategy is pursued both in legislative bodies like the U.S. Congress and in academia. But such committees are often more quasi-judicial and passive than regulatory in that they monitor only those violations brought to them by plaintiffs willing to go through a grievance or investigatory process. Rarely do such committees scan the environment for long-standing violations about which no one is willing to grieve.

Tenure also pushes university administrators toward consensus, muting somewhat the check hierarchial structures have on departments. Administrators who systematically overturn faculty decisions may experience the costs of discontent, discord, and dissension. While administrators may impose bureaucratic merit norms and ethical standards on any specific situation, a pattern of doing so regularly, or frequently may entail high costs.

CONCLUSION

This chapter explored the meaning of ethics in academic institutions and in faculty-student relationships. The standards of competence and fairness were identified as crucial to judging such relations and professorial performance. The implementation of these standards is complicated and at times confounded by the professional nature of being a professor, by pressures in the academy to use an industrial rather than a medical model for dealing with students, by legislative decision making at the department level in universities and colleges, and by academic tenure. No easy solution exists for the problems in implementating ethical standards. The boundaries are fuzzy between ethical and unethical behavior, and determination of whether boundaries have been inappropriately crossed is situational. Perhaps the best safeguard against ethical violations, given the above constraints and challenges, is for professors to have internalized the standards of competence and fairness to a high degree.

REFERENCES

Astin, Alexander W. 1993. *What Matters in College: Four Critical Years Revisited.* San Francisco: Jossey-Bass Publishers.

Audi, Robert. 1990. "The Ethics of Graduate Teaching." In Cahn, Steven M., ed. *Morality, Responsibility, and the University: Studies in Academic Ethics.* Philadelphia: Temple University Press, pp. 119–33.

Barr, Margaret J. 1988a. "Legal Organization and Control of Higher Education." In Margaret J. Barr and Associates, eds. *Student Services and the Law: A Handbook for Practitioners.* San Francisco: Jossey-Bass, Publishers, pp. 16–24.

Cahn, Steven M., ed. 1990. *Morality, Responsibility, and the University: Studies in Academic Ethics.* Philadelphia: Temple University Press.

———. 1994. *Saints and Sinners: Ethics in Academics,* revised edition. Lanham, MD: Rowman & Littlefield Publishers, Inc.

Cody, W. J. Michael, and Richardson R. Lynn. 1992. *Honest Government: An Ethics Guide for Public Service.* Westport, CT: Praeger Publishers.

Dressel, Paul L., and William H. Faricy, with the assistance of Philip M. Marcus and F. Craig Johnson. 1972. *Return to Responsiblity: Constraints on Autonomy in Higher Education.* San Francisco: Jossey-Bass.

Kadish, Mortimer R. 1991. *Toward an Ethic of Higher Education.* Stanford: Stanford University Press.

Kohlberg, Lawrence. 1981. *The Philosophy of Moral Development: Moral Stages and the Idea of Justice.* San Francisco: Harper & Row.

Lipson, Leslie. 1993. *The Ethical Crises of Civilization: Moral Meltdown or Advance?* Newbury Park, CA: Sage Publications.

McDowell, Banks. 1991. *Ethical Conduct and the Professional's Dilemma: Choosing Between Service and Success.* New York: Quorum Books.

Mount, Eric, Jr. 1990. *Professional Ethics in Context: Institutions, Images, and Empathy.* Louisville: Westminister/John Knox Press.

Pellegrino, Edmund D. 1991. "Trust and Distrust in Professional Ethics." In Pellegrino, Edmund D., Robert M. Veatch, and John P. Langan. 1991. *Ethics, Trust, and the Professions.* Washington, DC: Georgetown University Press, pp. 69–89.

Piper, David Warren. 1994. *Are Professors Professional? The Organisation of University Examinations.* London: Jessica Kingsley Publishers.

Rich, John Martin. 1984. *Professional Ethics in Education.* Springfield, IL: Charles C. Thomas, Publisher.

Riesman, David. 1980. *On Higher Education: The Academic Enterprise in an Era of Rising Student Consumerism.* San Francisco: Jossey-Bass Publishers.

Walter, Gordon A., and Mary Ann Von Glinow. 1987. "Fundamental Means to Ethical Teaching." In Payne, Stephen L. and Bruce H. Charnow. *Ethical Dilemmas for Academic Professionals.* Springfield, IL: Charles C. Thomas, Publisher, pp. 21–32.

Whicker, Marcia Lynn, and Jennie J. Kronenfeld. 1994. *Dealing with Ethical Dilemmas on Campus.* Newbury Park, CA: Sage Publications.

Whicker, Marcia Lynn, Jennie J. Kronenfeld, and Ruth Ann Strickland. 1993. *Getting Tenure.* Newbury Park, CA: Sage Publications.

White, Louis P., and Kevin C. Wooten. 1986. *Professional Ethics and Practice in Organizational Development: A Systematic Analysis of Issues, Alternatives, and Approaches.* New York: Praeger Publishers.

CHAPTER 15

The Ethics of Graduate and Professional Advising

GEORGE H. COX, JR.

Advisement is about relationships. A faculty member or university staff member is placed in a relationship with a graduate or professional student for the purpose of providing information and counsel. The desired outcome of advisement is a new member of the discipline who is both well educated and well socialized for the career that lies ahead.

Ethical advisement includes sufficient self-awareness in the relationship to safeguard the autonomy and integrity of both parties (Brown and Krager 1985, p. 404). It involves conscious and voluntary restraints on the part of the advisor, because that party is more empowered and intellectually mature than the advisee (Booth 1994, p. 32). It also involves awareness and consideration on the part of both parties as each tries to avoid seeing in the other a means to some personal end (Audi 1994, p. 36). An ethical advisement relationship is one that is wise enough to maintain balance and just enough not to allow exploitation. It is a specialized professional relationship which is often meaningful and rewarding to both advisor and advisee. Quality advisement is essential to the future of the profession.

The purpose of this analysis is to explore the expectations and assumptions that constitute the faculty advisor and graduate or professional student advisee relationship. Specific attention will be given to the ethical questions that arise in these relationships. The analysis may help faculty advisors see the advisement situation more clearly from the "potential victim's perspective" (Lewis, 1991: 120) and look to their own needs for congruence and peace of mind in advisement relationships (Booth, 1994).

FRAMEWORK FOR ANALYSIS

The structure of the analysis involves four dimensions of the advisement relationship and its ethical concerns. First, several typical functions of graduate and professional advisement are outlined. Second, the specific roles attending these functions are explored. Third, several core values of advisement are identified and applied to the advisement roles in which the advisor and advisee find themselves. Finally, the specific ethical threats that attend the roles are detailed (see Table 15.1).

Advisement Functions

Faculty advisors provide several instrumental functions within an academic department. Some authors devote considerable attention to detailing the instrumental duties of outstanding graduate and professional advisors (Cox 1992a, 1992b; Brown and Krager 1985).

Table 15.1. Advisement Roles and Ethical Threats

Functions	Roles	Core Values	Ethical Threats
recruitment orientation coursework problems exam preparation	teacher/pupil	concern and credibility	indifference
coursework planning professional counseling placement	mentor/protege	trust and authenticity	intimacy
research activities internships/practical service activities	artisan/apprentice	collegiality	exploitation

Briefly, advisors recruit new graduate and professional students, orient new students, and coach students in their coursework selections. Additionally, faculty advisors assist graduate and professional students with coursework problems and try to make certain that their advisees have programs of study that adequately prepare them for comprehensive or terminal exams. Advisors are often involved with the capstone experiences of graduate and professional education: thesis or dissertation and internship or practicum. Finally, it is often the faculty advisors who counsel the completing graduate and professional students in developing and implementing job placement strategies.

It is interesting to note what accrediting bodies have to say about graduate and professional advising activities. In 1993 a national survey was conducted that asked regional and professional (specialized) accrediting bodies about their advisement standards (Cox, Bradshaw, and Perry 1993). None of the regional institutional accrediting bodies goes beyond a passing mention of advisement services. For example, the Middle States Association of Colleges and Schools refers to advisement in its section on student services and emphasizes respecting the maturity level of the student (Cox, Bradshaw, and Perry 1993, p. 3). Generally, these organizations emphasize ensuring human dignity and justice in advisement relationships.

There is much more interest shown among some of the specialized accrediting bodies that oversee professional fields such as teacher education, business education, and education for the public service. Roughly half of the professional accreditors include advisement as a topic in their standards, that is, they give advisement extensive or limited treatment (selected functions) (see Table 15.2). For example, Standard 7.1 of the Standards of the National Association of Schools of Public Affairs and Administration (NASPAA) calls for "Strong and continuous program advisement, career guidance, and progress appraisal . . . from the point of admission through graduation." Several of the professional bodies, including the American Psychological Association (APA) and The National Council for Accreditation of Teacher Education (NCATE), itemize specific advisement functions. Many agencies, including NASPAA, emphasize placement counseling; others, such as NCATE, concentrate on support for interns.

Table 15.2. Advisement Functions: Frequency Response of Specialized Accrediting Bodies

Category	Number	Percent
General	7	28%
Basic	5	20%
Limited	3	12%
Extensive	10	40%
SUBTOTAL	25	100%
Not Reporting	13	—
TOTAL	38	—

Source: Cox, Bradshaw, and Perry 1993, p. 4.

Across varied functions, faculty or professional staff advisors develop advisement relationships with students. The advisor is recruiter, orienter, coursework counselor, and research guide. In many situations and settings, the advisor/advisee relationship informs and directs the neophyte's approach to the new profession.

Advisement Roles

There are at least three basic roles in the relationship between faculty advisors and their graduate or professional student advisees: (1) teacher/pupil, (2) mentor/protege, and (3) artisan/apprentice. These roles often develop chronologically as the student progresses through his or her academic program of studies. In this regard, the evolution of these three roles parallels the chronology of most of the instrumental functions of an advisor. However, each of these roles in the relationship between faculty advisors and their graduate student advisees portends specific ethical content. That is because key values are implicit in each role.

(1)   Teacher/pupil: Advisement is not the same activity as classroom teaching or even seminar interaction. Nevertheless, the legitimacy of counsel given to the graduate student advisee stems from the advisor's faculty status (Ryan 1992, p. 4). Many explicit and implicit advisement cues are given the graduate student in class, after class, or as a direct outgrowth of instruction. It is therefore prudent to make this dimension of the advisor/advisee relationship explicit. It is the most simple yet basic building block of the advisement relationship.

(2)   Mentor/protege: Many graduate and professional students gravitate to one or a few faculty members because of shared interests, charm, or personality of the instructor in class (Booth 1994, p. 33). Some are impatient to "get on with it" and prepare for a well paid vocation. They seek advice outside the classroom in an effort to move efficiently into their chosen profession. The faculty member-turned-advisor takes on the role of a mentor when he or she actively provides information, feedback, and counsel keyed to professional success (Winston and Polkosnik 1984, p. 300; more generally Murry and Owen 1991).

(3)   Artisan/apprentice: In academic circles, the term *apprenticeship* is sometimes used to convey the sense of advisement in which the student wants to "learn the trade" from a faculty member (Audi 1994, p. 28). Apprenticeship differs from mentoring in that the work that the faculty member and the student do together is the "live work" of normal scientific inquiry under the paradigm operative in the discipline at that time. It leads to concrete products in terms of grant reports, government documents, professional papers, and publications.

These three role pairs describe types of relationships. In none of the three is the student passive. What we study in graduate and professional advisement are the interactions of the two parties with each other. Students and teachers play off each other's cues. Proteges and mentors posture when they seek and give advice. Apprentices and artisans negotiate a balance of work demands and expectations. Both parties are investing, and both parties have vulnerabilities that must be respected.

Substantive advisement is an "ideals-guided" enterprise as contrasted with a "rights-driven" approach to higher education (Audi 1994, p. 36). It is in the protracted personal interactions of two people over time that values get expressed and that ethical dilemmas arise. Ethical concerns within the academic community require that members of the community have "moral character" (Booth 1994, p. 32) and that core values be recognized and respected.

Core Values in Advisement

The advisement literature is limited in its treatment of graduate and professional students' relationships with their advisors. There is correspondingly little in the way of ethical analysis of graduate and professional education; most of the literature that does exist addresses doctoral students (Selke 1994; Heinrich 1991; Winston and Polkosnik 1984; Barger and Mayo-Chamberlain 1983). Welcome exceptions to the paucity of broad ethical essays are Glyn Roberts' "Ethics in Professional Advising and Academic Counseling of Graduate Students" (1993) and Robert Brown and LuAnn Krager's "Ethical Issues in Graduate Education: Faculty and Student Responsibilities" (1985).

A "Statement of Core Values of Academic Advising" was published by the National Academic Advising Association (NACADA) in September, 1994. This statement posits students as responsible, deserving consumers (my term) who need competent instrumental and developmental advising in order to maximize the value of their educational experience. NACADA emphasizes the concern and credibility (or competence) of the advisor. This focus on concern and credibility is therefore an important consideration as faculty advisors are selected and trained. But we must also remember that graduate and professional education relies on one-to-one relationships between faculty members and students in its function of perpetuating disciplines and professions (Selke 1994, p. 11–13).

Consider the proposition that each of the three roles in the advisor/ student relationship—teacher/pupil, mentor/protege, and artisan/

apprentice—has incumbent core values. This fact would combine the developmental perspective on academic relationships (Ender, Winston, and Miller 1984) with the core values approach to ethical analysis (Brown and Krager 1985). As the relationship between advisor and student grows, new opportunities and new ethical threats emerge. The core values may overlap; they may even be additive. Nevertheless, there do seem to be specific values at work at specific times in the relationship. If the relationship is short-lived, the value issues of only one relationship type may pertain. For example, a relationship may never develop beyond the teacher/pupil level, or a student may apprentice him or herself to an individual artisan after previous mentoring relationships with other faculty. In any case, the core values approach may be viewed developmentally to the extent that long-term advisor/ student relationships often include a progression through several roles with a single pair of players or multiple pairings of advisors and advisees.

Concern and Credibility.   The key advisement values expressed in the teacher/pupil relationship are concern and credibility. These two values act as gatekeepers to other, deeper advisement relationships. An advisement relationship that extends beyond getting signatures on registration forms requires that mutual concern and credibility be demonstrated.

Concern for the individual graduate or professional student advisee can be expressed in many ways. It is painful to note that many graduate students report that the quality of their relationships with faculty members is the single most disappointing aspect of their graduate education (Bargar and Mayo-Chamberlain 1983, p. 407; less definitively, see Selke 1994, Table 10). Some faculty advisors show a lack of concern for their advisees in many ways, ranging from inaccessibility to patronizing forms of address to unwillingness to help with career planning (Cox 1992a, pp. 12–13). Concern is expressed in quality, worthwhile exchanges that over time signal commitment to the individual (Audi 1994, p. 34). A concern for the individual student, usually first revealed in the classroom, can be carried forward into a productive advisement relationship with both parties maintaining autonomy

(Brown and Krager 1985, p. 403) and respect for each other's time and talents (Bargar and Mayo-Chamberlain 1983, p. 430).

Credibility in a graduate or professional education advisor involves an understanding on the part of the faculty member of the personal and educational demands in the student's life (Brown and Krager 1985, p. 406). The ability to give good advice requires focused thinking that can counsel for a balance of work and school, academic and practical interests, and short-term versus long-term investments within the academic program. Each student is different as well as autonomous, but respect for autonomy does not suggest detachment, neglect, or neutrality by the advisor. Meaningful advisement requires a commitment to helping graduate and professional students make good decisions.

When the relationship between the graduate or professional student and the faculty member spills over outside the classroom, an essentially teacher/pupil relationship may evolve into a mentor/protege relationship. The occasion of sharing a directed readings experience or exploring reactions to an interesting conference often leads to a situation in which the faculty member models the professional lifestyle for the student (Roberts 1993, p. 80; Winston and Polkosnik 1984, p. 300). When the serious student wants to break free of the structure of the classroom and go straight to the source—the professor as knowledge producer—the stage is set for a mentoring relationship to be launched. Yet remarkably little is known about why "mere instruction is not enough," despite the recognition that mentoring a student one-to-one is often needed to satisfy the conditions of learning and academic community (Booth 1994, p. 30).

Trust and Authenticity. The mentor has to make decisions regarding what to talk about with the protege, what positions to take on the issues that they discuss, and what demeanor to adopt with the student protege. What are one's prejudices as opposed to one's reasoned judgments? What are the shortcomings of our own education for people entering the profession today? What are the proper motivations and expectations for a professor who accepts a student as a protege? Bargar and Chamberlain have called the inner dialogue in which a faculty member explores direct personal relationships with students one of the "best-kept secrets in graduate education" (1985, p. 417).

The protege also bears unclear motivations and expectations. Why am I really trying to show interest in this material or person? Am I looking for an easy inside track to professional advancement? Do I expect my workload to be heavier or lighter as a result of the counsel given by this faculty member? Students often "want to be like" a certain professor (Booth 1994, p. 32). They therefore tend to adopt the interests, techniques, and even the style of the mentor in an effort to be more like the person they admire. Unless great care is taken by the mentor to present the protege with valued alternatives, the protege may mimic the mentor and risk losing his or her autonomy (Brown and Krager 1985, p. 409). The relationship can then become the topic of cruel gossip within the university.

Just as the teacher has to feel and show real concern for the students, the mentor has to gain the trust of the protege. A student will not (and should not) accept counsel about critical professional decisions unless he or she is confident that the advisor has his or her interests at heart (Roberts 1993, p. 78). Based on what we know about successful mentoring relationships, the trust must be invested in the commitment of both parties to the creative dynamic. Neither party must be wedded to the specific predispositions that he or she had when they entered the relationship.

The purpose of the advisement relationship is professional development, not personal affirmation, and certainly not personal friendship (Audi 1994, p. 32). You trust a friend to keep your secrets and to confide theirs, to accomodate your biases and shortcomings, to support you in times of personal pain, and to seek you out when they are in pain. You trust your mentor to tell you the truth when you are on-track or off, working hard or loafing. The protege must trust the mentor to provide essential professional feedback, because to do less would be to show little concern. This is possible because mentors " . . . have a good understanding of the student as a person and a potential scholar" (Brown and Krager 1985, p. 409). By the same token, the mentor must be prepared to be obsolete or ill-informed about new issues in the field. The protege may have to teach the mentor new information technologies or data analysis methods. By identifying and repairing deficiencies, all scholars—mentor and protege alike—develop intellectually. Caring that prevents candor is a serious breach of trust for both (Audi 1994, p. 34).

This brings one to the issue of authenticity. An authentic relationship is true to its nature; it does not create within it the seeds of its own demise. This potential premise is consistent with Peter Markie's analysis of why professors and students cannot be friends. Markie argues that "engaging in an activity [that] is likely to limit severely our ability to honor one of our moral obligations" represents "a prima facie moral obligation not to engage in that activity" (Markie 1990, p. 141).

An authentic mentoring relationship must be true to its purpose and its sanctioned place in the academic community. Friendly feelings and a friendly demeanor notwithstanding, mentors and their proteges must not be friends. They must not place the imperatives of friendship—caring, support, and empathy—in conflict with the imperatives of their mentoring relationship. To do so sets up a potentially unethical situation for the mentor. The protege is then susceptible to a corresponding breakdown in the form of an unwillingness to receive constructive feedback. Audi refers to this problem as being "unable to receive friendly commentary as professional criticism" (29).

Collegiality.   A colleague is someone with whom we work to produce authentic works of professional scholarship. Collaboration is common in conducting research, writing and presenting professional papers, and publishing the best of one's work. The research and publication process is costly in terms of time and ego investment, and scholarship is constrained by canons of honesty and integrity that are themselves part of the professional socialization process (Roberts 1993, p. 84). The way in which we treat student collaborators is therefore a serious professional and pedagogical matter.

Collegiality is a core value that is highly revered but often troublesome in academia. The collegiality challenge is to balance contributions and credits such that a true and honest reflection of authorship is represented. To fail to represent or to underrepresent an individual's contributions does violence to the integrity of scholarly work (Roberts

1993, p. 84). Student apprentices are particularly vulnerable to abuse because they lack knowledge about fair treatment and have little leverage with which to assert their rights. Sometimes apprentices are exploited for their labor with little or no credit for their contributions to a project. Unscrupulous professors may even steal the work from the very students to whom they are supposed to teach ethical research practices. Let the apprentice object, and the threatened faculty member may strike back from his or her position of advantage and power.

One observer has asserted that "Our students' only hope of release from the oppressive use of power is thus the moral character of individual teachers" (Booth 1994, p. 32). The same could be said about most collaborative research efforts. Those of us who are far enough along in life to discern the moral competence of others will avoid collaboration with questionable colleagues. Nevertheless, we cannot expect student apprentices to be experienced and discerning in such matters.

There are then five core values that can be associated with the three sets of roles of advisor/student relationships. They are concern and credibility (teacher/pupil role), trust and authenticity (mentor/protege role), and collegiality (artisan/apprentice role). These are selected core values; many others are noted in the advisement literature. For example, we have not discussed fairness or justice, that is, allowing all students equal opportunities for professional development (Markie 1990; Brown and Krager 1985). The question of whether it is fair or not to take someone as protege and not offer everyone a mentor is a valid question and is discussed in the literature.

The principle for inclusion of the five core values of concern, credibility, trust, authenticity, and collegiality is that all relate to our developmental model of graduate and professional education. We assume that it is ethical to allow efficacious students to self-select into a relationship or series of relationships that enhance their academic and professional development (Winston and Polknosnik 1984, p. 294).

There are yet other perspectives from which to explore ethical concerns in advisement. Brown and Krager (1985) formulate ethical grids which articulate faculty and student responsibilities by faculty role (advisor, instructor, curriculum planner, researcher, and mentor) and several ethical principles (autonomy, nonmaleficence, beneficence, justice, and fidelity). Audi looks at ethical threats by applying three moral standards (being fair, respectful, and attentive to duty) to four models of teaching (didactic, apprentice, collegial, and friendship). The three-role developmental schema simply seems to describe graduate and professional advising issues most directly.

CONCLUSIONS

The five core values must be prevalent for the developmental advising relationship to work. They cannot be honored in the breech. To fail in upholding the positive value that each represents leads to ethical pitfalls that can greatly harm both parties. The prize of the long-term, successful advisement relationship is won only through knowledge of and respect for the serious pitfalls that often damage people and relationships along the way.

Ethical Threats to Advisement Relationships

It will not be possible for professors or graduate or professional students to conduct complicated ethical analyses every time an advisory situation occurs. Neither can the subject be avoided. Graduate and professional students cannot become ethical and moral practitioners unless they work with ethical responsibilities along with faculty in their discipline (Brown and Krager 1985, p. 417). Faculty and students need some guideposts to warn them when advisement relationships are out of balance (Booth 1994, p. 34) or beginning to cross boundaries of propriety (Markie 1990, p. 147). One approach to this need for simplicity is to make explicit the ethical threats that flow from the core value issues involved in the teacher/pupil, mentor/protege, and artisan/apprentice advisement roles. Each role has a broad ethical threat—indifference (teacher/pupil), intimacy (mentor/protege), or exploitation (artisan/apprentice)—that is apparent when core values are exercised in the everyday functions of advisement.

Indifference.   If a faculty member has advisement responsibilities, then it is ethically wrong to be indifferent to students. Even though a professor might be able to point to an advisement center or identify an advisor of record for graduate and professional students, the fact of life is that most faculty members are expected to advise students as a condition of employment (Ryan 1992, p. 4). The rare exception is the faculty member who is appointed to a research chair at a major university or an individual who has been bought out of teaching responsibilities by a grant.

The point of balance in the teacher/pupil role is between indifference on the one hand (Ender, Winston, and Miller 1984, p. 22) and excessive attention and charm on the other (Booth 1994, p. 34). A lack of concern can be detected by students when the faculty member avoids substantive interaction with them in the classroom. In didactic pedagogy, the professor has the questions as well as the answers, and the students are expected to absorb all that they can in class (Audi 1994, p. 28). Unless the students' passive acceptance or admiration, on the one hand, and benign tolerance or acceptance by the professor, on the other, is considered a relationship, there is none established where there is no sincere concern.

Students can tell the difference between a professor being charming and a professor showing a more open-ended concern with their educational experience (Booth 1994, pp. 33–34). They can tell when the professor does not think that their educational and professional concerns are credible, for example, when their concerns are trivialized consistently over an extended period of time. However, students can also "run all over" a professor who is so concerned with student educational needs and professional concerns that she or he is incapacitated as a teacher. The professor harms the student when educational needs are made slave to the social and emotional needs of student interaction (Booth 1994, p. 34). A balance must be struck somewhere in between the two extremes: indifference to student concerns, on the one hand, and unlimited concern for and credibility with students, on the other.

The consequences of indifference toward graduate and professional students can be cumulative across professors and across time in an academic department. Poorly advised students may claim that they have been treated unfairly by their university (Winston and Polkosnik

1984, p. 291); deans and university administrators can become concerned with resultant poor recruitment, retention, and graduation rates (Cox 1992a, p. 13). Yet the real consequence of indifference is the harm brought to the discipline or profession. A teacher has hurt his or her discipline in immeasurable, long-term ways when enthusiastic and talented students are lost to the profession. We live in an age in which efficacious consumers demand and get quality services in a competitive marketplace, and academia cannot hide from this reality. The indifferent professor is a menace to his academic community.

Intimacy. Mentors and proteges often get to know each other very well. "They have mutual affection that consists in their enjoying each other's company and valuing each other's welfare because of whose company and welfare it is" (Markie 1990, p. 138). The bond between the mentor and protege can become quite deep if the relationship (like all others) survives the disclosure of human frailties that time brings. A trusting and authentic mentoring relationship is a pearl of great price.

Recall that the trust that the mentor and protege share is a trust in the creativity and openness of the intellectual relationship. It is trust in candor and a mutual confidence in building better professional futures. Mentoring is not friendship, because it does not place the values of traditional friendship first (Markie 1990). Mentoring is certainly not love, at least not love in the nonacademic senses of the word. It is a bond that feels attraction and steadfastly channels the feeling into legitimate professional support (Heinrich 1991).

Affairs between mentor and protege are betrayals of trust, because they choose romantic or sexual expression over authentic mutual support. "In situations of full intimacy, neither the learner's nor the listener's mind is fully engaged with the material to be learned" (Booth 1994, p. 34). The regard in which the mentor and the protege hold each other is not inferior to or superior to the regard of good friends or ardent lovers, but it is clearly different from those kinds of personal regard. To be authentic, and therefore to be ultimately trustworthy, it must be chaste. To entertain thoughts of other contemporary or future relations with a mentor or protege is to court disaster. "I can, to be sure, face such a conflict between friendship and professional duty and still act professionally. But how do I know that, when I am in such a situation, I will always face the conflict?" (Audi 1994, p. 32).

The only way to safeguard the relationship is to place a taboo (Heinrich 1991, p. 533) on friendly or sexual intimacy. As a taboo, it needs to be understood by all in the academic community and supported by all who profess that community's value.

Exploitation. There are few core values that are more important to academic communities than is the value of collegiality. We are essentially a nonhierarchical association of scholar-teachers and neophyte students. We deal with complex and ever-changing subject matter and knowledge technologies that make our mutual protection through legalistic rules inadequate and perhaps undesirable (Audi 1994, p. 36). Our customs, conventions, and traditions are our guides even as we constantly discuss how future shock makes us update them. We must therefore be very careful what we teach and what we model in our collegial practices lest we reap a generation of abusive and corrupt future colleagues.

We must therefore treat our graduate and professional student colleagues with the greatest respect. We must encourage the apprentice in identifying and completing distinctive tasks which mark his or her direct contributions to a mutual project. We must make our own contributions as artisans transparent to the apprentice so that process learning can take place. We must take time out to explain specific conventions, such as the protection of human subjects and the avoidance of sexist and handicappist language, to apprentices. But most importantly, we must teach and model the positive values of collegiality, such as supportive cooperation, constructive criticism, and deference to the community of opinion (e.g., the blind review [sic] of article drafts). Unless the craft is made overt and explicit, the apprentice may not learn to be a nonexploitative colleague within the discipline or profession.

Perhaps we can remember and apply the three simple admonitions of ethical advisement: to struggle against indifference, to bracket intimacy, and to avoid exploitation. To the extent that advisors can integrate these admonitions into their daily practices, we may safeguard the advisement process from doing harm to those whom we seek to help. Perhaps then graduate and professional students will not perceive their personal relationships with faculty members as the most disappointing aspect of their academic experience.

Implications for Disciplines and Professions

It is sometimes difficult to remember the stakes that are involved in graduate and professional advising. Day after day, students make demands on our precious discretionary time. It is tempting to minimize time spent advising them because we have so many other responsibilities. But from their point of view, these are really important moments. Unsure of their scholarly focus, insecure in their status within the department, and mystified by the career paths of the profession or academe, graduate and professional students are ripe for neglect or abuse. They are vulnerable. But they are also the future of the profession or discipline. When we neglect them or take advantage of them, we do so at our own peril. We violate our own core values. We commit intellectual suicide.

REFERENCES

Audi, Robert. 1994. "On the Ethics of Teaching and the Ideals of Learning," *Academe*, 80:5, pp. 27–36.

Bargar, Bobert R., and Jane Mayo-Chamberlain. 1993. "Advisor and Advisee Issues in Doctoral Education," *Journal of Higher Education*, 54, pp. 407–32.

Booth, Wayne C. 1994. "Beyond Knowledge and Inquiry to Love, or: Who Mentors the Mentors?" *Academe*, 80:6, pp. 29–36.

Brown, Robert D., and LuAnn Krager. 1985. "Ethical Issues in Graduate Education: Faculty and Student Responsibilities," *Journal of Higher Education*, 56, pp. 403–18.

Cox, George H. Jr. 1992a. "Enhancing Graduate and Professional Advisement." Paper presented at the 16th National Conference of the National Academic Advising Association, Atlanta, Georgia.

———. 1992b. "Increasing Advisement Power in Graduate Public Administration Programs." Paper presented at the 15th National Conference on Teaching Public Administration, Charleston, South Carolina.

Cox, George H. Jr., Wilson G. Bradshaw, and Tammy L. Perry. 1993. "Graduate and Professional Advisement and Its Linkage to Program Accreditation." Paper presented at the 17th National Conference of the National Academic Advising Association, Detroit, Michigan.

Ender, Steven C., Roger B. Winston, Jr., and Theodore K. Miller. 1984. "Academic Advising Reconsidered," in their *Developmental Academic Advising*. San Francisco: Jossey-Bass, pp. 3–34.

Heinrich, Kathleen T. 1991. "Loving Partnerships: Dealing with Sexual Attraction and Power in Doctoral Advisement Relationships," *Journal of Higher Education*, 62, pp. 514–38.

Lewis, Carol W. 1991. *The Ethics Challenge in Public Service: A Problem-Solving Guide*. A Publication of the American Society for Public Administration. San Francisco: Jossey-Bass.

Markie, Peter J. 1990. "Professors, Students, and Friendship" in Steven M. Cahn, ed., *Morality, Responsibility, and the University: Studies in Academic Ethics*. Philadelphia: Temple University Press, pp. 134–49.

Murry, Margo with Marna A. Owen. 1991. *Beyond the Myths and Magic of Mentoring: How to Facilitate an Effective Mentoring Program*. San Francisco: Jossey-Bass.

National Academic Advising Association (NACADA). 1994. "Statement of Core Values of Academic Advising," *Academic Advising News*, 16:4 (insert).

Roberts, Glyn C. 1993. "Ethics in Professional Advising and Academic Counseling of Graduate Students," *Quest*, American Academy of Physical Education, 45, pp. 78–87.

Ryan, Carol C. 1992. "Advising as Teaching," *National Academic Advising Association Journal*, 12:1, pp. 4–8.

Selke, Mary J. 1994. "Doctoral Attrition: Insight for Advisors." Paper presented at the 18th National Conference of the National Academic Advising Association, Las Vegas, Nevada.

Winston, Roger B. Jr., and Mark C. Polkosnik. 1984. "Advising Graduate and Professional School Students," in Winston, et al., *Developmental Academic Advising*, pp. 287–314.

CHAPTER 16

Ethical Principles for Public Administration Research

JERRY MITCHELL

Public administration research and analysis involves ethics. This is evidenced by newspaper headlines questioning the veracity of government reports and by legislative hearings on research misconduct in public agencies. But perhaps the best indicator of the heightened interest in ethical issues is within the public administration academy. It is now easy to find books and articles that have examined, for instance, whether value-neutrality should be a viable ethical principle for research and analysis. Should a study of "workfare" focus exclusively on the processing of welfare clients, or should it also make value judgments about whether people who fail to get a job might go hungry if they lose their benefits?

Even though ethical issues loom large in public administration research, there have been few efforts to identify systematically the specific ethical principles that researchers might follow. Ethical issues have certainly been discussed in texts on administrative management and policy analysis, but in a more general sense and without reference to a specific set of standards that students can be taught and public administrators might look to for guidance. As such, the purpose of this chapter is to draw from the existing literature four ethical principles for the conduct of public administration research: truthfulness, thoroughness, objectivity, and relevance. The intent is to first describe each of these ethical ideas and then to consider some problems in putting them into practice. The assumption is that a better understanding of ethics is essential for not only improving the integrity and utilization of public administration research, but also for enhancing the potential for research to fulfill democratic ideals.

The scope of this inquiry is broadly conceived. The emphasis is on public administration research because most of the studies in the policy process are agency-generated. Nonetheless, the discussion is relevant to the research undertaken by politicians, lobbyists, lawyers, journalists, and even academicians, including what is published in journals like *Public Administration Review*. There is no particular attention to any one level or branch of government or to any particular area of public policy. Research is assumed to encompass several approaches, such as social science, policy analysis, and program evaluation. Various methodologies are also pertinent, including surveys, experiments, cost-benefit studies, and risk assessments. Most important, ethics is considered an issue no matter whether the purpose of the research is to describe problems, predict outcomes, evaluate solutions, or assess organizational performance.

BACKGROUND

Ethics is a part of public administration research and analysis because of the history of the research enterprise. As research has become more prevalent in its uses both to support and to oppose public programs, attention has been drawn to its ethical character. For example, when administrators continually design research that strongly supports their own programmatic activities, questions are necessarily raised about whether this is appropriate behavior or not. Because of the way studies have been used in the political process, the unquestioning acceptance of research and analysis has become a thing of the past.

Historical Context

The origins of modern-day government research can be found in the Progressive Era of the early 1900s. During this period, people first began to think that the scientific method could fundamentally improve society. As one writer put it, the analytical methods of modern science were expected to "transform almost beyond recognition the most familiar aspects of the physical and social scene" (Nagel 1952). Applied to public problems, the assumption was that the newly discovered social sciences of sociology, psychology, economics, and political science could emulate the successes of the "hard" or natural sciences of medicine, engineering, chemistry, and physics. As the hard sciences were curing diseases and helping people to travel faster, the social sciences were expected to improve social relations and solve policy problems. If, for instance, diplomats were to obtain a body of empirically tested propositions about the concepts and variables that cause political revolutions, it was expected that they could utilize such data to help contain or promote revolutions.

After two world wars in which research and analysis played a large part in the design of weapons systems and the distribution of troops, it was not until the presidency of Lyndon Johnson that the activity really took hold. In the 1960s, all kinds of research was widely celebrated as the proper basis for government decision making. As one leading scholar of the period noted, "research was touted as a determinant in and of itself of new policy directions, or at least as an input with a presumed special claim and higher standing than others in the policy-making process" (Nathan 1989). Many of the programs of the Great Society and War On Poverty were highly influenced by, if not in some cases directly developed by, researchers (deLeon 1989). Consider, for example, that the federal Head Start program was created because studies showed early education could release poor children from the grip of poverty, and vocational rehabilitation was greatly expanded because research indicated that for every dollar of cost there were ten dollars in benefits to society.

By the 1970s, practically every government agency in the nation had staff functions for planning and analysis. Amassing information about programs, services, and agencies had become the full-time job of many public administrators, as well as for private consultants and think tanks working under contract for the government. The assumption was that rigorous analysis could produce informational flows capable of improving public organizations. At the same time, legislators enacted laws with provisions for the periodic review of programs, which in turn further strengthened the need to upgrade and expand research staffs at every level of government. Even the legislative branch itself became a major source of research and analysis. For instance, Congress's independent agency for auditing and evaluation, the General Accounting Office, was expanded greatly and given additional authority to assess the executive branch's programs and agencies.

The emergence in the 1980s of the conservative administration of Ronald Reagan and his "mandate" to eliminate big government brought forth a different focus for research and analysis. Taking their cue from liberal Democrats who had long been using research as a strategic tool, particularly as manifested in the Great Society programs, conservatives put research to a new purpose—to eliminate public programs, often the very same ones earlier analysis had helped to create. For example, during the 1980s the President's Office of Management and Budget (OMB) required most government regulations to undergo a cost-benefit analysis (Byrne 1987). If the benefits of a regulation did not outweigh the costs, the OMB recommended its elimination.

The upshot in the 1990s is that research has gained a political aura. Studies can be found which both defend and attack privatization support and oppose reinventing government and clarify and complicate health care reform. Courtrooms are replete with "hired scientific guns" who say whatever they are paid to say. Official government statistics are a significant measure of society's well being, but they are also the subject of much debate in newspapers and on television. Does the census, for example, really count all Americans? While there is generally agreement that the scientific analysis of public problems and politics is good, there is a degree of uncertainty about whether the enterprise can leave up to the "public interest" ideals first put forth during the Progressive Era.

Current Problems

It is in the context of a relatively new, rapidly growing, but often controversial enterprise that ethical issues come to the fore. As administrators, politicians, scholars, the media, and average citizens have grown more familiar with research and analysis, it has become easier to notice problems with not only the conduct and conclusions of studies, but also the overall objectivity and relevance of research. Several problems have been identified.

First, there is a sense that some portion of government research is intentionally deceptive, if not factually false. Scholars have noticed an increase in cases where fraudulent research has been used to advance personal careers and political objectives (Nelkin 1994). Newspaper stories about cheating in federally funded medical studies contribute to the impression that fraud is a pervasive problem. There have been four major congressional hearings since 1990 concerning the integrity of research findings in the public sector (Woolf 1994). One writer concluded that society's overall trust in science has been eroded because of "charlatans misusing public funds for falsified and plagiarized research" (Woolf 1994, p. 83).

Second, there are doubts about the findings of government studies because of the way research is conducted. A sizable amount of public administration research could be characterized as sloppy. It seems as though the rigors of the hard sciences are rarely applied to the research undertaken in government (Crossen 1994). It is not difficult to find studies which have undefined terms, uncontrolled variables, poorly developed samples, extremely low response rates, and questionable interpretations. To cite one example, serious methodological flaws have been found in the National Household Survey of Drug Abuse, widely recognized as the government's best measure of the war on narcotics (*Washington Post* 1993). The Survey, for instance, claims a refusal rate of 1 percent, but it routinely excludes truants and other absentees, which account for 20 percent of all students.

Third, the blatantly political use of data by both conservatives and liberals has caused people to question the objectivity of research. It seems as though fewer studies are being done to get information, and more are being done to substantiate a claim or accomplish a particular promotional goal (Crossen 1994). It has been suggested that no science is "uninfluenced by politics" (Tesh 1988, p. 177). In 1994 the National Academy of Public Administration even went so far as to publicly criticized the nation's leading research organization, the U.S. General Accounting Office, for becoming too involved in policy advocacy (*New York Times* 1994).

Finally, a significant amount of research and analysis is perceived as irrelevant. Much of the research generated by agencies is focused on measurable variables and arcane statistics. Values are studiously avoided. The problem is that the issues addressed by government agencies are often less statistical and more matters of principle (Crossen 1994). Freedom and property rights are only two examples. But even when researchers attempt to examine values, such as in cost-benefit studies, the problem is not resolved, because the effort is to arbitrarily assign numerical scores to things like natural beauty and life itself. Not surprisingly, the underutilization of research has been attributed to its lack of relevance (Chelmisky 1987; Mitchell 1990). As one government official put it, everybody is for research and analysis, but few expect much from it.

ETHICAL PERSPECTIVES OF RESEARCH AND ANALYSIS

The criticisms of public administration research reflect ethical problems. The underlying focus is on what is right and wrong. To complain about fraudulent research is to think that truthfulness should be an ethical standard; to question the technical integrity of research is to believe that thoroughness should be an ethical aim; to fault public administration research for engaging in policy advocacy is to suggest that objectivity should be an ethical principle; and to lament the inability of researchers to study meaningful issues is to recommend that relevance should be an ethical goal.

It is relatively easy to discuss problems with public administration research and to propose simple solutions, but not as simple to define specifically what is meant by ethical behavior, especially when public administrators are involved in so many diverse activities. It is even more difficult to indicate how ethical principles should be put into practice. Keeping this context in mind, the remainder of this chapter will more fully examine four ethical principles for public administration research: truthfulness, thoroughness, objectivity, and relevance. After describing each of these principles, and identifying problems with their application, the concluding section will consider three ways to introduce ethics into the profession of public administration.

Truthfulness

A widely accepted ethical principle for public administration research is the prohibition against intentionally lying or otherwise engaging in fraud. This may take several forms. First, there is fabrication, such as reporting a survey response rate of 80 percent when it is actually 50 percent, or giving a cost-benefit ratio of 1.5 when it is really .05. Second, there is plagiarism, such as using language and data from previous research without attribution. Third, there is trickery, such as lying about the purposes of a study in order to obtain particular responses. Lastly, there is the failure to fully inform research subjects of the risks they may face by participating in a study.

The deliberate misrepresentation of a fact is an ethical problem because of a general prohibition against lying in a civilized society. Sissela Bok (1977, p. 20) in her book *Lying* concluded that a society "whose members were unable to distinguish truthful messages from deceptive ones would collapse." She accepts Aristole's position that "truthful statements are preferable to lies in the absence of special circumstances" (Bok 1977, p. 32).

While it is clear that it is unacceptable for an administrator to lie when conducting and reporting research, there is less certainty about the legitimacy of using fraudulent research produced by others. Can an administrator knowingly use a interest-group study which contains inaccurate data if the purpose is to obtain increased funding for an important program? Is this an example of the special circumstances that Bok mentions? There are several standards upon which the decision to use fraudulent research could be made, including whether the costs outweigh the benefits and whether the use of the research could withstand public scrutiny.

Another problem is the assumption that some research cannot be conducted without deception. Researchers often feel that they have to hide their intentions, because if the subjects knew about them they might respond accordingly. Researchers try to counter the "Hawthorne Effect." One book on research ethics has concluded, for instance, that it is entirely appropriate to deceive subjects, that is, if one can rationalize the deception in terms of informed consent and the balancing of costs and benefits (Kimmel 1988).

Truthfulness is thus a basic standard for research, as well as for most other human endeavors, but it nonetheless could be modified by particular circumstances in light of an acceptable rationale.

Thoroughness

A second ethical principle is that public administration research should be methodologically thorough. The fundamental expectation is that researchers should fully consider and divulge all practices. At a minimum, a study should define its key concepts, select appropriate samples, encourage empirical replication, and identify any limitations of the basic research design. For a specific methodology, such as a survey, a researcher should guarantee confidentiality to respondents and pretest the survey instrument; report the response rate, sample size, margin of error, and time frame; and if possible, provide examples of questions and response categories and the valid and raw statistics.

An argument can be made that thoroughness is not an ethical issue. The claim is that a study can be methodologically sloppy and still be ethical if the researcher is truthful about the way the research is conducted. This argument rests on a limited sense of what constitutes ethical behavior, but certainly it is one that is common in research methods texts (O'Sullivan and Rassell 1995). However, most people would probably agree that the outcomes of public administration research have moral implications for society. In this sense, the way research is accomplished is ultimately of ethical importance because of its consequences in public policy.

A formidable problem scholars encounter is the inability to specify exactly how far a researcher has to go in order to be thorough. Is it appropriate to ask a survey question with a three-point scale as opposed to a five-point scale? How many opportunity costs should be calculated for a cost-benefit analysis? Exactly how long should an experiment last before the conclusion is reached that a program is a failure? There are no unqualified answers for such questions, it all depends on what is being examined, the level of funding, the need for quick results, and the basic competence of the researcher. While there is some point at which a study becomes methodologically flawed, it is difficult to know precisely where that point is.

Another problem in judging thoroughness is that the terminology in public administration research is often inexact. There are no precise meanings for such terms as *citizen satisfaction, efficiency, effectiveness, benefits, unemployment,* and *accountability.* It doesn't matter which methodology is used, or even how it is used, if the terms and assumptions that underlie the research are ambiguous. Consider, for example, the use of race as an independent variable, such as in studies which measure the distribution of public funds and evaluate the representativeness of congressional districts (Wright 1994). In an increasingly multicultural society, how should researchers classify children whose parents are from different races? Are they the race of the mother? Are they multiracial? But then what happens when multiracial people marry one another and have children? While it is difficult to answer such questions, it is clear that the inherent ambiguity of race and other complex social and political terms can routinely compromise the thoroughness of public administration research.

In short, thoroughness is evidently at the core of methodology; the ethical problem is in defining exactly what thoroughness means in the actual conduct of research.

Objectivity

A third ethical principle is that public administration research should be objective. The idea is that a researcher should not allow his or her personal feelings or beliefs to contaminate a study. For instance, the selection of independent variables should not reflect various ideological and political perspectives. In addition, the methodology employed by a researcher should be free of bias and should not promote particular conclusions. For example, a researcher should not ask a question in a survey in such a way that it will elicit a particular response.

The principle of objectivity is derived from the theory of positivism. Positivism holds that there is a separation between facts and values. Value choices are understood to be matters of personal conviction, taste, or faith, and are therefore beyond the reach of science. It is

possible to investigate scientifically aspects of value statements, such as
the conditions that lead to the adoption of specific values or value systems, but there is no way of scientifically establishing the categorical truth
of a value judgment. Objectivity is thus equated with value neutrality.

Objectivity is not easy. At every level of government, examples
can be found where researchers have been less than objective. For
instance, the U.S. General Accounting Office (GAO) in 1987 asked
state rail safety administrators this question: "In your opinion, if Federal Railroad Administration (FRA) funds were completely eliminated,
how likely (if at all) is it that your state would decrease the number
of inspectors?" Administrators obviously need federal funds, and so
83 percent of the respondents said they would decrease the number of
inspectors if FRA funds were eliminated. This GAO finding was used
in a congressional hearing to support continued federal funding of rail
safety. At the state level, the New York State Comptroller's Office
conducted a survey in 1992 in which they asked a series of questions
about state government, including this one: "Do you think the state's
political leaders will reform how the state government operates themselves, or do you think they will have to be pressured from the voters
and press to do so?" Not surprisingly, 94% of the respondents said it
would take public pressure. This fact was reported in several newspapers across the state. At the local level, the Coalition of Greater Minnesota Cities (1994) conducted a survey which asked city administrators
to respond with a "yes" or "no" to this question: "Will you support a
program that requires the state to pay 50 percent of the cost of compliance with state and federal water quality mandates?" Of course, all
of the respondents said yes. The Coalition supplied this information in
1994 to every candidate running for public office in Minnesota.

One problem with objectivity as an ethical standard is that it is
difficult for researchers to divorce themselves from their own values. Is
it reasonable to expect that a conservative who believes in the potential
of private markets to ever produce a study which shows that privatization
is a failure? Even more problematic are instances where a researcher's
own sense of right and wrong must be set aside. When examining the
cost effectiveness of a military weapon, for instance, should an analyst
consider who will be killed, such as civilians or soldiers?

A second issue is the impossibility of separating methodology from normative theory. For example, cost-benefit analysis is derived from the theory of utilitarianism and the assumption that humans seek pleasure over pain. From a strict utilitarian perspective, practically any social welfare program is not cost-beneficial, because the majority of average citizens pay the costs and a small number of disadvantaged people reap the benefits (Jorgenson 1986). Cost-benefit analysis simply has no mechanism to recognize social compassion as an important value. But it is not just cost-benefit analysis that is conceptually biased; similar philosophical and sociological critiques have been made of surveys, experiments, and risk assessments (Tong 1986).

Perhaps the most troublesome problem with objectivity in a democracy is that the concept itself is politically biased. In the positivist tradition, politics is seen as subjective and irrational field that is manifestly inefficient and nonscientific. This leads easily to the argument that the political process itself must be changed to better accommodate objective research and analysis (Heineman, Bluhm, Peterson, and Kearny 1990). Using this line of reasoning, one of the cherished principles of American government—the system of checks and balances—can be thought of as a hindrance to objectivity and rationality, and therefore something to be eliminated rather than enhanced and improved.

Objectivity is perhaps the most heralded aspect of the scientific method overall, yet at the same time it is a standard that presents troublesome conceptual problems when applied to social and political reality.

Relevance

A final ethical principle is relevance. It requires that research address questions that people want answered. Common sense suggests that there would not be much point in research if it did not help people to discover truths about important matters. It can furthermore be argued that in a democracy, research has a moral responsibility to be understandable to people and useful in their endeavors. Ultimately, empirical facts are worthless unless placed in the context of democratic values.

The intellectual basis for relevance as an ethical standard is derived from an alternative conception of what it means to be "rational."

Jurgen Habermas (1968), a German philosopher, has suggested that a comprehensive concept of rationality involves three levels of reasoning: empirical, interpretative, and critical-reflective. Empirical knowledge is useful for comprehending reality, but it is has no intrinsic meaning unless it is considered in relation to basic norms and values. But even interpretative knowledge is not enough to be rational, because to truly understand something requires reflection on what is known in light of cultural and intellectual developments. In short, empirical research cannot be relevant unless it is integrated with social, political, and cultural values—or what Lance deHaven-Smith (1988) has termed "policy frameworks."

There is clearly a practical urgency for research to become more normatively relevant. With enormous budget deficits, widespread child abuse, increasing teenage violence, and the scourge of AIDS, America is said to literally confront a "crisis of values." Solutions to these deeply entrenched problems often raise questions about the configuration of social and political values underlying contemporary society more than they do technical matters about institutional processes and program design. It may be important to know whether welfare recipients are efficiently processed through the government bureaucracy, but it is also worth understanding the extent to which a "culture of dependency" is produced by the system. John Wallis, in his book the *Soul of Politics* (1994: p. xvii), has argued that without clarifying the essential moral issues at stake in any political discussion, "political life degenerates into public corruption, cultural confusion, and social injustice."

The problem for researchers is how to be relevant, to address both facts and values, while also remaining thorough and objective. One approach has been to find ways for research to produce "usable knowledge." If decision making and evaluation were in a more mutually supporting relationship, then research should be more relevant (Lindbloom and Cohen 1979). The idea is to develop ways to make empirical analysis directly applicable to the concerns of decision makers. For instance, investigators should try to more carefully integrate the needs and interests of so-called "stakeholders" into research designs (Kelly and Maynard-Moody 1993). The problem is that it is hard to know which stakeholders are important and to come up with guidelines for the examination of stakeholder values.

A second approach is to change positivism. Since the fundamental problem in research is the neglect of normative concerns, the critical aim is to bring facts and values together into a more systematic mode of analysis and deliberation (deLeon 1994; Fischer 1990; Jenkins-Smith 1990; Majone 1989; Tribe 1972). This movement is termed "postpositivism." While postpositivism has not been entirely thought through as a single coherent strategy, one idea is to develop participatory research projects in which randomly selected citizens are allowed to join in the design and interpretation of research (deLeon 1994). The basic assumption is that through democratic participation citizens can tell researchers what values are important to them, and then the researchers can incorporate these values into their empirical analysis. The problem with this approach is that many "average" citizens are too apathetic to participate and are no more interested in research than they are in politics as a whole. It is also very likely that any citizen participation will be co-opted by researchers.

Relevance, like any other ethical standard, is an overall goal that researchers are supposed to achieve, but which is not easily formulated or implemented.

PUTTING ETHICS INTO PUBLIC ADMINISTRATION RESEARCH

Dilemmas exist for every ethical principle in public administration research. The difficulties do not end with the individual principles however. There is also the overall problem of how to bring a discussion of research ethics into the public administration academy.

In many respects, ethical reflection has not been important to public administration research. The data are supposed to be objective and not in need of ethical examination. Perhaps more so than any other aspect of public administration, researchers believe in the dichotomy between politics and administration. Researchers like to see themselves as mere technicians far removed from the dilemmas confronting other administrators (Amy 1987). The tendency is to dismiss the increasing criticisms of the research enterprise as empirically unfounded or to assume that the inferior parts of research and analysis are the fault of a few methodologically bad apples.

It is nonetheless clear from this essay, as well as from several recent books and articles, that ethical issues are important for public administration research. While the task is difficult, there are three possible ways to bring ethical concerns forward. First, ethics can be part of research methods courses in Master of Public Administration programs. Case studies of research ethics can be developed, and the responsibility of managers to use research properly can be explored. Second, research ethics can become a part of the ethical codes of professional organizations, such as the American Society for Public Administration and the International City/County Management Association. By identifying ethical principles, professional associations can increase their members' awareness of ethical problems when conducting and reporting research. Third, administrative agencies can create special offices to monitor research ethics. Offices of research integrity, some of which already exist at the federal level, can conduct ethical checks of research in the public sector.

Overall, there is a greater need to think intelligently about ethics in public administration research. What does deception mean? How can terms be better defined? When should value neutrality be less important? Who should studies be designed for? Research ethics has to be more than the conclusion of a survey research text, which noted tersely that "there are few methodological decisions that a researcher could make that could be labeled categorically as wrong" (Fowler 1993, p. 137). While the issues are conceptually problematic, the choices made by public administration researchers cannot be simply dismissed as amoral. Ethical principles are building blocks that can first improve the substance of research, then make it more relevant and interesting, and in the end, enhance the overall integrity of government in a democratic society. As Carol Lewis (1991, p. 17) observed, "democracy is sustained by public trust, a link forged by stringent ethical standards."

REFERENCES

Amy, Douglas J. 1987. "Can Policy Analysis Be Ethical?" In *Confronting Values in Policy Analysis: The Politics of Criteria*, Frank Fischer and John Forester, ed. Newbury Park, CA: Sage, pp. 45–67.

Bok, Sissela. 1978. *Lying: Moral Choice in Public and Private Life*. New York: Vintage Books.

Byrne, John. 1987. "Policy Science and the Administrative State: The Political Economy of Cost-Benefit Analysis," in *Confronting Values in Policy Analysis: The Politics of Criteria*, Frank Fischer and John Forester, eds. Beverly Hills, CA: Sage, pp. 70–93.

Chelmisky, Eleanor. 1987. "Linking Program Evaluation to User Needs," in *The Politics of Program Evaluation*, Dennis Palumbo, ed. Newbury Park, CA: Sage, pp. 100–45.

Coalition of Greater Minnesota Cities. 1994. *Issues for 1994 Candidates.*

Crossen, Cynthia. 1994. *Tainted Truth.* New York: Simon and Schuster.

deHaven-Smith, Lance. 1988. *Philosophical Critiques of Policy Analysis.* Gainesville: University of Florida Press.

deLeon, Peter. 1988. *Advice and Consent: The Development of the Policy Sciences.* New York: Russell Sage.

deLeon, Peter. 1994. "Democracy and the Policy Sciences: Aspirations and Operations," *Policy Studies Journal* 22 (Summer), pp. 200–12.

Fischer, Frank. 1990. *Technocracy and the Politics of Expertise.* Beverly Hills, CA: Sage.

Fowler, Floyd J. 1993. *Survey Research Methods.* Beverly Hills, CA: Sage.

Habermas, Jurgen. 1968. *Toward a Rational Society.* Boston: Beacon.

Heineman, Robert A., William T. Bluham, Steven A. Peterson, and Edward N. Kearny. 1990. *The World of the Policy Analyst: Rationality, Values, and Politics.* Chatham, NJ: Chatham House.

Jenkins-Smith, Hank C. 1990. *Democratic Politics and Policy Analysis.* Pacific Grove, CA: Brooks/Cole.

Jorgenson, Dale W. 1986. "Efficiency versus Equity in Economic Policy Analysis," In *Essays in Economics*, Michael Szenberg, ed. Boulder, CO: Westview Press, pp. 105–21.

Kelly, Marcia, and Steven Maynard-Moody. 1993. "Policy Analysis in the Post-Positivist Era: Engaging Stakeholders in Evaluating Economic Development Programs," *Public Administration Review* 52 (September/October), pp. 135–42.

Kimmel, Allan J. 1988. *Ethics and Values in Applied Social Research.* Newbury Park, CA: Sage.

Lewis, Carol W. 1991. *The Ethics Challenge in the Public Service.* San Francisco: Jossey-Bass.

Lindbloom, Charles, and David Cohen. 1979. *Usable Knowledge*. New Haven: Yale University Press.

Majone, Giandomenico. 1989. *Evidence, Argument, and Persuasion in the Policy Process*. New Haven: Yale University Press.

Mitchell, Jerry. 1990. "Policy Evaluation for Policy Communities: Confronting the Utilization Problem," *Evaluation Practice* (June), pp. 109–14.

Nagel, Ernest. 1952. "Automatic Control," Reprinted in *Great Essays in Science*, Martin Gardner, ed. New York: Washington Square Press, pp. 164–70.

Nathan, Richard P. 1988. *Social Science in Government: Uses and Misuses*. New York: Basic Books.

Nelkin, Dorothy. 1994. "The Public Face of Science: What Can We Learn From Disputes?" in *The Fragile Contract: University Science and the Federal Government*, David H. Guston and Kenneth Keniston, eds. Cambridge: MIT Press, pp. 101–17.

New York State Comptroller's Office. 1992. *A Study of the Views of New York Voters Concerning the State Economy*.

New York Times. 1994. "Study Criticizes Objectivity of U.S. Accounting Agency," (October 17), p. B10.

O'Sullivan, Elizabethann, and Gary R. Rassel. 1995. *Research Methods for Public Administrators*. White Plains, NY: Longman.

Tesh, Sylvia Noble. 1988. *Hidden Arguments: Political Ideology and Disease Prevention Policy*. New Brunswick: Rutgers University Press.

Tong, Rosemarie. 1986. *Ethics in Policy Analysis*. Englewood Cliffs, NJ: Prentice-Hall.

Tribe, Lawrence. 1972. "Policy Science: Analysis or Ideology?" *Philosophy and Public Affairs* 2, pp. 66–110.

U.S. General Accounting Office. 1987. *Rail Safety: States' Reaction to Proposed Elimination of Inspection Funding*.

Wallis, John. 1994. *The Soul of Politics*. New Haven: Yale University Press.

Washington Post. 1993. "Validity of Drug Use Survey Questioned," (August 8), p. A3.

Woolf, Patricia. 1994. "Integrity and Accountability in Research," in *The Fragile Contract: University Science and the Federal Government*, David H. Guston and Kenneth Keniston, eds. Cambridge: MIT Press, pp. 82–100.

Wright, Lawrence. 1994. "One Drop of Blood," *The New Yorker* (August), pp. 46–55.

CHAPTER 17

The Ethics of Consulting in the Public Administration Academy: Mapping a Black Hole

THOMAS H. ROBACK

Increased attention to questions of professional ethics has become an important theme in the public administration literature over the past decade. This attention has tended to focus on career civil servants and the values that guide their professional work (Denhardt 1988; Tong 1986). This chapter provides an examination of the ethics of consulting in the public administration academy, which has received scant attention in the public administration literature. Because the unique values of the discipline are linked to providing professional norms in studying and working in support of the public service, this topic raises important questions.

Of course, all public and private sector members of the academy should follow the highest legal and ethical standards. The public administration literature simply has examined ethical questions of members of the bureaucracy and public service. Public administration academics are no different from other public employees in the ethical standards and values that have been developed for public sector employees. However, public administration scholarship has generally not examined itself in its consulting employment practices under ethics and value normative guidelines. The academy is required to follow university consulting procedures but has not specifically developed a more complete ethics policy under the American Society for Public Administration (ASPA) code. It appears to have developed a wide range of ethical consulting standards that would fit many different nonacademic university employees.

It is the intent here to provide a preliminary mapping of the organizational and ethical terrain within which the academic public administration professional operates. Since the academic field has developed an active scholarship area in general ethics, it would appear that this specific research area needs to be explored.

BACKGROUND

A key ethical problem to be examined deals with the public academic who is employed by a public agency as a private consultant. The reasons for these role differences are normative and derive from the employee's multiple obligations and concerns, including the public interest, constitutional values, statutory duty, public service, public obligation, and a vision of a shared common weal. While the literature on ethics lacks theoretical consensus, the argument can be made that public administration and government service should still demand a high standard of conduct (Rohr 1989).

While the individual universities examined in this study have rules on consulting and outside employment, the resulting codes and standards have a tendency to be legalistic, procedural, and often written in general language that simultaneously encourages and constrains faculty engaging in consulting activity. From an ethics and values perspective, academic public administration consultants who look to either their universities or to ASPA for ethical direction might be left with imprecise terminology such as "undue personal gain," "professional development," "highest standards," "official duties" and "conflict of interest." As one might expect, ethical conduct is generally left to the values and discretion of the individual academic consultant to make personal decisions throughout the consulting process.

The following ethical questions will be discussed in this study:

(1) What are the primary conceptual and organizational roles of public administration consultants in university settings?

(2)   What are the ethical difficulties that describe each role category when academics must simultaneously play both their consultant and academic roles?

(3)   Is the ethical guidance provided by the standards of professional associations adequate? Is mere compliance all that is necessary, or are higher-order standards of governance required of the public service consultancy?

(4)   What is the future market for consulting by the public administration academy in a rapidly changing public sector world?

The public administration academic consultant has a large number of complex organizational and ethical situations from which to choose. Indeed, value and ethical considerations are inherent in making the decision whether to consult. A decision to consult beyond one's full-time academic employment raises considerations of time allocation to serve students, research, and collegial obligations, legal and professional responsibilities, and moral obligations in relationships with clients and family.

A large number of complex consulting permutations come into play when describing these organizational relationships. This analysis will utilize a multidimensional approach to describing public administration consulting. Such an approach goes beyond the single, individual consultant-client relationship and includes a number of dynamic and overlapping types of organizational arrangements. The academic who simultaneously serves the academy and a public agency develops a set of professional relationships that integrates technical expertise, instructional skills, political acumen, and the public-private dimension.

There are several major roles that the public administration academy plays in performing consulting activity. These roles will be differentiated according to the following variables: funding and compensation source; personnel status; degree of occupational autonomy; public service motivation; and potential for ethical misconduct.

In this broad definition of *academic consultant* there are four major roles and functions by which public administration consulting activity is performed:

(1) The Academic Contractor as "Lone Ranger"

(2) The Sponsored Research Principal Investigator as "Rainmaker"

(3) The Public Service Center Academic as "Salaryman"

(4) The Academic Public Service "Altruist"

The following section presents these roles and examines their characteristics.

THE ACADEMIC CONSULTANT PLAYING FIELD

Table 17.1 describes the consulting roles according to the variables described above. These role categories are Weberian "ideal types" but do depict authentic consulting roles for the public administration academy. The typology is meant to range theoretically from the traditional contractor-client arrangement to the purely civic duty of giving a luncheon speech to the local Rotary Club or giving expert testimony to a school board or a legislative committee. It is important to remember that academic consulting can provide valuable services to the public sector. However, the typology will identify and put more focus on the ethical dilemmas that can face academic consultants.

It is important to understand that the dynamic flow of public administration consulting in each of these roles constitutes relationships and activities that often overlap and form symbiotic professional, social, and political networks. This study adopts such a multidimensional approach because it seems to best represent the grounded world of public administration that I have observed. However, for purposes of description, I will describe the attributes and some broad ethical parameters as discrete categories.[1]

The Lone Ranger

This role fits the most common definition of consulting as a work relationship between an individual agent and an external organization that falls outside the personnel policies of the university. The academic consultant becomes an independent contractor by making a

Table 17.1. Typology of Academic Consulting Roles

Consultant Role	Funding Source[a]	Autonomy[b]	Personnel Status[c]	Primary Motivation[d]	Ethical Misconduct Potential[e]
Lone Ranger	External	High	Moonlighting Contractor	Material	High
Rainmaker	External with Internal Control	Moderate	"Bought-Out" Faculty	Material Solidarity	Moderate
Salaryman	Mixed Internal-External	Low	Full-Time Faculty/Staff	Solidary Purposive	Low to Moderate
Altruist	None or Expenses	High	Full-Time Faculty	Purposive	Low

[a] The primary source of funding for project as either internal to the university or from an external agency or jurisdiction.

[b] The degree to which an academic consults independently of the university.

[c] The extent to which consulting is part of an academic's job description.

[d] The seminal incentive categories of political motivation derived from (1961). Material incentives refer to financial compensation. Solidary incentives pertain to professional networking and affiliation. Purposive incentives refer to public service and ideological motives.

[e] The likelihood that financial allocation of time and general conflict of interest abuses might occur.

formal agreement with an agency to which the university is not a signatory. These agreements can range from providing broadly written contracts for personal services to detailed contracts where products and deliverables are required within specific time frames. Under these circumstances, the university normally will provide an oversight function according to its formal "consulting policy."

Table 17.1 outlines the following attributes of the academic Lone Ranger. Such a role is funded from an external source; enjoys maximum autonomy outside of regular university employment; is primarily motivated by material incentives; and presents a higher potential for ethical misconduct than other consultant roles.

The sources of consulting opportunities for the Lone Ranger are manifold. First, they may be unsolicited and external and stem from scholarly reputation, panel participation at professional association annual meetings or agency-sponsored symposia. Second, serendipitous opportunities may evolve from the academic's normal duties as a teacher or researcher in academic programs offered to public agencies. Consulting can develop from relationships between academic departments and agencies that begin in instructional or service programs focusing on in-career students who may hold mid- to high-level government positions. These official university-agency relationships may grow into the private employment of faculty or staff to meet an agency's need for professional expertise. Such arrangements may be solicited by either party but have a high potential to approach both the legal or ethical misconduct demarcation lines.

A third source of individual consulting is the entrepreneurial model whereby the academic creates an incorporated consulting firm or is employed by a firm as a part-time "gun for hire." This can be done by ignoring university consulting policy or by informing the university and following permissable guidelines.

Each of these types of relationships creates ethical choices for the public administration consultant that involve questions of disclosure, conflicts of interest, financial misconduct, and the proper balance between responsibilities to the university, the client, and individual needs and values. For example, the consultant may have to choose between evaluating a student's class performance while simultaneously being offered a personal contract to work for the agency of that student.

In any of these cases, violations of existing legal and ethical standards would be both tempting and legally dangerous for the reckless consultant. The ASPA Ethics Code does not deal with such problems. When a consultant looks to the Code, Rohr's "low road" of mechanical compliance and negative sanction never has appeared lower (Rohr 1989).

The Rainmaker

The Rainmaker role portrays the activities of the academic principal investigator (P.I.) in acquiring and administering sponsored research projects. In this case, the funding source is external but is channeled through the university in the form of contracts or grants. In either case, the P.I. often performs consulting activities but must operate under the internal administrative, personnel, financial, and ethical policies and procedures of the university. This reduces professional autonomy and transforms regular faculty personnel status since the P.I.'s time is usually "bought out" by the sponsor.

The motivations underlying sponsored research for the Rainmaker are mixed but consist largely of professional and material incentives. While some personal financial benefit is involved (for example, maximum summer pay), the consultant as P.I. develops university organizational influence and political power by attracting the sponsor, building the research team and generating direct and indirect monies. This process involves a web of internal beneficiaries including research faculty, graduate students, support staff, and university administrators who constitute a complex organizational system.

The ethical misconduct risk is moderate due to internal university controls that remove some discretion from the consultant as P.I. Nonetheless, considerable latitude for independent decision making remains that could create ethical dilemmas. Common vehicles for potential misconduct can include travel abuses, doublebilling, improper use of time, and the distribution of political pressure patronage in *quid pro quo* arrangements with professional colleagues and "exploitation" of graduate students. In such cases, university policies can have the potential to be either paid lip service or conveniently ignored. A conflict of interest could exist in these relationships that could be problematic unless stronger university rules and standards were enforced. Obviously, following the rules and ethical values is the best strategy for the consultant as P.I.

The Salaryman

Employees of university public service centers and institutes play their consultant roles as salaried experts whose sole function is to provide assistance to governments. Funding comes from either state line-item appropriations or contracts with other public agencies and local jurisdictions. Some land-grant universities also have extension units that provide such services. Under this rubric, the university expert can provide individual technical services, training, and organize and monitor conferences and symposia. The Salaryman has little individual autonomy in controlling the terms and conditions of consulting and is bound to university policy as a salaried employee on work assignment and compensation.

The motivational framework that operates for consultants in such public service units tends to lean toward solidary and purposive incentives. While contracts and funding must often be generated by such centers, consultants cannot receive extra compensation and primarily derive rewards from the work itself, social and professional interactions, and the reward of public service. Providing competent job performance enhances a consultant's professional reputation and ensures future organizational opportunities with satisfied clients.

Ethical misconduct potential is lower because of the legal and organizational requirements of university employment that reduce individual discretion. Financial compensation and reimbursement policies are determined by rigid internal procedures and a position classification system, and while opportunities for misconduct are possible, the projects are closely monitored. The ethical compass of the Salaryman is most affected by personal judgments about quality of work performance, confidentiality, and judgments about political agendas that might influence and compromise the honest findings of the final consulting effort.

The Altruist

The public administration academy consultant as Altruist comes closest to being the ethically pure public servant of folklore. The level of autonomy and discretion is high, but usually no sources of funding or compensation exist (except perhaps for expenses). Responding to purposive incentives related to societal, political, and public service values best describes the motives of the consulting activity of this final academic role. Altruists are compelled to perform public service because of their intrinsic moral and social beliefs.

While enhancement of professional reputation might be involved, this form of consulting is usually performed as university "public service" activity and rarely involves ethical misconduct or potential for conflict of interest. Such activity may be "expected" of most faculty but may not be recognized as much as research or teaching. It is usually done out of a willingness to serve the public or agency or for internal political reasons within the community or university.

Each of these consultant roles is discrete and provides an array of activities on a continuum ranging from individual self-interest to pure public service. The remainder of this analysis will primarily emphasize the Lone Ranger and the Rainmaker roles because of their relative vulnerability to ethical concerns.

CONSULTING AND THE PUBLIC ADMINISTRATION ACADEMY

The ethical questions faced by public administration faculty who consult can be analyzed as part of a general normative ethics orientation that governs the discipline. However, it must be recognized that a paradigmatic framework for public administration ethics has failed to achieve consensus among scholars (Denhardt 1988). It is not my intention to analyze or resolve this theoretical dilemma, but it points up the complexity of dealing with this unexplored consulting issue by the academy.

Ethicists have proposed an array of often complex definitions and concepts surrounding virtue, moral consequences, moral responsibility, and principles around which public administrators can find guidance. This has not prevented ASPA from developing the official *Code of Ethics of the American Society for Public Administration*. Cooper and others have complained about a "lack of coherent ethical identity for public administration" in ASPA's code, which contains no statement of the "internal goods from which particulars are derived and around which practice ought to be formed" (Cooper 1992). While this normative quest provides academics with interesting research material, ASPA's *Code of Ethics* and the standards of other practitioner-oriented professional associations should be supported for throwing an ethical "life jacket" to public administrators who face daily ethical questions.

It is in this interaction with public administrators that the ASPA code is made relevant and operational for public administration faculty who consult. They clearly are bound by the ethical prescriptions of their universities, but in the consulting act they become bound by both the university codes and the codes of professional societies. This normative arena is the "third sector" of ethical responsibility. It is different from the behavior of the academic "as university administrator or subordinate" and the academic "as research scholar studying and teaching about public organizations and administrators."

ASPA's code appears to be directed toward practitioners in real-time public agencies and provides minimal assistance to the academic consultant who must traverse an ethical minefield of disclosure, compliance, and conflicts of interest issues. Academic consulting needs a professional dialogue that would help clear the "ethical air." This need is acute for the public administration academy because of its proximity to public-sector consulting, which includes a public-private dimension of divided loyalties, ambiguous statutory domains, and political issues surrounding the value to universities regulating the consulting activity of faculty.

Lone Rangers and Rainmakers in Academe

It is in these two consulting roles that the dimensions cited above provide an opportunity to explore the ethical briar patch of public administration academic consulting. First, existing university standards for consulting approve and regulate essentially private sector activity by faculty.

As Lone Rangers, faculty who are public employees are working for public agencies as private sector employees. With broadly written permission and disclosure requirements, the university potentially gives the consultant carte blanche as to setting conditions of employment. Potential ethical problems are left to the common sense and value discretion of the faculty member who must weigh a set of obligations to oneself, the university, students, colleagues, family, the client, and the public interest.

For certain kinds of unethical behavior involving statutes and rules, "unambiguously wrong" activity includes violations under "waste, fraud, and abuse" statutes, misuse of funds, graft, peddling contracts for political influence, gratuities and gifts, or deliberate unprofessional research misconduct in completing projects. On the other hand, there are "ambiguously wrong" behaviors that consultants might perform that involve deception, silence, lying, and minimal compliance with disclosure or conflict of interest regulations.

The consultant roles of Lone Ranger and Rainmaker involve ethical decisions that consist of both unambiguous and ambiguous value situations. It is clear that independent public administration consultants have more discretion to make normative choices than do principal investigators in sponsored research projects. The formal legal regulations and community values in the university keep Rainmakers from agonizing over many ethical questions that confront Lone Rangers.

It is recognized that differences between these roles exist, but in working with public agencies the roles often overlap. Both types of consultants must deal with many similar ethical dilemmas in professional relationships with students, colleagues, university administrators, clients, and with government institutions and agencies.

Academic Relationships and Ethics

In the case of student relationships, consultants and principal investigators have to be sure that they provide sufficient time for their students' academic needs. This means adequate preparation for teaching, thesis or dissertation direction, and advising in spite of consulting.

The choice of guiding paper assignments to topics related to the Lone Ranger's consulting task is problematic. This can lead to uncompensated student labor and involves deception, abuse of power, and unprofessional behavior. These situations involve "ethical mismatches" (Burton 1990), where the disparity in professional status, expertise, and power precludes any equitable negotiation between faculty and students. If such activity exists, it should be made clear to students and be compensated. Of course, all academic assignments should be based on the curriculum and not the consulting agenda.

The Rainmaker has a better opportunity than the Lone Ranger to provide meaningful learning and research opportunities for students. In this case, sponsored research offices provide management procedures that remove many ethical decisions from the table. The faculty member as P.I. exchanges professional expertise and opportunities for student learning experiences, future employment opportunities, and financial compensation through assistantships.

In a "worst case scenario" that is possible in off-campus and in-service programs, a regular teaching assignment can lead to consulting or contractual relationships with government managers who are enrolled in public administration degree programs. Ethical questions can easily be raised when the faculty member is dealing simultaneously with a manager who is both student and consulting client. This is an ethically sensitive situation that conflict of interest laws or university codes may not always mention. Obviously, in such cases, the academy needs to provide unequivocal guidance that regulates such relationships. There are many variations on this theme, and conditions and protections for both the academy and the public agency need to be developed. Relationships with academic colleagues can also be affected by consulting and sponsored research contracts. Again, improper allocation of time can affect the orderly business of the public administration department. The allocation and control of overhead funds can cause tensions and petty feuds that may weaken departmental missions.

I have observed that creating a departmental team approach to providing services to a public agency removes some of this dissension and provides collaborative research opportunities. Universities increasingly encourage grant and contract activity, but as public agencies "down-size" and "restructure," such management consulting and training opportunities for the public administration academy may be decreasing. In the future, Lone Rangers may be forced to work directly for consulting firms.

The ethical relationship between university administrators and the public administration faculty member who plays the Rainmaker and Lone Ranger roles is complex and multidimensional. First, these roles are evolutionary, and independent consulting and contracts and grants activity may feed off each other. Graduate teaching programs with public agencies might lead to either individual consulting opportunities or university contractual arrangements. Sometimes such dual consulting activity may exist simultaneously. This is not necessarily unethical, but what should university administrators do in such situations? At minimum, there need to be disclosure mechanisms that protect all parties involved. There are few à priori reasons to preclude such university-principal investigator and consultant-client-agency relationship webs from operating, if compliance with the legal, procedural, and ethical questions is resolved in advance. If such standards cannot be met, these arrangements are clearly improper. Public administration consultants who find themselves in such ambiguous positions should take the ethical lead in such cases.

Faculty members who are balancing sponsored research funding and entrepreneurism may do so at their own peril. A recent case in a public university in Virginia illustrates an illegal or unethical conduct violation that was uncovered and publicized. This case involved a Rainmaker who was being investigated for embezzlement, allegedly selling state property to an agency of a foreign government. Audits, search warrants, and seizure of office documents have all been part of a full-fledged investigation. While criminal charges are pending, the faculty member went from a position of longstanding university prominence to the subject of a criminal investigation.

A last admonition for the public administration consultant is that the reward system in the university may not always adequately recognize prowess in acquiring contracts and grants. Unless one's department and college attach weight to strong sponsored-research performance, such activity may not be useful in gaining tenure or promotion.

A final relationship involves the university consultant's ethical posture toward the client public agency. This relationship involves a set of professional and ethical obligations to the agency that includes a number of base-line prescriptive elements. In this case, the consultant owes the client agency the highest standards of honesty, effort, and professional integrity in completing the statement of work. The client should be presented a complete record of professional qualifications to judge the consultant's competence. Fees and charges should be reasonable and reflect market value. Confidentiality about the agency and data results needs to be maintained under the agreement, but the consultant should not be immune from taking moral responsibility when the advice and recommendations become public.

The deliberate act of giving the agency "what it wants" in terms of findings is another problematic area, because it may stretch fundamental professional and ethical standards and can put in jeopardy the function of being an objective researcher. This may be one of the most difficult judgments that the public administration consultant must make, because this may be where personal self-interest needs and broader public-interest values may collide.

In this case, the consultant must deal directly with agencies and indirectly with a notion of the "public interest." This puts an additional burden on the consultant, because the consultant role is often played as change agent for the client. Kelman cites two dangers that face consultants in influencing the client toward change:

> one is the failure to recognize that the consultant is engaged in the control of the client's behavior. The other is the intoxication with the goodness of what he is doing for and to the client, which in turn leads to a failure to recognize the ambiguity of the control he exercises (Kelman 1965).

In the case of working for public agencies, resistance to manipulating the client by substituting your own values and needs for the client's values as the dominant criterion for change should be encouraged. The public administration academic consultant should carefully formulate a conception of the public interest that goes beyond merely "helping" the client solve a specific management problem that has ambiguous moral implications. This approach involves an internal value system that formal ethics codes and criminal statutes usually do not affect. The discretionary nature of the academic consultant's role can become seductive and requires much greater attention to such matters. Clearly, further development of Kohlberg's higher levels of moral reasoning orientation applied to the academic consultant role could yield interesting research results (Kohlberg 1984).

CONCLUSION

The nexus between public administration academic consulting and the contemporary decline of political support of government bureaucracy is somewhat paradoxical. At the same time that downsizing of the public sector is increasing, the need and demand for government consulting should be rising. What will be the role of the public administration academy in providing such a consulting cadre? The reinvention, restructuring and re-engineering "gurus" either are not attached to the academy or bring distinctly think-tank or private-sector orientations to their consulting roles in public service. Many elected officeholders appear poised to reduce the size of the career bureaucracy while increasing the role of consultants and private contractors.

In an era when an antigovernment mood exists and the public sector is shrinking, the academy's consulting activity may find itself under even tighter conflict of interest rules and more rigid accountability standards. It is precisely at this time that the public administration academy that is grounded in notions of the public interest and civic obligation should be utilized to diagnose and design the emerging deregulated and reinvented bureaucratic institutions of the future.

Under these circumstances, mapping the "black hole" of future academic consulting trends will become even more difficult. According to the Consultants Bureau, there are an estimated 70,000 management consulting firms and 100,000 independent consultants in the United States. The bureau estimates that private industry and the nonprofit sector together spend eighteen to twenty billion dollars a year for consulting services, and the trend is increasing (Odd Jobs 1995).

Private consulting by the academic may be ethical if it provides institutional support for becoming an outstanding teacher or scholar. The practice of the public administration academic (teacher, scholar, public servant) is embedded in the bureaucratic and institutional structure known as government and consulting for money alone may be problematic unless its justification is based on internal standards of administrative excellence. The ability to criticize and also to advance the state of the art that contributes to the public interest and efficient management practices would appear to justify consulting employment.

The distinction between the public and private roles of the public administration academic consultant needs professional clarification. It is important to remember that academic private consultants often receive public employment because of their public academic roles. The consulting compensation for time and effort often has public roots, which means that the consultant should remain an ethical "agent" held morally responsible, especially when a public client is involved. The public employee "hat" cannot be taken off so easily when one moves into private consulting. In reality, however, the consultant may be guided by ethical codes, but personal and moral decisions appear to be most influential in choosing to consult.

Will the consultant fail in ethical misconduct choices from time to time? Yes, but the public consultant is always morally accountable to do the best job possible according to professional standards of technical expertise. Expert opinion and performance are not practiced in a normative vacuum, because the moral ends and goals of the consulting effort are always relevant. Simply being an amoral "Lone Ranger" consultant does not absolve the public administration consultant from ethical responsibility to individual, university, and professional society ethical and value standards.

In the interim, more rigid standards, disclosure burdens, and conflict of interest statutes will do little to make academic consulting more ethical. The public administration academy and the professional societies need to recognize the scope of academic consulting activity and clarify the moral expectations and value premises of this uniquely public-private vocation. Clearly ASPA should continue to play a greater role in providing ethical guidance to its academic membership when consulting problems arise.

NOTE

1. The faculty procedures and policies manuals of three large public universities in Virginia were used to analyze such consulting codes. They are not meant to be a random, scientific sample of all U.S. universities but probably share many attributes of comparable institutions.

REFERENCES

Burton, Lloyd. 1990. "Ethical Discontinuities in Public-Private Sector Negotiation." *Journal of Policy Analysis and Management*, 9(1), pp. 23–40.

Clark, Peter B., and James Q. Wilson. 1961. "Incentive Systems: A Theory of Organizations," *Administrative Sciences Quarterly*, 4 (September), pp. 129–66.

Cooper, Terry. 1992. "Hierarchy, Virtue, and the Practice of Public Administration: A Perspective for Normative Ethics." In William Richter, Frances Burke, and Jameson W. Doig, eds., *Combating Corruption, Encouraging Ethics: A Sourcebook for Public Administration Ethics*. Washington, D.C.: ASPA.

Denhardt, Kathryn. 1988. *The Ethics of Public Service: Resolving Moral Dilemmas in Public Organizations*. New York: Greenwood.

Kelman, H. C. 1965. "Manipulation of Human Behavior: An Ethical Dilemma for the Social Scientist." *Journal of Social Issues*, 21(2), pp. 21–46.

Kohlberg, Lawrence. 1984. *Essays in Moral Development: The Psychology of Moral Development* (Vol. 2). New York: Harper and Row.

Odd Jobs. 1995. (January 8). *Washington Post*. p. H4.

Rohr, John. 1989. *Ethics for Bureaucrats: An Essay on Laws and Values*. New York: Marcel Dekker.

Tong, Rosemarie. 1986. *Ethics in Policy Analysis*. Englewood Cliffs, NJ: Prentice Hall.

About the Contributors

James S. Bowman is professor of the Askew School of Public Administration and Policy at Florida State University. Noted for his work in ethics, Dr. Bowman has also done extensive research in total quality management. Bowman is the author of nearly 100 refereed articles as well as several books. He was recently appointed as the first editor-in-chief of *Public Integrity Annual*, a journal cosponsored by the Council of State Governments and the American Society of Public Administration.

Willa Bruce is a professor in the Department of Public Administration at the University of Nebraska at Omaha. Her research interests include administrative ethics, job performance and satisfaction, mediation, and dual career couples. She is a member of the editorial boards of *Public Administration Review* and *Public Voices*. She is author or co-author of four books and numerous articles.

George Cox is professor of public affairs at Georgia Southern University. He now chairs NACADA's Commission on Graduate Advising and has authored a set of national standards to assist graduate advisors and accrediting bodies. He has published articles and book chapters in the areas of public policy, state government administration, and program evaluation.

Henry T. Edmondson III is associate professor of political science and public administration at Georgia College in Milledgeville, Georgia. His articles have appeared in *Policy Studies Review*, *PS: Political Science and Politics*, and an edited volume, *Teaching Public Policy: Theory, Research, and Practice*.

Charles J. Fox is professor of political science and Director of the Center for Public Service, which grants a Master of Public Administration degree, at Texas Tech University. Originally trained in political philosophy, Dr. Fox has published widely on ethics, public administration theory, public personnel administration, and public policy implementation. He is, with Hugh Miller, the author of the book *Postmodern Public Administration: Toward Discourse*.

John Holcomb is associate professor of legal studies in the Daniels College of Business at the University of Denver. He is published widely in the areas of corporate and government relations in such journals as *Business and the Contemporary World* and *Electric Perspectives*.

Bruce Hutton is professor of marketing in the Daniels College of Business at the University of Denver. He has numerous professional publications, and his areas of research interest include consumer research and public policy, with special emphasis on environmental issues and strategic corporate social responsibility.

Alfred G. Killilea is professor of political science at the University of Rhode Island. He teaches political philosophy and is particularly interested in questions relating to the political implications of human mortality and also ethics in public life. The author of *The Politics of Being Mortal*, he is the co-director of the J. H. White Center for Ethics and Public Service at the University of Rhode Island. He is also co-editor of the book *Ethical Dilemmas in Public Administration*.

Jeffrey L. Mayer is Director of Policy Development at the Economics and Statistics Administration of the U.S. Department of Commerce. Prior to that, he was Associate Professor of Government and Politics at King's College, Wilkes-Barre, Pennsylvania.

Ronald L. McNinch is a doctoral candidate in political science at Georgia State University. His dissertation is on the selection of higher civil servants in Taiwan. He has published in *Public Voices*.

Donald C. Menzel is a professor of public administration and political science at the University of South Florida at Tampa. He has published articles on the ethical environment of local government managers, ethics stress in public organizations, and ethics education in MPA programs. He has recently published an edited volume *The American County: Frontiers of Knowledge*. His current research interests are in the areas of ethics education, administrative ethics, and world wide web survey research methodology.

Jerry Mitchell is an associate professor of public affairs at Baruch College, The City University of New York. A member of the editorial board of the *Policy Studies Journal*, his research focuses on nontraditional public administration, such as public enterprises and government boards and commissions. He is the author of *American Government in the Nation and New York* and the editor of *Public Authorities and Public Policy: The Business of Government*.

Dalmas H. Nelson is Professor Emeritus of Political Science, University of Utah. He authored *Administrative Agencies of the U.S.A.: Their Decisions and Authority*; coedited (with Richard L. Sklar) *Essays in Law and Politics*, by Francis Dunham Wormuth; and co-edited (with Richard L. Sklar) *Toward a Humanistic Science of Politics: Essays in Honor of Francis Dunham Wormuth*. His authored and coauthored articles have appeared in a variety of political science, public administration, and other professional journals.

Donald R. Nelson is associate professor of legal studies in the Daniels College of Business at the University of Denver. He is former president of the Academy of Legal Studies in Business. He has numerous professional publications in journals such as *American Business Law Journal* and the *Journal of Business Ethics*.

Lloyd G. Nigro is professor of public administration in the School of Public Administration and Urban Studies at Georgia State University, Atlanta, Georgia. In addition to articles on administrative theory, administrative ethics, and public personnel administration, his publications include *The New Public Personnel Administration*, *Modern Public Administration*, and *Decision Making in the Public Sector*.

David T. Ozar is professor of philosophy, Director of the Center for Ethics, and Co-Director of the Graduate Program in Health Care Ethics at Loyola University Chicago. He has written numerous articles and book chapters on topics in health care ethics, professional ethics, and ethics education, as well as *Dental Ethics at Chairside: Professional Principles and Practical Applications*.

Lynn Pasquerella is a professor of philosophy at the University of Rhode Island and an adjunct Professor of Medical Ethics at the

Brown University Medical School. She has published extensively in the areas of theoretical and applied ethics, public policy, and the philosophy of law and is co-editor of *Ethical Dilemmas in Public Administration.*

Jeremy F. Plant is professor of public policy and administration, School of Public Affairs, Penn State Harrisburg, where he teaches graduate and undergraduate courses in Public Administration and Public Policy. He is the author of numerous articles on public ethics and is the co-author, with David S. Arnold, of *Public Official Associations in State and Local Government.*

John G. Pomery is associate professor of economics at the Krannert Graduate School of Management, Purdue University. He has published on topics in international economics in the *Journal of International Economics,* the *Handbook of International Economics,* and *The New Palgrave: A Dictionary of Economics,* and his Ph.D. dissertation was published in Garland's Second Series of *Outstanding Dissertations in Economics.*

William D. Richardson is associate professor of political science and public administration at Georgia State University in Atlanta, Georgia. His articles on aspects of American political thought and ethics have appeared in numerous journals and books, including *Administration and Society, Public Administration Review, Polity, Interpretation,* and *Public Voices.* His most recent book is *Public Administration, Character, and the American Regime.*

The late **Thomas H. Roback** was associate professor of public administration in the Center for Public Administration and Policy at Virginia Polytechnic Institute and State University. His publications include articles in *Administration and Society, Public Administration Quarterly, Public Personnel Management, Journal of Politics, Polity,* and a number of articles in edited books. His major areas of concentration were public personnel management, patronage-merit system reform, and organizational behavior.

Robert A. Seidel is Lecturer and Administrator for Teaching Programs at the Institute for Policy Studies of Johns Hopkins University. He has worked in policy education since 1973.

Robert W. Smith is a Ph.D. candidate in public administration at the University at Albany, a Senior Budget Examiner with the New York State Division of the Budget, and an adjunct lecturer at the College of St. Rose and at the University of Albany. His primary research interest is institutional methods employed by governments to enforce or encourage ethical behavior.

Peter J. Van Hook directs Nonprofit Management Programs at the Center for Organizational Programs and Professional Development at the University of Utah. He is the author of forthcoming articles in the *International Encyclopedia of Public Policy and Administration*, one of them on ethics in nonprofit organizations. He served for twenty years as a parish pastor, spending a good deal of his time helping people with ethical issues.

Michael Vocino is professor of library science and an adjunct professor of political science at the University of Rhode Island. He is Interim Dean of the University of Rhode Island Libraries and teaches in the Rhode Island Master of Public Administation Program and the Graduate School of Library and Information Studies. He is co-author of *Labor and Industrial Relations Journals and Serials: An Analytical Guide* and co-editor of the book *Ethical Dilemmas in Public Administration*.

Marcia Lynn Whicker is a professor in the Graduate School of Public Administration at Rutgers University, Newark. She has published fourteen books and numerous articles in the areas of public policy, public administration, the presidency, leadership, and American national politics. Among these is *Dealing with Ethical Dilemmas on Campus*, co-authored with Jennie J. Kronenfeld.

Dennis Wittmer is assistant professor of management in the Daniels College of Business at the University of Denver. Recent publications appear in *Public Productivity and Management Review*, *Journal of Public Administration Research and Theory*, and *Information Systems Research*. He also has a chapter on "Ethical Decision Making" in *Handbook of Administrative Ethics*.

Louis C. Zuccarello is professor of political science and chair of the department at Marist College in Poughkeepsie, New York. He has published articles on the history and politics of the Catholic Church in the mid-Hudson area and has also conducted numerous workshops dealing with ethics and technology, and ethics and public service.

Index